Photograph on page 58 © Jack Gescheidt; on page 90, courtesy of Jay F. Kainz; on page 176, courtesy of Jan Kunz. All other interior photographs © 2008 by Bart Yasso

Rodale books may be purchased for business or promotional use or for special sales. For information, please write to: Special Markets Department, Rodale, Inc., 733 Third Avenue, New York, NY 10017

Runner's World is a registered trademark of Rodale Inc.

Printed in the United States of America
Rodale Inc. makes every effort to use acid-free ♾, recycled paper ♻.

Book design by Susan Eugster

Library of Congress Cataloging-in-Publication Data

Yasso, Bart.
    My life on the run : the wit, wisdom, and insights of a road racing icon / Bart Yasso, with Kathleen Parrish.
        p.   cm.
    Includes index.
    ISBN-13 978-1-59486-941-9 hardcover
    ISBN-10 1-59486-941-3 hardcover
    1. Yasso, Bart.   2. Runners (Sports)—United States.   3. Marathon running—Anecdotes.   I. Parrish, Kathleen.   II. Title.
GV1061.15.Y37A3   2008
796.42092—dc22
[B]   2008006928

Distributed to the trade by Macmillan

    4   6   8   10   9   7   5   3   hardcover

We inspire and enable people to improve their lives and the world around them

For more of our products visit **rodalestore.com** or call 800-848-4735

TO MY MOM,

Rose Marie Yasso,

AND LATE BROTHER,

George B. Yasso,

FOR SHOWING ME THE WAY

Bart and his mother, Rose Marie Yasso at
Trevi Fountain during Rome Marathon, 2001

Bart above tree line
on Kilimanjaro with
the snow-peaked cap
in the background

CONTENTS

ACKNOWLEDGMENTS

Writing a book is similar to running a marathon—it takes a lot of hard work, stamina, and belief in oneself. There are hills and straightaways, days of headiness and exhaustion and a sprint to the finish. It also takes encouragement and support from family and friends, and I'd like to thank those who helped make this literary journey possible.

To my late brother, George, for encouraging me to take up road racing and for his steady guidance throughout my life. Without him, there wouldn't be a book.

To my wife, Laura, for her patience, understanding, encouragement and editing help throughout the process, especially when I hit the wall at page 200.

To my mom and dad, Rose Marie and the late George F. Yasso; siblings Anne Marie, Gerry, Spud, and Mimi; sisters-in-law, Jean, Amy, and Cinda; brother-in-law James Freed; and my nieces and nephews. You guys are the greatest.

To the Rodale family, who have made me feel like a part of their family during my 21 years at *Runner's World*.

To *Runner's World* publisher Andy Hersam, editor in chief David Willey, associate publisher Sue Hartman, and editor at large Amby Burfoot for their belief and enthusiasm in the book. This project would not have been possible without their support. Because of their expertise and care, *Runner's World* is one of the most successful fitness publications in the world.

To Rodale director of fitness and health Budd Coates for helping me take my running to the next level.

To all my colleagues at *Runner's World*, present and past, who share my passion for a healthy life through running. Our love for the sport is reflected in the pages of the magazine each month.

To past *Runner's World* colleagues, George Hirsch, Vern Walther, Bob Wischnia (Wish), Jane Serues, and Claudia Malley. We spent countless hours traveling to races together for the magazine. We ran lots of miles, shared smiles and ate tons of good food, thanks to George Hirsch whose affinity for a good meal was rivaled only by his enthusiasm for running. George knew at dinner where we would be eating breakfast the next day.

To Kevin Smith, Rachelle Laliberte, Cristina Negron, Tish Hamilton, Charlie Butler, and Kathy Reinhard for their keen eye and editorial expertise.

To Neal Novak, Fred Reichenbach, and the entire Lehigh Valley Half-Marathon committee. I consider having turned a local race into a nationally renowned half-marathon in the backyard of *Runner's World* one of my proudest accomplishments. I could not have done it without the dedication of the race committee.

To Dave McGillivray, race director of the Boston marathon, and the hardest working person in the running industry.

To my agent, Stephen Hanselman of Level 5 Media, for making it happen.

Many thanks and appreciation go to the following people for having a positive influence on my life: Bob Babbitt, Dick Beardsley, Marty Eddy, Paula Fahey, Jerry Friesen, Joe Gaffney, Jeff Galloway, Jack Gescheidt, Thom Gilligan, Jay Glassman, Karl and Sara Glassman, John Q. Griffin, Ryan Hall, Nick Herman, Joe Henderson, Shay Hirsch, Nancy Hobbs, Ron Horn, Steve Jones, Scott Jurek, Don Kardong, Dean Karnazes, Khalid Khannouchi, Gail Kislevitz, Dave and Linda Kresge, Mike Kresge, Bob Larsen, Dottie Lessard O'Conner, Greg Meyer, Billy Mills, Mojave the Cat, Paul Perrone, Rob Powers, Larry Rawson, Mike Reilly, Sarah Reinertsen, Steve Repasch, Roger Robinson, Bill Rodgers, Tracey Russell, Bill Serues, Frank Shorter, Kathrine Switzer, Jeffrey Timm, Grete Waitz, and Tom and Tammy White.

Bart Yasso, chief running officer at *Runner's World* (left), and Amby Burfoot, winner of the 1968 Boston Marathon and editor at large, *Runner's World*

FOREWORD

For the past 20 years, I have worked side by side at *Runner's World* magazine with Bart Yasso—fact-checking historical running events, doing clinics at various marathons, running workouts together, collaborating on training articles, and just gassing on about our favorite races, runners, movies, and vegetarian restaurants. From this observation post, I can honestly say that few others, if any, have done as much as Bart to personify and inspire *Runner's World*'s mission—or to unite all parts of the national and international running communities. Most important, it has been a privilege and a pleasure to have this association with Bart. He makes everything easy—and fun.

The exercise physiologists who poke and prod runners in basement laboratories often speak of something called running economy, which can vary widely from one individual to the next. Some runners burn a lot of oxygen while running at a steady pace. Others—generally the best distance runners—burn relatively little oxygen. These lucky few have a superior running economy.

In this sort of treadmill test, Bart wouldn't score very well. He's an awkward, ungainly, knock-kneed runner, if you must know the truth. He doesn't win marathons so much as brute-force himself through the 26.2-mile distance. However, Bart's skill and economy in so many other areas are where he tops the charts. I'm thinking particularly of his talents at an expo booth, in race directing, and in organizing running adventures.

I get exhausted simply thinking about the huge 2- and 3- and sometimes 4-day expos that accompany big road races. You have to stand on a concrete floor behind a row of tables, smile as constantly as a morning-TV host, try to remember the names of the people streaming past and answer questions like "Can I use my Argentinean Banco Populaire credit card to order next year's *Runner's World* calendar?"

I usually hit the wall in just an hour or two and begin fantasizing about a nap in my hotel room. Bart? He can go hour after hour, even day after day, without showing any signs of fatigue. Not only that, but he seems to remember the first names of about 75 percent of the people who approach him to say hello—and their marathon PR time to boot. It's no wonder so many of his friends call him the Mayor of Running. He's shaken more hands, exchanged more pleasantries, and probably kissed more babies than any other runner I know.

Bart no longer holds the title of race director for the Lehigh Valley Half-Marathon, but he filled that post for many years and is more responsible than anyone else for the event's past and continuing success. Since I've never had to put on a big race myself, I'm sure I don't know the half of what he does. But I've seen him work with volunteers, police, media, timers, announcers, hotel staff, caterers, clinic speakers, and more, and he never loses the smile on his face and the chipper tone in his voice.

Almost every year, someone approaches me at the last minute with an entry request—months after the field had officially filled and registration was cut off. But I try to be a nice guy, and the person is always terribly sincere and has good excuses. You know, it's a long-lost college teammate who just moved to Pennsylvania from New Mexico, and his heart transplant has finally kicked in, and he's up to 15 minutes of walking once a week, and he says that running a half-marathon would mean so much to him. So I creep toward Bart's office and knock timidly on his door and ask how he'd feel about just one more entry, and, by the way, could my friend also have a ticket to the sold-out pasta party?

Anyone else would explode over these ridiculous requests, and I wouldn't blame him for a moment. But Bart doesn't even grimace or emit a low whistle. He says, "Sure, that's no problem. I can take care of it easy." And he does.

Bart has captained a number of *Runner's World* teams at the Hood to Coast Relay in Oregon. Several Augusts ago, I got the chance to join up and experience the snow-to-surf race. It was better than I had heard, for two principal reasons: First, the concept, scenery, and organization were superb. Second, Bart took care of all the details. Give me the choice of any tour leader in the world—at a road-relay event, on a runners' cruise, or while driving around Los Angeles to preview the marathon course—and I'll pick Bart every time. He knows how to drill down and get all the details just right. Without this, any adventure trip would quickly turn chaotic. Just as important, he does the right stuff without seeming to sweat the details.

Like I said at the start, Bart has a balance and economy about so many things. He's biked across the country, climbed Kilimanjaro, completed the Ironman, run through Death Valley to the top of Mount Whitney, and on and on and on . . . more than I can possibly mention here. But he's done all this without chest-thumping or braggadocio—and without the isolated, sometimes alienated persona of many endurance athletes.

Indeed, Bart is a friend and coworker first and a cardio champ second. He's fun to be around. He's fun to work with. He's not just the Mayor of Running and Chief Running Officer at *Runner's World*; these days, we don't always think highly of politicians and corporate mavens and don't always trust them. But Bart you can trust, from first step to last. He's got the marathon mentality, combined with the good-neighbor helpfulness.

I hope we go another 20 years together. We might not log as many miles as we have the past 2 decades, and they certainly won't be as fast. But we've still got miles to go, things to accomplish, and good times to share.

Amby Burfoot

EDITOR AT LARGE,
RUNNER'S WORLD MAGAZINE

Bart poses at Mount Everest
Base Camp in Nepal, 1996

INTRODUCTION

I've been presenting a slide show I call "Never Limit Where Running Can Take You" for the past 20 years. It's a collage of photos from races I've done across the globe and I show them at pasta dinners mostly to entertain runners who need a distraction from the next day's race. There are shots of me on Mount Kilimanjaro, facing a disgruntled rhino in Chitwan National Park in Nepal, and running sans clothes across the finish line at the Bare Buns Fun Run.

Afterward, someone will invariably tell me that they want to read my book—but up until now, I didn't have one. It's not that I didn't have anything to say, I just didn't have the time to write it all down.

My Life on the Run is an expansion of my slide-show message of not limiting yourself in running and life. I think a lot of people become complacent, or maybe just too comfortable, with their choices and don't feel the need to shake up things or seek new experiences. I could have chosen that path, and for the first 20 or so years of my life I did. I didn't go to college, and I drove a delivery truck for a pharmaceutical company. I spent a lot of time on a cracked leather stool at the same bar drinking cheap beer because it was all I could afford. But then I started running. And when I started running, I started dreaming. It couldn't be helped. The mind works as hard as the body does during exercise. It knows its role during these lonely interludes—to inspire, analyze, and fantasize. I did a lot of the last. *If only I could get a job that allowed me to travel and run,* I thought as I ran on college tracks, the narrow streets of Bethlehem, Pennsylvania, and wooded trails.

And guess what? I did. But it took more than a dream. It took a lot of hard work, determination, and, yes, luck. I know that last bit can't be scripted, but the philosopher Joseph Campbell once said: "If you do follow your bliss, you put yourself on a kind of track that has been there all along, waiting for you, and the life that you ought to be living is the one you are living. When you can see that, you begin to meet people who are in your field of bliss, and they open the doors to you."

In committing myself to becoming a better runner I met Budd Coates, director of fitness and health at Rodale, who helped me get hired by *Runner's World* magazine. He opened the door and I sprinted through, surrounding myself with like-minded people who loved to run as much as I did. Then I met George Hirsch, the avuncular publisher of *Runner's World,* who took a shine to me and opened the doors of travel. Again, I didn't stop to ring the bell before crossing the threshold.

As a breed, runners are a pretty gutsy bunch. We constantly push ourselves to discover limitations, then push past them. We want to know how fast we can go, how much pain we can endure, and how far our bodies can carry us before collapsing in exhaustion.

But I'm urging you to take it a step further and test the boundaries of life, not just your physical prowess. You already know the rewards of putting one foot in front of the other. Sure, it's hard at first, but who hasn't looked back and wished they had done it sooner or been baffled that they were ever afraid or hesitant in the first place? Moving outward is an act of courage, and in my life, running has also been a vehicle of introduction—to people, places, cultures, and animals. I have run on all seven continents, but it's not the details of the races I recall or the images I project in my slide show at a pasta dinner. And it's not what's made my life book-worthy. The interesting stuff, the humorous stuff—memorable, life-affirming, and worth-reading stuff—is the meeting of a stranger, the stamp on a passport, the glimpse of a never-before-seen sight, the outlandish adventure.

Running may be the connective tissue, but the true essence of the sport is a passage to a bigger world. So open the door and run through. Just don't be surprised if you arrive in a place you only dreamed existed.

Bart

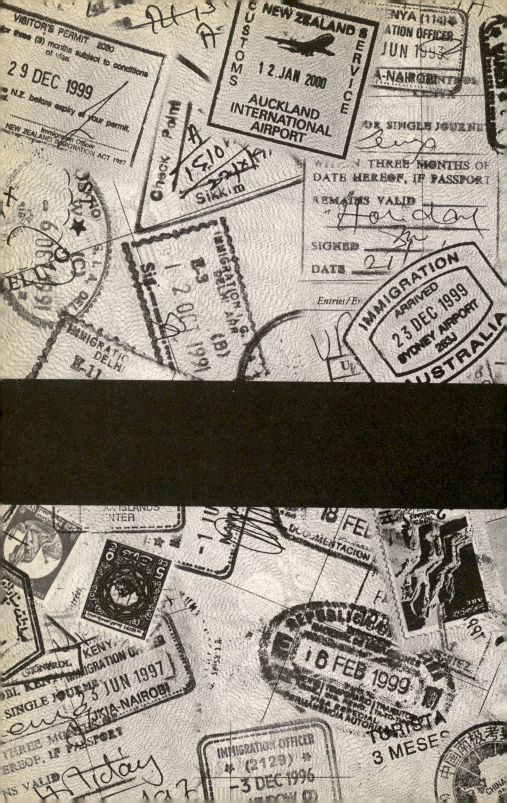

PART ONE
My Life

KILIMANJARO NATIONAL PAR
MARANGU ROUTE.

PLACES.	E.T.A.	ALTITUDE.	VEG.ZO
MANDARA	3HRS	2700M	FORES
HOROMBO	5HRS	3720M	MOORLA
KIBO	5HRS	4703M	ALPINE DE
GILMANS	5HRS	5685M	ALPINE DE
UHURU PEAK	1½HRS	5895M	ICE CA

Bart at the start of the Marangu
or main trail to the summit of
Mount Kilimanjaro, 1997

Chapter 1

MOUNT KILIMANJARO

I was two-thirds of the way up the highest mountain in Africa, and I couldn't see out of my right eye.

But that was the least of my problems. The fever that had started several days before during a layover in Cairo, Egypt, burned with the intensity of scalding coffee through my veins, melting my 160-pound frame into a pool of delirium. At first I thought it was altitude sickness. After all, I was almost 16,000 feet above sea level on a craggy slope of Mount Kilimanjaro in Tanzania, only a few miles from the snow-ringed summit.

Altitude sickness can overtake even the most seasoned climber, which I was not, but at the time—June 1997—I considered myself to be one fit dude. Being in shape was part of my job. I had been race and event promotion director at *Runner's World* magazine since 1987, and my fortitude had been tested on some of the toughest terrain in the world—Death Valley, the Himalayas, and Pikes Peak in Colorado.

By some genetic twist, I had been given a body that was indefatigable. I could run across the Mojave Desert while others were reduced to crying like newborns on the side of the road. My pain threshold was incredibly high and had been tested many times while playing chicken with a cigarette as a teen. This was the game: You and a buddy each place one of your forearms on a table, side by side. Lay a lit cigarette in the crevice between the arms and see who can withstand the pain the longest. It was a torture test I never lost.

Even if what I've started is a sick game of self-abuse, I firmly believe in not giving up.

But as I stood roughly 6 miles from the roof of Africa, I thought about calling it quits. For the first time in my life, I felt helpless, buffeted by forces greater than my iron will.

A few days earlier, I had arrived in Cairo with my friend Paula Fahey. We were part of a tour group scheduled to first climb Kilimanjaro and then run the Mount Kilimanjaro Marathon. I had met Paula at the Twin Cities Marathon in Minneapolis, where she was on the race committee and I had just been hired by *Runner's World*. Over the years, she dated Fred Lebow, the late founder and race director of the ING New York City Marathon, and our paths would often cross at races. When I mentioned I was going to Tanzania, she asked if she could come along.

I certainly understood the pull of East Africa. As a kid, my all-time favorite television show was *Mutual of Omaha's Wild Kingdom*. Every week the hosts—the graying, mustached Marlin Perkins and his youthful sidekick, Jim Fowler—would be in the plains of Africa or some other exotic location, tooling around in a jeep spotting zebras, lions, and rhinos. Jim was my favorite, probably because Marlin was older, or was it wiser? Jim was the one who got up close and personal with the animals and once was even chased by startled elephants. I wanted to be Jim.

When I finally went to Africa, it was everything I had imagined and more. This is where Darwin's survival-of-the-fittest theory is played out day after day in real-life Technicolor. This is where man stood erect for the first time to claim his spot at the top of the animal kingdom. This is where a trail of footprints dating back 3.5 million years was discovered in Tanzania's Olduvai Gorge, the birthplace of distance running. This is where 1.7 million wildebeests pass through the high grass of the Serengeti to Kenya's Masai Mara in the largest annual animal migration on the planet. And this is where Mount Kilimanjaro rises from the earth in majestic splendor.

More than anything else, Paula wanted to scale Kili, as it's affectionately known by the thousands of people who have ascended its peak. It's a manageable 3- to 4-day climb to the top and one that can be done without special equipment or tons of experience. It's also near the equator, so the climate is balmy compared to that of other mountains, such as Pakistan's glacial K2, making it an adventure junkie's dream. But the broad shoulders of the mountain, once an extinct volcano, can be deadly, too. Two weeks after Paula and I returned home from Tanzania, a friend's wife died suddenly only miles from the top of the mountain from a pulmonary embolism brought on by altitude sickness.

The plane trip to our layover in Cairo was uneventful. I felt weak and run-down, but I dismissed it and blamed it on the 12-hour flight from JFK International Airport in New York. For the past few months, I had been traveling to overseas races pretty extensively. In fact, I'd returned to the states from Peru only a few days before. I had nothing a good night's rest couldn't cure, I thought.

I couldn't have been more wrong.

The next morning, I awoke in a swamp of sweat, but instead of feeling hot, I was freezing. It didn't make sense. My room was on the 30th floor of a mid-class hotel, and the air-conditioning was broken. I couldn't stop shaking, not even beneath the weight of five blankets, so I did what I always do when I'm feeling out of sorts. I went for a run, thinking a jog near the banks of the swirling Nile would rejuvenate me. I didn't get very far. After about 1½ miles, pain flashed through my legs before settling into a steady throb. My body felt spent, as if I had just run a marathon.

I walked back to the hotel, climbed into bed, and fell asleep for a few hours. When I awoke, my fever had broken and I was famished. I made plans to join Paula and the others for dinner.

There were about 24 of us in the tour group, all runners who'd gathered from around the globe in hopes of securing Mount Kilimanjaro bragging rights—*hope* being the operative word. Forty percent of all climbers who attempt an ascent turn back at some point, usually after succumbing to altitude sickness, which can cause fatigue, vomiting, headaches, and sleeplessness.

As the only runner in the group who had climbed the mountain before, I was the center of attention, and the others peppered me with questions.

"How tough was it?"

"It was a lot harder than I thought," I said. "You don't get much time to acclimate to the elevation, and the altitude really takes a toll."

"Is it cold?"

"At the top it is, but if you didn't bring enough warm clothes, you can rent them from the guides."

I saved my best advice for last: "Don't be a runner on the mountain. Be a very slow walker. Save the running for the marathon."

The next day we caught a plane to Nairobi, then rode a bus for 8 hours into Tanzania, where we spent the night in a lodge at the foot of Kili. It was 25 miles to the top, although you couldn't see it from the staging area. It was hidden by a curtain of fog like nature's own Wizard of Oz, but I already knew the secret: The reward is completing the climb, not the fleeting view of the panoramic scene below.

The first day I was weak but felt well enough to start the climb, and Paula and I walked side by side through the rain forest on a dirt trail. About an hour into the trek, the trail became an overgrown path that followed a babbling stream. Monkeys yammered, and moss dripped in long strands from the trees. But they don't call it a rain forest for nothing. It was wet in this lush, green bubble, and the soft drizzle bathed our faces in a warm mist. I was thankful when we emerged a few hours later into a meadow of high grass.

The air was cool, and the breeze felt good. Our shorts and T-shirts quickly dried in the sunny field. It didn't feel like I was on a mountain at the moment, the peak obscured by clouds. This was good. I tricked myself into believing my final destination was our sleeping quarters in the Mandara Hut and not the top of a once-mighty volcano that was a 2-day hike away.

That night Paula couldn't stop talking about the beauty of the mountain. "It's like being in paradise," she said. "The clear streams . . . the trees so green and lush."

"It's the only place in the world where you pass through five ecosystems," I said, repeating information I had heard on PBS's *Nature* show, my second-favorite TV program behind the Weather Channel.

"This is the best day of my life," she said.

Soon after, a New Jersey lawyer crashed into camp swearing like Tony Soprano. "This sucks," he said, pulling off his boots to reveal painful blisters. "I didn't know there was going to be this much walking."

Did the guy think there was elevator service to the top?

Paula and I laughed, not at the guy's misery, but at the stark contrast to her cheery disposition.

Somewhere between Mandara and Horombo Huts on the second day, I started to wonder if I was going to make it to the top.

The altitude at 9,000 feet started to affect me, and I was having a hard time catching my breath in the thin air. Paula was struggling, too, and the pain in my legs that I had been trying to ignore since Cairo returned like an unwanted houseguest. The slope became steeper as we scrambled over lava ledges. The air was colder. To keep warm, I was forced to pull out my sweater, then gloves, and finally, my hat.

Dinner that night was chicken, but neither Paula nor I ate it. She had witnessed its neck being snapped at the base of the mountain and didn't trust a 2-day-old meal. "I saw that chicken when it was alive," she said, reaching for the jar of peanut butter and crackers she had stashed in her bag. For my part, I'm a vegetarian. I unwrapped a PowerBar.

But at least the chicken was dead. The rats that scurried beneath our picnic table were very much alive and hungry.

We spent the night at Horombo Hut, 12,300 feet above sea level. The clouds were spread below our feet like dollops of whipped cream. It was ethereal, but all I wanted to do was go to bed.

Paula sensed my exhaustion. "I don't think we should run the marathon," she said.

"We'll see how I feel when we get off this mountain."

With the rats still vivid in Paula's head, she grabbed an upper bunk. I took the one below and fell asleep in minutes. Cold wood slats never felt better.

The next morning we departed for Kibo Hut, where we would rest a few hours before attempting to summit. Each step was a struggle, and I had developed a rash. I thought it could be caused by brush scraping my bare legs, although I wasn't sure. I didn't want to ruin the trip for Paula, so I kept my mouth shut, but I knew something was terribly wrong with me.

The terrain was different here, as though we were on the moon or some windswept lunar crater. The dirt was red. There were no trees or grass, just rocks, and the going was slow. We didn't talk much, both of us focused on navigating the steep path to Kibo.

Paula could tell I was hurting. "Let's go back," she urged. "If we turn around now, we can make it to Horombo before sunset."

"No," I said. "The distance back is the same forward."

But I was not stupid enough to believe I could make it to the top. I told Paula that when we reached Kibo, I would rest, and she could make the push to the summit with the others.

She agreed, albeit reluctantly. "Take these," she said, handing me walking poles that I had teased her for bringing.

"Thanks," I muttered, angry at my body for failing me. Never before in my adult life had I needed someone to take care of me. It was a new experience, and I didn't like it.

Eight hours later we reached Kibo, and I immediately hit the sack. It was bitter cold, and there was no heat source. I was wearing everything I'd packed—a fleece pullover, wool tights, and a turtle-neck. I even slept with my balaclava on.

The group awoke at midnight to start the 6-hour journey to the summit. They wore headlamps to illuminate the path. As I sat up to wish Paula good luck, I noticed my vision was blurred. "I can't see out of my right eye," I said.

"What do you mean?" she said.

"I don't know. Everything is kind of blurry."

I stood up, pitched to the side, and fell down.

Paula ran to help me up. "Your face," she said. "It's drooping."

I tried to blink, but my right eye stayed open. Nothing moved on that side of my face. It was paralyzed.

"Maybe you were bitten by a spider," Paula said.

I was freaked out, really freaked out, and I wasn't buying her spider theory. "You go," I said. "I'll stay here until you get back. Then we'll walk down together."

"No," she said. "I'll stay here with you."

"That doesn't make sense," I said. "I don't want to leave until it's light out anyway, and I want to rest some more. You've come this far. It would be a shame if you didn't summit. I'll be fine."

Eventually she agreed and headed into the darkness with the others.

The next time I saw her she was nudging my shivering body. Paula had turned around at 17,500 feet after developing a severe headache from the altitude. She never made it to the summit.

"Let's go," she said, her voice thick with concern.

It was 7:00 a.m., and the sky was filled with a pink and orange glow.

We started walking down, but the lid of my right eye wouldn't close, and volcanic ash and red dust irritated my retina. My eyes wouldn't produce tears, and it felt as if my eyeball was shriveling like a November leaf. I covered it with the fleshy part of my palm, which helped relieve some of the eye pain, but I soon developed a throbbing headache.

A little while later we saw a porter wheeling a climber down the mountain in what looked like a jogging stroller. Porters not only carry supplies but also transport people to the bottom who get sick or can't make it on their own.

"We need to get you one of those," Paula said.

"I am not coming down the mountain in a baby stroller," I said, my pride clearly interfering with my better judgment.

I hadn't seen myself. I didn't pack a mirror, and Paula didn't have one, either. But she did tell me that I looked like Popeye with a squinty eye and slanting mouth.

"Is there any chance I resemble Clint Eastwood?" I asked. "Maybe a little?"

"No," she said.

Even the porters wanted no part of me. They were scared and thought I had been possessed by an evil spirit.

We made it down to Marangu Gate at the bottom of the mountain in just 9 hours, a trip that takes most climbers 2 days because they stop for the night. There wasn't much there—just an information booth, general store, and a few benches. With no public transportation, we had no choice but to hang out until our hotel shuttle showed up. We weren't alone. Two other climbers came back early, too. One was having trouble breathing, and the other had lost a few toenails scrambling up rocks on the ascent.

Paula made friends with the guy at the general store, and he jotted down the address and phone number of a local hospital. In return, he wanted her to send him some Madonna CDs. "Go here," he said.

A few hours later, the shuttle arrived, and we headed back to our hotel in Moshi, where we showered off 4 days of grit and stink. Then I collapsed on the bed, and Paula called a cab driver she had met at the orientation before the climb. As Americans, we commanded a certain interest among the locals hoping to earn some cash.

His name, he told us, was Ringo. It means "stick" in Swahili, he said, holding up his finger in case there was a problem in translation. We immediately thought of Ringo Starr and associated the name with drumsticks. He told us to call him if we had any problems.

Mayday, mayday, Ringo, and bring the band.

A little while later, he arrived in front of our hotel in a small blue car without a meter. He took one look at the scrap of paper scrawled with our destination and shook his head. "That place is no good," he said. "I know where to take you."

I didn't argue. Paula was calling the shots now. I was never one to be fussed over, and she knew it, but I was letting her take care of me because I no longer could. This unspoken admission worried us both.

Eventually, we arrived at the hospital, a one-room concrete outpost in the middle of nowhere. Steel bars guarded the pharmacy, and the nurses wore crisp white uniforms and stiff hats. They looked like characters in a Bugs Bunny cartoon, but there was something about their starched efficiency that instilled confidence.

Ringo asked Paula if we had money.

"I have a credit card," she said.

"They do not take credit cards," he said.

"How about American money?"

"No. You need Tanzania currency."

"But we don't have any."

"Come with me," Ringo said. "But do not tell anyone I am doing this. It is illegal."

While the doctor examined me, Ringo drove Paula through the back alleys of Moshi in search of black-market shillings. They arrived at a run-down garage on the outskirts of town. Inside, a large, wrinkled woman sat on a chicken crate. Paula handed her $200 in exchange for a wad of Tanzania shillings. The transaction complete, they returned to the hospital, where my doctor delivered his diagnosis.

"We have never seen anything like this," he said.

"What should I do?"

"Get to Nairobi as quickly as possible."

We took his advice and arrived in Nairobi 8 hours later, in the midst of a government-enforced lockdown.

George Yasso (left) and brother
Bart drink some beers in the yard of
their parents' home in Fountain Hill,
Pennsylvania, in 1976.

Chapter 2

BATTLING LYME DISEASE

Her screams pounded in my head with the force of a nail gun, making it feel like my brain would explode. She was only a child, an 8-year-old who had fallen out of an acacia tree and broken her arm, but she was shrieking like a banshee on the table next to mine at Nairobi Hospital. I felt sorry for her, but I wanted her to stop.

A day after getting off Mount Kilimanjaro, I was finally in a modern medical facility and about to be examined by a doctor trained in Western medicine. I was fortunate to be there. As our tour bus from Tanzania had crossed into Kenya at Namanga Gate, we were met by a chaotic carnival of peddlers, swindlers, and customs officials, which was disorienting enough, but then our driver received a call on the radio and made an announcement.

"Nairobi is under lockdown," he said of the frenetic city populated by 2 million people. "Once you arrive at your hotel, you cannot leave."

Apparently, this had been happening all summer. Kenyan president Daniel arap Moi had been cracking down on protesters demanding political reform, and sometimes the demonstrations turned violent. The night before, there had been an uprising.

This wasn't good, not only for the state of democracy but also for my health. I still had a fever, my one eyelid was frozen open, and the right side of my face drooped. The glands in my throat were so swollen that I hadn't eaten anything for 3 days. The doctor in Tanzania had said Nairobi Hospital was my best chance for figuring out what was wrong with me, and now I couldn't even get there. The lockdown may have been a regular occurrence in Kenya's capital, but it was my first brush with dissidence. I didn't know what to expect, but it wasn't this—darkened streets devoid of people or cars. The silence was eerie as the bus made its way to our hotel.

Once we arrived, Paula called a friend from Minnesota who had married an Indian from Kenya and was now living in Nairobi. The woman was a nurse by training, and she understood the severity of my situation. Because her in-laws were also well connected to the political elite, she was able to arrange for a cab to take us to the hospital, Nairobi's largest and most reputable. No exchange of cold cash for black-market shillings would be needed this time. Credit cards were accepted. The waiting room was gleaming white and clean, and even though there was a wait, I was immediately ushered into the emergency room and given a gurney next to the screaming girl.

A few minutes later, a doctor in a white coat pushed aside the curtain and looked at me. "How are you?" he asked.

"Not good. I have this weird rash, and my right eye won't close."

"You are an American?"

"Yes, from Pennsylvania. I'm a long way from home."

He could tell I was anxious and tried to put me at ease. "Do not worry," he said, peering at my disfigured face. "We have some of the best doctors on the continent here." Still, he looked puzzled. "I want a neurologist to look at you."

A short while later, another doctor came by to examine me. I explained my symptoms, and he did a quick check of my reflexes. My right side was noticeably weaker, as if the paralysis had spread to my lower extremities.

"You have Bell's palsy," he said, explaining the reason for my facial paralysis. "I do not know what's causing it or why you have a fever and rash. But I do know that whatever it is, you didn't contract it in Africa."

"What should I do?" I asked.

"I strongly recommend that you return to the United States as soon as possible. "

My flight wasn't scheduled to leave for another 5 days, but the doctor believed it was imperative I get on the next plane home. "If you can't, we will treat you here," he said. "We will do what we can. We are not throwing you out the door."

I appreciated the offer, but I, too, felt the best place for me was back home. Paula and I rushed back to our hotel, grabbed our bags, and headed to the airport.

As I stood in line to change the return date of my ticket, I started talking to the guy in front of me. He noticed I couldn't blink. Turned out he was an ophthalmologist.

"You should tape your eye shut," he said. "That way you won't get dirt in it and damage your cornea."

He also assured me that 90 percent of people who develop Bell's palsy make a full recovery. His intent was to cheer me up, but it had the opposite effect; I felt sure I was among the 10 percent.

When I reached the airline counter, I asked the reservation attendant for a piece of tape.

"Sure," she said, handing me the dispenser.

I ripped off several pieces and bandaged my eye. I must have looked strange, because other passengers avoided me and tried hard not to stare. But I understood why they did. It's not every day that you see a guy with Scotch tape plastered over half his face.

It was an 8-hour flight from Nairobi to Cairo, then another 12 hours to JFK International Airport in New York. I was too worried to sleep on the plane, so I put on my Walkman and listened to my Bruce Springsteen tape. A dose of the Boss always did me good.

Paula sat next to me but said little, too exhausted by the ordeal.

When we arrived at JFK, my savior Paula escorted me to the cabstand, where we hugged good-bye. She needed to board another plane for Minneapolis, and I was heading for the Port Authority Bus Terminal. I planned to take a bus home to Bethlehem, Pennsylvania, a 1½-hour ride.

I slipped into a cab and told the driver to take me to Port Authority. But halfway there, I had a change of heart and asked the driver to instead head downtown to the satellite office of Rodale, the parent company of *Runner's World*. I thought the sight of a familiar face would ease my rising panic. The first person I saw when I got there was George Hirsch, the magazine's publisher and a good friend who treated me like his own son.

"Bart," he said, "you look terrible! Let me take you to a hospital."

"No," I said. "I'm going home."

"Well, how are you getting there? Let me call you a cab."

"I'm going to take the bus," I said. "It'll be quicker."

Then I called my older brother, George, who told me a bus was leaving for Bethlehem in the next half hour. "Get on it, and I'll pick you up," he said.

I staggered out the door. Port Authority was only about a mile away, but it was rush hour, and I couldn't find a cab. I started to walk but quickly grew tired from lugging my backpack, which weighed at least 40 pounds. I considered ditching it. It contained clothes and toiletries, stuff I could easily replace, but for some reason I hung on to it. Secretly, I had always wanted to be a Sherpa. I liked the idea of carrying heavy bags up and down mountains. During hikes with my girlfriend, Marty Eddy, I would sometimes stuff my backpack with rocks to increase the load. I had no interest in being a Sherpa right now, though. I could barely walk a straight line. I focused on the cracks in the sidewalks, counting each one I passed. Sweat rolled down my face and pooled in the hollow of my rash-stained back.

I made the bus with just minutes to spare and collapsed in the seat. I closed my eyes but couldn't sleep.

When the bus arrived in Bethlehem, George was waiting. He gasped at the sight of me. "Come on, get in the car," he said. "We'll go to the hospital and get everything straightened out. Don't worry; I'll take care of you."

I didn't mind letting him take charge. I never did. He was the ultimate big brother. The second oldest of seven siblings, George was more of a father figure to me than my real dad, a stern disciplinarian whose expectations I could never quite meet. We raced to Saint Luke's Hospital in Fountain Hill, Pennsylvania, and once again I found myself on a cold table, wearing a green paper gown.

I repeated my story of fever, fatigue, joint pain, and paralysis, hoping someone could give me a prognosis that didn't involve "worst-case scenario, you have 2 months to live."

"The doctor in Kenya doesn't think I got this in Africa," I told the new doctor.

"Don't be so sure," he said. "It could be anything. You've done a lot of traveling to remote places."

They drew vials of blood. Then they admitted me for the night so they could insert an IV and rehydrate me.

The next day, the doctor explained what had caused the Bell's palsy. "You have Lyme disease," he said, handing me a paper cup containing two pills, the first of many antibiotics I'd be ingesting over the next few weeks.

My Kenyan doctor had been right. Lyme disease is an infection spread by deer ticks, and there aren't any in Africa. I had probably been bitten while running the trails of eastern Pennsylvania or walking through the fields of the 200-acre farm in Virginville, Berks County, where I lived.

I was released from the hospital the next day with strict orders to rest. My Lyme disease had advanced to the second stage because I had waited too long before receiving medical attention. My high pain threshold was the culprit. I hadn't been feeling well for months but had ignored my symptoms, preferring to tough it out rather than seek help. Still, I felt lucky. Not much was known about Lyme disease at the time, and many people were misdiagnosed. At least my ailment now had a name and my girlfriend had its number. Marty spent the next few days pulling recipes from holistic cookbooks in hopes of restoring my strength with organic meals.

Marty's cooking, combined with the meds and rest, must have jump-started my recovery. I began feeling a little better on the third day home, so I decided to ride my bike to work, a 25-mile one-way trip to *Runner's World* headquarters in Emmaus, Pennsylvania. I hadn't been there for 3 weeks, and I missed the place. I have the coolest job in the world, and I thought the commotion of the office would distract me from my discomfort. I was going stir-crazy sitting at home, and I knew my voice mail and the inbox of my email were piling up with messages from race directors around the country who relied on me for *Runner's World* sponsorship of their events, ensuring they received goodie bags, pace charts, and bib numbers.

The morning was overcast, but I decided to take a chance that it wouldn't rain. For the first time in over a month, I climbed on my bike and started pedaling on the winding roads. Soon, it started to rain—not a light misting but heavy drops that blinded my one good eye. I still couldn't close the other one, and it was patched anyway. Soon I couldn't see beyond my handlebars, so I stopped to wait out the storm beneath someone's garage overhang.

Two hours later I arrived at work, soaked and shaking like a mangy dog.

"What the hell are you doing here?" asked Amby Burfoot, executive editor of the magazine.

"You look like crap," deputy editor Bob Wischnia chimed in.

"Nice to see you, too," I said.

"How did you get here?" Amby asked.

"I rode my bike."

"You did what? Are you nuts?"

I didn't answer. I wasn't feeling well, so I just walked past them, entered my office, and closed the door. It felt good to be back. It was where I belonged. Staying home felt like defeat. I had already beaten drugs, alcohol, and aimlessness. Lyme disease was not going to keep me down. Sitting at my desk on a rainy Wednesday was the best tonic in the world. The only way I could stay positive about the outcome of my illness was to keep busy and stick to my normal routine. Only then could I believe things would be okay.

Later that morning, as I was listening to numerous messages on my office phone, Amby walked in to remind me that before I had left for Africa, I had agreed to lead the fastest pace team at the Chicago Marathon. The race was 13 weeks away. "I don't want you to do it," he said. "I'm going to send someone else. You're off the hook."

"No way," I said. "I can do it. It will force me to get back in shape."

He shook his head and walked away. He knew better than to argue with me, especially about a physical challenge. I could tell he was worried, not only about my health but also about the runners who counted on me to lead them to a 3-hour finish. This was only the third time in race history that pacers would be used to lead runners in a marathon to a desired finish. It was a runner's version of cruise control. Amby came up with the idea of using *Runner's World* pace teams 2 years before to get as many runners as possible at the St. George Marathon in Utah qualified for Boston. Our staff acted as pacers the following year at the Dallas Marathon, and the magazine received so much praise from runners that we decided to do it again for the popular Chicago Marathon.

But pacers couldn't screw up. They had to finish under the desired time so runners in their group would hit their goal.

Amby had good cause to worry. I had lost 15 pounds since leaving for Africa, most of it muscle, as I had very little body fat to begin with. Plus, I hadn't trained for about a month.

I tried to run later that week but only made it one mile before collapsing in a heap of misery. My joints ached with such ferocity it felt as if someone had injected battery acid into my bones and then lit a match. It suddenly occurred to me that I might never run again. Lyme disease causes arthritis, especially in the knees; chronic muscle pain; memory loss; and concentration difficulties.

Running was my livelihood. It gave me focus and a direction I hadn't found in any other pursuit. My brothers were star athletes on the football field and basketball court. They made my father proud, and he showered them with an affection he had never shown me. I was a scrawny teen who didn't excel at sports. I wasn't good at school. In eighth grade, I was expelled from Saint Ursula's Catholic Grade School for being a troublemaker and sent to public school. I graduated from Liberty High School in Bethlehem, but barely. Dull textbooks and the strict confines of the classroom didn't interest me. I preferred cigarettes, booze, and dope, although I got high only once in my life: from 1970 to 1977.

Then I discovered running. It rescued me from my demons and gave my father a reason to be proud. We were never close, but I still craved his respect.

Now there was a chance my gift of late-blooming athleticism would be taken away by a tiny deer tick. I became depressed and decided that if I had any shot of recovery, I would have to take it easy and rest like the doctor had ordered. I started marking off the days on the calendar until I finished the antibiotics and could once again lace up my running shoes.

My plan worked. After 3 weeks, I started feeling like my old self again, and the inflammation in my joints subsided. Still, I took it slow, running 2 or 3 easy miles every other day. My body quickly responded to the familiar motion, and I regained my endurance. Just to make sure I was ready for Chicago, I ran the Oley 10-miler in Berks County, Pennsylvania, in under an hour, posting sub-6-minute miles. I was back!

The Chicago Marathon is one of the largest races in the United States, attracting elite athletes from around the world and amateurs of all stripes. In 1997, 16,000 runners registered for the marathon, a number that grew to 45,000 in 2007.

The race expo opened at a fancy downtown hotel 2 days before the Sunday marathon, and the 3,000 runners who had signed up for a pace group were invited to meet their leaders at one of two sessions. The idea was to instill confidence in the pacers' ability to bring the runners across the finish line at a predetermined time.

Since I would be leading the 3-hour marathoners, the fastest group, Amby, who was master of ceremonies, started with me. I expected a brief introduction before he handed me the microphone, but I was wrong.

"Thirteen weeks ago, Bart was so sick he couldn't walk to the copier," he said. "He had a fever that lasted 3 weeks, and he was blind in one eye!"

"What is he doing?" I whispered to Adam Bean, who was managing editor of *Runner's World* at the time and the 3:10 pace leader.

"I don't know," he said, "but no one's going to want to run with you. They're going to bail before the race."

"Dude, tell me about it."

Amby continued his sermon on my miracle comeback. "He was

really sick, and no one thought he would ever run again, especially me, but here he is, leading the fastest pace group," he said. "It's unbelievable."

This was his idea of confidence building?

Amby handed me the microphone, and I stared out into the slack-jawed faces of the 150 men and women who had signed up for the 3-hour pace group. The room was completely silent.

"Okay, everything Amby just told you is true, but I know I can do this on Sunday," I said. "We're going to have a perfect race."

I don't think Amby realized he was creating anxiety in the runners, many of whom desperately wanted to run a sub-3-hour marathon so they could qualify for Boston. He was just amazed by and proud of my resilience. Afterward, I asked him to tone down the intro for the next day's session.

"But I want people to know what you've gone through to get here," he said. "It's inspiring."

"Maybe if I was the 5-hour pace leader," I said, "but these guys don't want to be inspired. They want results. They're scared I'm not going to make it to the start line, let alone the finish."

"Okay," said Amby. "I'll see what I can do."

It wasn't much because the next day he didn't leave out a single detail: "He was paralyzed, he couldn't see—give it up for your pace leader, Bart Yasso."

Adam and I rolled our eyes. I've always said Amby is a genius, but his IQ suddenly must have dropped a few points. His behavior was so out of character. Amby is a serious guy. He spent time in the Peace Corps in El Salvador, and as a public speaker, his demeanor was reminiscent of a slightly stodgy college professor. Yet here he was recounting my return from what he described as near death with the zeal of a revivalist preacher.

Except that none of the congregants assigned to my group were impressed. Concerned? Yes, just not about my health.

"Dude, are you sure you can run 2:59:30? Because I have to break 3 hours," one runner asked. "It's my lifetime goal."

"Don't worry," I said. "Running is my job, and Sunday will be just another day at the office for me."

But well-meaning Amby had shaken my confidence. I went to bed that night doubting my abilities. Adam, who was leading the 3:10 pace group, offered to switch pace teams. "Are you up for this?" he asked.

One of *Runner's World's* rules is that pace leaders must be in shape to run the marathon 15 minutes faster than their assigned race-time finish. That meant as the 3-hour pace leader, I had to be in shape to run a 2:45 marathon so I would have enough wind power to "coach, entertain, and encourage" the other runners along the way. But was I? I had thought so before the weekend, but now I wasn't so sure.

I didn't get much sleep that night.

It was sunny and cool the next day, perfect weather for a marathon. My group and I gathered at the start line. I programmed my watch to beep every 6 minutes 51 seconds, our per-mile pace time.

The first mile we hit it on the nose.

"You the man," came the chorus from behind.

We arrived at the second mile 2 seconds off pace. The gang groaned. "You're going too slow," they yelled.

"Relax," I told them. "We have 24 more miles to go. I think we can make up 2 seconds."

And we did. From there on out, our splits varied between 6:50 and 6:51. I didn't stop for water, holding the middle of the road as if I were leading a flock of geese south for the winter.

The pack had thinned by mile 23, but we were still 75 strong, and our feet pounded the road like drums. We were catching runners who'd started out too fast, engulfing them in our mass and then passing them in a final surge toward the finish. But the last

3 miles of any marathon are all about guts and inner strength. Training, adrenaline, and a dependable pace leader can only take you so far.

"All right, guys," I told them. "Everyone in this race is hurting. You have to mentally stick it out the next few miles. The pain you have now is temporary, but the memory of breaking 3 hours will last the rest of your life."

Then I threw out some of my favorite aphorisms for good measure.

"Run on the edge of death."

"Lay it on the line."

"Run until you puke."

No one did, but a few runners sped up.

One mile before the finish, it became apparent we would make our goal time. Suddenly, I was everybody's best friend, and promises of massage certificates, rounds of golf, and Caribbean vacations were proffered in gratitude.

Then it was over. I had crossed in 2:59:30, just like I said I would. A few runners shook my hand, but the majority got caught up in the moment of cheering fans, finishers' medals, and photos with friends.

I was *so* last mile.

I had done it but at a price. My vision was blurry and my legs throbbed—symptoms of Lyme disease—so I popped a few aspirin for the joint pain. It had been fun helping people reach their marathon goal time, but I vowed the next race would be for me. I had gone through too much since Mount Kilimanjaro to let other people's goals define my relationship with the sport.

I chose the Smoky Mountain Marathon in Tennessee as my next race. I had always wanted to run along the ridgeline of the Smokies and decided a trip there in February 1998 would make a nice vacation. I picked this course for its scenery, not because I wanted to post a fast time. Those days were over.

In some ways, getting sick was a blessing. I had taken running for granted or at least put too much emphasis on the wrong things. I had never won a race of the mythical 26.2-mile distance, and at the age of 43, I probably never would. It was time to appreciate the sweaty exertion for what it was—an affirmation of life. Running was magic, and I never wanted to lose my ability to conjure up that altered state again. In my teens and early twenties, I had turned to alcohol and pot for sanctuary, but running had replaced those vices. I had traded addiction for a healthy lifestyle, and it held me tight in my dependence.

So I slowed things down. I trained hard but not as often, and some days I left my watch at home. I started noticing the foliage along the running trails of Lehigh Parkway in Allentown, Pennsylvania. It was the end of October, and the leaves glowed amber and red. I kicked the crumbled leaves that huddled in piles along the path, thinking they were an apt metaphor for my once fragile state. It was a thought that carried me through the snows of winter until February's first thaw.

I decided to drive the 10 hours to Knoxville, Tennessee. Flying reminded me of work, and I was on vacation. At dinner later that night, I met some guys from Michigan who had driven the marathon course to get a feel for the terrain. "It's going to be tough," one said. "There's a monster hill at mile 21."

The old Bart would have been out the next day measuring the grade of the incline and monitoring the Weather Channel for wind speeds. The remainder of the day would have been spent resting my dogs in bed, but this was the new me. I went hiking instead.

It was misty and cool the next morning, about 56°F. The first part of the course was an out-and-back loop along country roads with the majestic Smokies veiled by the clouds. I crossed the start line near the front of the pack and settled into a 6:20-minute-per-mile pace. There were about 10 runners in front of me, but I didn't try to pass them. I held pat, conserving my energies for the hill. Without a conscious effort, I began passing runners one by one until mile 20, where I took the lead. The only one in front of me was a Tennessee state trooper, and he was eating a doughnut while driving the lead vehicle.

Then came the hill. I didn't slow my stride, and by the time I crested it, the closest runner was several minutes behind. I felt triumphant, not only because I was in the lead but also because I was running fast on a tough course. The last 3 miles were a blur, a cinematic screening of the past year's struggles. Scenes of writhing in pain after attempting to run, struggling to stand from my office chair, and enduring acupuncture for facial paralysis flashed through my head.

All that was behind me and now, at the age of 43, I was poised to win my first marathon. A few months earlier, this day had never seemed possible, but running is the ultimate faith healer, restoring belief not only in oneself but life's possibilities.

The first thing I did when I crossed the finish line was call Bob Wischnia. "I won the Smoky Mountain Marathon!" I said.

"You won your age group?" he asked.

"No, the race."

"What do you mean you won the race?'

"I was the guy behind the cop car. They call that the overall winner."

"No kidding," he said.

No kidding indeed. I had been deluding myself for years that the purpose of running was to win races, that if I trained hard enough and smart enough and pushed my body beyond all limits, I'd somehow come out on top. It took finally winning a race to expose the flaws of my logic.

Winning is a nice reward—don't get me wrong—but glory isn't the payoff. This may sound cliché, but the reward is living the lifestyle and embracing the journey. It's not only about finishing, it's about moving forward. It was a lesson I took to heart, and I was glad I did.

Little did I know a more devastating bout of Lyme disease would strike 3 years later, forcing me once again to redefine myself and my love for the sport.

Bart as a fifth-grader at Saint Ursula's Catholic Grade School in Fountain Hill, Pennsylvania

Bart and his father, George F. Yasso,
after the Boston Marathon, 1982

Chapter 3

GETTING STARTED

Standing in the doorway of his hospital room, I could see my best friend since grade school, Michael Johnson, lying in a coma with tubes sprouting from his bandaged form. His parents sat by his side and his mother stroked his hand as the heart monitor emitted a steady beep, beep, beep.

Days before, on Christmas Eve, he had walked out of a bar at closing time, stepped off the curb into a busy street, and been hit by a car. He wasn't expected to make a full recovery. His bones were broken, his brain was bleeding, and his breath was shallow.

He was only 22.

It could have been me.

I started drinking large quantities of beer and Boone's Farm apple wine in the woods as a freshman at Bethlehem Catholic High School in Pennsylvania in 1970. We smoked weed there, too, usually before school, and cigarettes in the bathroom between classes.

I grew up on the gritty streets of Fountain Hill, a small borough outside Bethlehem, where the hulking form of the steel mill stood like a behemoth against the skyline. Everybody's father, uncle, and grandfather toiled in the mill, turning hot molten steel into I-beams and H-beams destined for the Chrysler Building in New York, the Golden Gate Bridge in California, and US battleships. My father was eventually promoted to foreman, and the money was good enough to support our large family.

But no one worked harder than my mother, Rose Marie Yasso. She had her hands full with seven kids, yet she made everyone who visited our home feel welcome and always offered to set an extra place at dinner even if she had to add more water to the soup. Our two-bedroom house was the neighborhood hub and I thought everyone wanted to live with us. Kids played ball in the street out front, hung out on our porch, and watched TV in our living room. Mom served Kool-Aid, broke up squabbles, and bandaged scraped knees. It was controlled chaos, and I felt like the luckiest kid alive, even though I shared a bedroom with three of my brothers—a bedroom so small that there was only room for two sets of bunk beds and not much else. The space was so tiny that if you left your jeans on the floor, there was no way to avoid stepping on them when it was time to hit the sack.

I started working at an early age not so I could buy clothes or sneakers or baseball cards, but because I enjoyed being productive and self-sufficient. When I was 9, I set up shop at the local country club as a "creek boy" and retrieved wayward golf balls from a stream. Golfers sometimes tipped me as much as 25 cents for my efforts. On good days I earned $1.

I graduated to caddy three years later, shouldering bags almost as heavy as my 65-pound self on weekends and warm days after school. It was worth the sore back and shoulders because caddies often earned $20 a day, a huge sum to a 7th grader in 1967. I also took on a paper route, rising at 4:00 a.m. every day to deliver newspapers to 60 families in my hilly neighborhood. I saved my loot, hoarding the shiny coins and crumpled bills in a glass jar.

Eventually, I had enough for a car, and when I turned 17 I bought my brother Gerry's 1968 Cougar XR7 and a motorcycle.

My adolescence arrived just as the psychedelic '60s finally made their way to the sleepy Lehigh Valley and student protests of the Vietnam War dominated the news. Older boys in my blue-collar neighborhood had been drafted, and everyone worried whom the war would claim next.

But that's not why I got high and drank and goofed off in class. As best as I can surmise, I was rebelling against my detached father, who mustered affection only for his sons who excelled on the athletic fields. I hadn't yet shown any talent for running.

It wasn't easy being the unexceptional middle child of seven. My oldest sister, Anne Marie, was the brain who earned straight A's. Then there was George, the embodiment of the brother in the movie *It's a Wonderful Life*. A scholar athlete, he got a full ride to Hofstra University in New York to play football. Gerry was a menace on the football field and basketball court. Born after me was Tommy, who died of spina bifida when he was 2 years old. I don't remember much from those years, just spending a lot of time in the playroom at Children's Hospital of Philadelphia while my weary mother sat teary-eyed at my brother's bedside.

The second youngest, James, earned an unusual nickname. As a child he begged to have his head shaved. My father agreed, and when he turned off the electric razor, James looked like Mr. Potato Head. We started calling him Spud, and the name stuck. He hasn't gone by James in at least 40 years. Then there was Mimi, my adorable baby sister.

I was short and skinny, with arms as thin as bamboo reeds. I got cut from my sixth-grade basketball team and 2 years later was asked to leave St. Ursula's for being disruptive and doing drugs.

I was the runt of the litter and, in the eyes of my hardworking Slovakian father, a failure. He never spoke those words, but it was evident, at least to me. I was never asked to join my brothers when my father took them golfing or to Philadelphia for baseball games. The man barely said two words to me, nor would he refer to me by my real name. He called me Alice, in reference to Alice Cooper, the heavy metal rocker, whose hair was as long as mine. I felt invisible.

So I drifted, retreating into an alcoholic haze until I turned 18, when I moved out of our twin home. I took the first job I could get, delivering shampoo, soap, and assorted sundries to area pharmacies for Allen Drug Company. I never drank or did drugs during work hours, but once I punched out the party started. All night long, people would stream in and out of the apartment I shared with my girlfriend. I routinely drank a half case of Pabst Blue Ribbon beer while smoking a bong until the wee hours of the morning.

Starting at age 14, I got drunk every day. I refused to acknowledge it at the time, but I was an alcoholic and a dope head.

Then I got busted. It happened after I drove a friend to buy marijuana from a dealer who turned out to be an undercover narcotics agent. We were arrested the next day at our places of employment, transported to the police station, booked, and fingerprinted. I was released without bail but charged with being a co-conspirator, even though I hadn't bought any drugs. A few months later, I appeared before Lehigh County Judge Lee Koch, better known as the hanging judge.

I wanted to plead not guilty, but my lawyer convinced me to plead guilty, saying the judge might show me some mercy. He didn't. Koch sentenced me to 2 years' probation and a $500 fine. My friend received a stiffer penalty and spent some time in county jail.

If relations between my father and me were difficult before, they grew far worse after my arrest. He refused to have anything to do with me. I'm sure he wished I would run away and disassociate myself from the family—or at least change my last name. Mine isn't exactly a common surname, so when news of my brush with the law made its way through our small town, everyone knew I was the son of George Yasso, Sr. I had embarrassed him once again. My status as the black sheep of the family was secure.

Being arrested scared the crap out of me. I knew if I ever got charged with a drug-related offense again, I'd end up in jail. I never wanted that address, so I stopped smoking pot. To compensate, I drank more. Much more.

Four years later, I watched my friend Mike, whose life had been so much like mine, from the safety of the hospital door frame. I stopped binge drinking and let a dog called Brandy, ironically enough, be my savior. Brandy was my girlfriend's dog, a rambunctious collie that needed a lot of exercise. I started taking her for walks through the woods, and when we arrived in a clearing, she'd take off like a rocket. I envied the sense of freedom and joy she derived from bounding through the grass. One day, I decided to try it myself. I ran a half mile to a local bar called the Zoo before collapsing on a stool. I downed two beers to celebrate, then walked home. I considered the jaunt a success and marveled at my willpower to leave before closing hour.

I continued to walk Brandy after work each night and run on my own. One morning as I was driving to the grocery store for milk and a newspaper, I spotted an old friend from grade school, Dick Metzger, running in the rain. It was 5 a.m. *Now that's dedication,* I thought.

I started following his regimen, rising early every morning to log 3 miles before work. I struggled at first. My lungs burned from smoking two packs of cigarettes a day, and my legs felt like cinder blocks. But gradually it got easier, and I began to relish the peace and stillness of dawn. These runs became a form of therapy, a time to sweat and breathe and disconnect from the distractions of life.

George supported my new healthy lifestyle by inviting me to join him in road races. He understood the redemptive powers of athletics and recognized the potential of my inner athlete, even when I didn't. I always said no to his offers. For me, running represented recovery, and I didn't need the hullabaloo of a race to crash my serenity.

But then George got tricky. He issued a challenge, thinking I wouldn't be able to resist a chance to beat my older brother. "Let's race," he said one day. "I'll bet I'll kick your ass."

"There's no way you would win," I said, intrigued. "You're built like a linebacker and I'm built like a runner, and linebackers don't beat runners in distance races."

"Does this mean you'll race me?"

"Sure," I said, "if only to teach you a lesson."

On a hot June Saturday later that month, we stood side by side at the Moore Township 10-K, trying to outdo one another in trash talk, the universal language of brothers.

Bang! The gun went off and I blasted forward, posting a 5:20 pace for the first mile. I quickly found myself near the front of the pack with George. *I must be in better shape than I thought,* I said to myself. *This is a piece of cake.*

And it was—until mile 2, when I thought I was going to puke. I developed a side stitch at mile 3 and was reduced to a jog. George, who had only been a few yards in front of me, quickly pulled away. Eventually, the stitch subsided and I was able to regain a good pace, but I never did catch George. Twenty minutes later I crossed the finish line thinking I had failed. I was humiliated, humbled, and hurting. So much for my theory that body type influences success at distance running.

But when the results were posted, I had done better than I

thought, finishing 40th out of 240. I was shocked. Maybe I did have an inner athlete, and with proper training and better pacing, I could coax it out.

I called my brother the next day.

"I want a rematch."

"Anytime, Bart."

It was on.

I was tired of being the runt.

I picked up a copy of *The Complete Book of Running,* by Jim Fixx, who is credited with popularizing running as a sport that even an out-of-shape former party animal could do. I also bought *Runner's World* magazine and studied its coverage of training techniques. I ran sprints to build speed, stretched my hamstrings and calves to discourage injury, and learned the secrets of pacing so I wouldn't crash and burn midrace.

Three weeks later, on a humid Sunday in July at a 10-K in Easton, Pennsylvania, the rematch went down. I kept the trash talk to a minimum. I had gained confidence in my abilities, but I also knew George was a worthy competitor.

This time I started slower, marshaling my strength until mile 5, where I passed George. I saw his blue shorts from the corner of my eye as I surged ahead. I didn't look back. At the finish line, we shook hands.

"Good job," George said. "You smoked me."

He knew my win was less about beating him and more about the rejection of my former life. I had purpose, and I embraced it with the gratefulness of a drowning man being thrown a life preserver.

"I really think you can take your running to the next level," George said later that day. "You have the ability, but it's going to take a lot of hard work. It's all up to you."

His words ignited a fire, and I set a marathon as my next goal. The following year I ran a 3:13 at the *Prevention* Marathon in Bethlehem.

Two months later, I lopped 6 minutes from my finish time at a marathon in Long Island, New York. I felt as if there was nothing I couldn't do.

So I put the daddy of all marathons, Boston, in my sights, but to qualify at the age of 25 I would have to run a 2:50. That meant I'd have to shave 17 minutes off my fastest marathon time. I upped my weekly mileage from 60 to 90, with a 20-mile run on Saturdays. I also started to lift weights.

In the fall of 1981, I ran the marathon in Philadelphia, home to the fictional Rocky Balboa, who by this time had become an American icon. During filming of the original movie, Sylvester Stallone runs through the Italian Market on South Ninth Street, passing tables topped with fruits and vegetables on a wintry morning. In an unscripted scene, a vendor throws Stallone an apple and he catches it. The marathon course threaded through the Italian Market at mile 23, and I couldn't wait to follow in Rocky's footstep. Surely, the vendors would be out cheering us on and blaring Rocky's theme song, "Gonna Fly Now," from boom boxes.

The vendors were out all right, but they weren't cheering. They were booing and hurling lettuce and tomatoes at us. The streets had been closed for the race, and the vendors were angry that their regular customers couldn't get through. Instead of a crowd giving me a much-needed boost 3 miles from the finish, the only jolt I got was from a flying head of lettuce to the arm.

I was on target to run a 2:50 race, but I knew I'd have to nearly kill myself the last mile. A few years ago, Boston was an unimaginable dream, and now here I was poised to qualify. *Just hang on, Bart,* I thought. *A little farther. Boston will be worth this temporary pain.*

I can see the finish line.

2:49:20.

My heart is going to explode.

2:49:49.

I can't feel my legs.

2:49:55.

I'm going to puke.

2:50:27.

I see my dad in the crowd.

2:50:56.

I crossed the finish line and made my goal by the smallest of seconds. I qualified for Boston. I punched the air with my fist.

I am so happy.

After catching my breath and drinking a bottle of water, I walked over to my dad, who had driven me to the race.

"How come you didn't win, Bart?" he asked. "You should have won."

"Did you just call me Bart?"

"It's your name, isn't it?"

"Yeah, but you've never called me that before."

"You can do better," he said. "You're going to have to step it up."

The Boston Marathon of 1982 will always be remembered as the Duel in the Sun, an epic test of Herculean will between hometown hero Alberto Salazar and Minnesota farm boy Dick Beardsley. Entire books have been written about this odyssey. It had all the elements of a Coen Brothers film; there was the kooky fan who tried to stuff dollar bills down the shorts of Salazar and Beardsley as they ran by, a pothole that Beardsley credits with freeing a muscle cramp after he stepped in it, and an inspiring sprint to the finish in which Beardsley was cut off by a motorcycle cop.

Salazar won by 2 seconds but collapsed at the finish and was taken to the hospital. He was dehydrated after not drinking for 26.2 miles.

I was about 50 minutes behind those guys, overwhelmed by

the heat and sights of Boston. But the race has a different significance for me. My parents, 83-year-old grandmother, and my younger sister, Mimi, were standing somewhere along Boylston Street. This was the first time the family had come to watch their middle son. I met up with them after the race, but it was not exactly a celebration.

My mother hugged me. "Congratulations," she said.

"Where the hell were you?" my dad said. "We didn't see you."

"I wasn't as fast as I thought I was going to be," I said. "The heat really weighed me down. But I gave it my best effort. Sometimes you have to be happy with that."

"I thought I told you step it up," he said.

Even though I did as well as I could, I knew what my mistake had been. I never trained during the middle of the day when the sun was hottest. I always ran in the morning before work, and then again at night. The Boston Marathon began at noon that year, and temperatures soared to 70°F by midday.

My father harbored unrealistic expectations for me, but on one level, he was right; I could do better. So I hooked up with Budd Coates, a 2:13 marathoner who had qualified for the men's Olympic Marathon trials four times. He was the director of fitness and health at Rodale and lived a few towns over. He knew his stuff, and on Wednesday nights he led a small group of us up hills, around college tracks, and through dirt trails. Becoming a successful runner takes more than training 2 or 3 hours a day, Coates said. It's a lifestyle that requires 24/7 dedication. From Coates I learned the importance of nutrition, rest and recovery, stretching, cross-training, weight training, and how to peak for a race. You must act like a runner, Coates said, even when you aren't running.

I took his message to heart, and in 1983 I ran a 2:40 at Boston, 19 minutes faster than the year before.

I called my parents that night.

"Did you win?" my father asked.

"Not this time."

"You need to train harder."

In 1985, Rodale purchased *Runner's World* and moved its operations to Emmaus, Pennsylvania, transforming the Lehigh Valley into a running mecca and attracting top editors, writers, and experts in the sport to the area. The Lehigh Valley's ribbons of scenic trails added to its reputation and encouraged an explosive growth in local running. I became vice president of the Lehigh Valley Road Runners, a local running club, and started organizing races that were always well attended.

I was still working as a pharmacy delivery boy, and that was fine with me. The 8-to-5 job paid the bills and gave me time to train, which I needed, considering the depth of talent in the Lehigh Valley. Case in point: Out of 4,000 runners at a New York City race, I would routinely come in 15th, but at a local 10-K, I had to fight to place 8th out of 300 runners.

Around this time, I started hanging out with a guy named Jeffrey Timm, who introduced me to the duathlon, a sport that combines running and bike riding. Timm was hard-core, and I had to pedal like a maniac just to keep up with him. I still ran, but I liked the diversity of the duathlon and started competing in races. In 1986, I did about 20 duathlons and in each one placed in the top five.

In 1987, I won the prestigious US Biathlon Association Long Course Championship at Harriman State Park, 30 miles north of New York City. The race started as a 6-mile run, followed by a 45-mile bike ride, and then another 6 miles on foot. I took the lead in the bike portion and held on to it at the start of the second run, but I kept hearing the footfalls of competitors behind me. I didn't know how many there were, but it sounded like a lot, so I went faster. I didn't realize that I was alone in front until I reached an orange cone representing the turnaround mark. The pounding of feet was all in my head, an echo of past races.

Breaking the tape at the finish line was exhilarating and unexpected. So was receiving a call from *Sports Illustrated* the next day. "I already get the magazine," I told the caller.

"I don't want to sell you a subscription—I want to do a story on you."

"Me? I think you have the wrong number."

"Did you win the Long Course championship yesterday?"

"I did! Right. That's me. I won."

I won.

I called my dad. "I won the Long Course championship, and *Sports Illustrated* is going to do a story on me," I said.

"Congratulations, Bart," he said. "I'm really proud of you,"

I now realized he had always had my best interests at heart. I was an underachiever by nature, and my father knew I was capable of more. With my athletic pursuits hitting new heights, I had finally gained his acceptance.

Plus, he was mellowing in his old age and relishing his role as grandfather to my nine nieces and nephews; we called him Pop Pop.

I'd also attracted the attention of *Runner's World* executives, who were looking for someone to work with race directors around the country, a sort of liaison between the magazine and the running community.

At 31, I was ready to stop coasting and start focusing on a career. With the help of my friend Budd Coates, I got the job. This is what it entailed: *Runner's World* would provide race bibs and bags to race directors, who in turn would supply the magazine with addresses of participants, whom we would target to sell new subscriptions. I would also represent the magazine at races around the country and brainstorm creative ideas for generating new revenue streams. I knew it was the opportunity of a lifetime, entry into the ivory tower of running, and I wasn't going to screw it up. I didn't want anyone to regret hiring a former lowlife who'd barely made it through high school. I vowed to be not only the hardest-working employee at *Runner's World* or Rodale, but also the hardest-working person in the running industry.

The first year my boss gave me a goal of procuring 250,000 names of potential subscribers. I secured one million names by creating the *Runner's World* Race Sponsorship Program.

The next year I upped those numbers to four million runners and 7,000 races. I also created revenue streams from companies such as Kellogg's and Breathe Right, who paid to have their names splashed across bib numbers.

As part of my job, I went to race expos, where I conducted seminars, solicited runners' opinions of the magazine, and engaged people in conversation about the sport. Runners considered me an expert and sought out my opinions on everything from what type of shoes to wear to what to eat the night before a race.

It was a new role for me. I had always been the student, the one in the background taking notes. Now I was being cast as a teacher, and I knew I had to tackle my fear of public speaking with the same determination I had employed in banishing the demons of drinking and listlessness.

On the inside, I was still the shy middle child of a hardscrabble steelworker, but to the outside world I was becoming the face of the most respected runner's magazine in the world. I would do everything it took, anything they asked, to stay in the game.

I would even run across Death Valley.

Bart runs across the desert floor of Death Valley during Badwater Ultramarathon 146, 1989.

Chapter 4

BADWATER ULTRA 146

People become famous for different reasons. Consider one of my idols, Captain Jacques Cousteau. He was the first to bring the wonder of the seas into people's homes through his daring documentaries and television shows.

Then there is my other hero, Chuck Bednarik, a hometown boy who played center and linebacker for the Philadelphia Eagles in the fifties and early sixties. He was the last professional football player to play both offense and defense at the same time for the entire game, earning him the nickname Last of the 60-Minute Men.

Me? I gained notoriety for running one of the craziest, most challenging races on the planet. It was 146 miles through California's Death Valley—in July, no less. The contest started in Badwater Basin, the lowest, hottest, driest place in the United States, and ended 14,496 feet atop Mount Whitney, the highest point in the contiguous United States.

This was before reality television turned ultra athletes into celebrities, and running 26.2 miles was considered extreme. It was also before the Internet was as ubiquitous as the cell phone, so the average person had no idea a race of this proportion even existed.

I got roped into doing it in 1989, when a group of us from *Runner's World* were at the Atlanta Super Show, the largest trade show for sporting-goods manufacturers. We met some folks from the Modesto, California, office of Hi-Tec, a California shoe company that had signed on the year before as sponsor of the Badwater 146 to promote its footwear. They even named a running shoe after the race.

None of us had ever heard of this crazy exercise in masochism. But George Hirsch, who was publisher of the magazine at the time, thought the race was too good to pass up—for me, that is. Part of my job was to, well, run marathons—or at least those that no one else was up for. I was George's whipping boy, but in the best sense of the word, and he loved to see how far I could push my physical and psychological limits.

"I think it's fantastic, and I'm personally volunteering Bart to do it," George said during a meeting with the Hi-Tec guys after they suggested *Runner's World* do a story on the race.

Everyone looked at me.

"Come on," said Amby Burfoot. "You're the only one who could do something like this."

"I am?"

"You are, because I'm certainly not doing it," said Amby. "You don't have to win the thing. Just finish."

What could I say? I didn't want to disappoint anyone, but if I had known how hot, high, and far the race was, I may have taken a few days to think about it. There were several problems. I had never run more than 26.2 miles at one time in my life. This race was 5½ times that distance, and it was across the floor of Death Valley, where daytime temperatures once soared to 134°F, the second highest ever recorded in the world.

The hottest place on the planet? That distinction belongs to a desert in Libya called El Azizia, but it beat Death Valley by only a mere 2°F. No one's thought to hold a marathon there yet.

The first thing I did when I returned from the Super Show was research the racecourse. Here's what I discovered: Badwater is a flat pan of crunchy salt that sits 282 feet below sea level. The few times it does rain, it leaves behind briny pools of water that evaporate quickly. The residual salt shines like diamonds.

From there, the course keeps going up and up, covering three mountain ranges. By the time you reach the peak of Mount Whitney, you've climbed a total of 19,000 feet in cumulative altitude gains and dropped 4,700 feet in a toe-smashing descent. It's like running up and down the Empire State Building 15 times.

Runners travel on roads that can radiate temperatures of up to 150°F, hot enough to turn the treads of running shoes into gooey taffy. The course passes through places with ominous names like Devil's Cornfield, Furnace Creek, and Stovepipe Wells. There's face-stinging wind, burning sandstorms, and occasional lightning strikes.

Oh yeah—and you have to bring your own crew, water, and support vehicle because there are no official aid stations along the way. No sane person could stand the elements while waiting for runners to pass hours and even days apart.

No one had tried running from Badwater to Mount Whitney until 1974. Even then it took the first man, Al Arnold, three attempts before he finally did it in 1977. In his youth, Arnold was a hulking brute who tried out for the Olympic boxing team, but he was fat and sedentary by his late thirties. Then a diagnosis of glaucoma scared him skinny, and he started lifting weights and running. The first time he gave the Badwater course a try, he was 46. He brought along a friend, David Gabor, who collapsed and went into shock 18 miles into the journey.

The next year, Arnold made it to the 36-mile mark before his knee gave out. He then decided if he was serious about doing this, drastic measures were in order. So, for the next 2 years, he rode his stationary bike in a 200°F sauna for 2 hours a day. He also ran between 200 and 250 miles a week without water.

By the time I came along in 1989, Badwater had been an official race for 2 years, and only nine people had completed it.

There was no way I was going to be able to replicate Arnold's training regimen: (a) I didn't have time, and (b) I didn't enjoy running in the heat, at least not at the time. I melted like an antacid tablet in water. But I did try—once. After donning a Gore-Tex running suit, wool hat, and gloves, I logged 8 miles on a 91°F day. The effort drained my strength. From then on, I stuck with what I did best—running 70 miles a week along Pennsylvania's shaded trails.

Besides, I had a plan. I asked a colleague, Cristina Negron, to custom sew a suit made from Coolmax, the latest wicking fabric. It was the runner's version of those robes worn by sheiks, and it was the first and last time I ever cared about what I was wearing.

My crew was first-rate and included my boss, Jane Serues, the magazine's promotion director, and deputy editor Bob "Wish" Wischnia. They would not only hand me water and PowerBars but also act as sports psychologists, medics, cheerleaders, and chauffeurs.

Jane had qualified for the Olympic trials in 1984. She was tough as Bethlehem Steel, a hard-core endurance athlete who had completed more than 20 marathons.

Wish was a top age-group runner and a really good writer who had been covering the sport for 20 years.

We flew to Las Vegas the night before the race, but there was no time to play the slots or hit a show. The gamble would be Badwater 146, and none of us knew what to expect. The next day we rose early, rented an RV, and loaded it with $300 worth of groceries, bags of ice, and 200 bottles of water for drinking, dousing, and sponging. My biggest fear was dehydration. It gets so hot in Death Valley that the sweat literally evaporates from your body before it beads.

By 5:00 p.m. we were in Furnace Creek for a meeting before the race. It wasn't hard to imagine how the town got its name. When I stepped out of the RV, a bellowing blast of hot air knocked me back as if I had been punched in the gut by a supernatural force.

"Whoa," said Jane. "This is brutal. I couldn't run 10 feet in this. You could die just standing here."

"It's like an oven," said Wish, heading back inside the air-conditioned RV.

After the brief meeting, at which we collected our bib numbers, heard the rules, and got last-minute instructions, we headed back to Badwater, population zero, for the start of the race. The only things in Badwater are a sign, which indicates that it's located 282 feet below sea level, and a metal garbage can.

Besides yours truly, there were five runners at the start line that year: 46-year-old female twins Barbara Alvarez and Angelika Castaneda, who carried their résumés to pass out to any spectators along the way; Jim Walker, who dropped out of the race in 1988 after completing 96 miles; Adrian Crane, who carried a modified set of skis on his back; and Tom Possert, who'd finished first the year before but was disqualified for unlawful assistance on the course after his crew was photographed dragging him up Mount Whitney. At the time, I didn't know anything about Possert's checkered past performance, but I certainly wouldn't have considered him a cheater. He was one tough athlete, and I admired his persistence. As to why race officials let him participate again, I can only surmise that they needed bodies. After all, there were only six of us.

Crane's plan was to ski across the salt flats and emerge later on the main road, shaving 20 miles from the course. He had attempted to walk across the salt bed the year before, but he crashed through the crust so many times that his legs were too lacerated to continue. Now he was leaving nothing to chance. He had topographical maps, lights, a compass, and a dozen bottles of water that he'd buried along the course a few weeks before. Still, no one thought he had a shot at winning.

I'm not sure why, but we all carried thermometers, the big plastic kind that float in swimming pools. We certainly didn't need them to tell us it was hot, so maybe they were talismans against heatstroke or solid assurance that Dante's *Inferno* was only fiction.

The race began at 9:00 p.m. on July 26, 1989, as temperatures dipped to a cool 117°F. It was the first year for a nighttime start, and purists protested that it lessened the torture fest. It was switched back to a daytime start in 1996.

In lieu of a starter's gun, race director David Pompel shouted "Go!" and we crossed the white line spray painted on the road.

Possert, who wore tinted sunglasses, surged into the darkness like it was a 5-K, blazing a 6:30 pace. Crane followed, disappearing into the desert. I was in third place, and the twins and Jim Walker trailed me.

I resisted the urge to chase Possert, but it was difficult because the pace was so slow. But I knew this distance required common sense. The first 18 miles from Badwater back to Furnace Creek were a steady climb, nothing too rigorous, but the night was stifling. It felt as if I was taking hits of hot air from a blast furnace. I carried a flashlight to illuminate the path, but it wasn't necessary. With few artificial lights interfering with the celestial sky, the stars blazed with the intensity of 200-watt lightbulbs.

Jane and Wish met me every mile with a bottle of water, pretzels, and an occasional melted PowerBar. The pit stops sustained me, and I tried to think of something funny to say at each reunion. I was feeling good, but they were having troubles on their end. They resisted turning on the air-conditioning in the RV because they were afraid of running out of gas before they could refuel in Lone Pine, an old mining outpost 120 miles away at the base of Mount Whitney. To make matters worse, the radio was broken and they were reduced to singing aloud to fill the time. Jane preferred show tunes, and Wish was a Grateful Dead groupie.

I was glad to be outside.

At midnight we passed Furnace Creek, the last vestige of civilization and the first checkpoint. There was no one there to meet us, but we celebrated anyway, slapping high-fives and hooting and hollering in the middle of the street.

"Eighteen miles down, 126 to go!" I said.

"One hundred and twenty-six?" said Wish. "It's stinking hot in this RV. I'm going to die."

"*You're* going to die? You've got a fridge full of Dos Equis. Give me a break."

Jane ran with me for the next few miles, and we discussed my competition. "All you have to do is finish in one piece," she said. "Don't get too competitive. It's only a *Runner's World* project."

"It's still a race," I protested. "What do you think ski boy's going to do?"

"That Adrian guy?"

"Yeah, the one with the skis on his back. What a nut!"

"How do you ski across a sand dune?"

"Maybe he thinks this is a cross-country ski race," I joked.

It's no coincidence that people who run ultramarathons are a little wacky; the sheer enormity of the distance requires a mind at odds with reality.

Exhaustion set in at mile 30. My crew made me pee in a cup to see if I was dehydrated. We tried to check my urine's clarity in front of the RV's headlights, but they weren't bright enough. We took the sample inside and examined it like it was some sort of science experiment.

"Looks like you're okay," said Jane.

It was pale yellow, so all was well. Coca-Cola–colored urine would have meant I wasn't ingesting enough fluids.

I wouldn't have minded staying inside the RV for a little longer. It was a lot cooler inside than outside on the asphalt.

"Sorry, Dude," said Wish, pushing me out the door. "It's time to run."

The next checkpoint was Stovepipe Wells, and we saw its glow about an hour before arriving. At first we didn't know what to make of the lights. Was it a glittering mirage? First castings of a distant dawn? A 7-11? When we arrived at 4:30 a.m., we were disappointed. There was nothing there except a few shuttered buildings and a closed gas station with its lights dimmed for the night. The glow had been emanating from a single parking-lot light.

Still, we were at mile 45.

Just then I saw piles of freshly baked banana bread on the road.

Banana bread? Maybe I was hallucinating. This was common in Badwater. The physical exhaustion, unrelenting heat, and altitude changes can wreak all sorts of psychological mayhem on runners. Turns out I was still lucid. Possert was throwing up bananas, which would then bake into neat mounds on the 160°F blacktop. I chuckled, knowing that Chiquita was his sponsor. Right now he was not making a good poster boy.

He desperately wanted to win the race, and his crew was pushing him. I knew I was getting close to him when I began to see piles of mushy bananas that hadn't yet been cooked.

Outside Stovepipe Wells, the Hi-Tec guys, who had been cruising back and forth in vans, dropped off Steve Flanagan, their East Coast sales director, who wanted to run with me for 15 miles. I was pretty chewed up at this point but welcomed the company. The temperature had dropped to 105°F.

"How ya feeling?" asked Flanagan as he matched my stride.

"Okay, considering I just ran 56 miles in this crazy place," I said.

"You look good, but Possert's still ahead of you. What, are you dogging it?"

"Dogging it! Let's see how far you make it," I said.

Flanagan was a world-class runner, and soon we were cruising at too fast a pace. Jane, who was watching like a mother hen from the window of the RV, became concerned that Flanagan was pushing me too hard. "Hey, slow down, you two," she yelled. "You've still got to climb the Panamints."

Flanagan had said earlier that the incline was only 3 miles, which didn't sound too bad—except Flanagan was full of shit. The mountain ascended for 17^1/$_2$ miles, and it was an elevator climb to the clouds. After a few miles, Flanagan bailed. "It's too hot, man," he said. "My shins are killing me. I'm going back into the air-conditioned van."

"What are you, a wimp? You said you were going to run 15 miles with me," I said.

"Yes, I'm a wimp. I'm going back into the van where it's cool and there's beer. See you later, Bart."

I think Jane must have felt sorry for me because she jumped out and started pacing me up the rise. We crested the mountain at noon after averaging 3 miles an hour. I was finally out of Death Valley, and I wasn't in a cedar box.

Next came a grueling 10-mile descent. On a bike, this would have been the greatest ride, but it was brutal on foot, and my quads screamed in protest. I gave in and decided to walk, which was a big deal for me. In the 1980s, no self-respecting marathoner would dare go slower than a trot. Walking was for wimps and would displease the gods of running, who had sanctified the sport thousands of years ago with the first Olympic flame. I fully expected to be struck by a lightning bolt for walking, but I didn't care. My legs hurt.

At the bottom of the hill was the largest dry lake bed in North America, a few miles from Edwards Air Force Base. A fighter jet blew past our RV, causing the windows to rattle and waking up Wish, who had been napping in the back. I knocked on the door to change my running shoes, Asics X-Caliber GTs. I had brought along seven pairs and exchanged them for a fresh pair every 10 miles because the midsoles got soft from the heat. I could wear the shoes again once they had been out of the sun and off the road for a few hours.

It was now 2:30 p.m. Thursday, and I had been running for more than 17 hours straight. I was at mile 75, and my crew decided I needed a rest before the next big push. "You're weaving across the road," said Jane. "Why don't you come in, and we'll put some ice on your legs."

My legs were burned, not from the sun, but the rising heat of the road. I also felt disoriented and dried up like a turkey left in the oven too long. I climbed into the RV, and Jane covered me in bags of ice.

"This feels great," I said. During the 17 hours I had been running, Jane and Wish had been handing me water, Fig Newtons, and PowerBars every mile or so, and they were pretty wiped out, too. We were all tired and cranky, so we decided to check into a motel in Lone Pine, about 53 miles away, and rest for a few hours. The race rules allowed for this detour as long as I resumed the run later at the exact point I had stopped.

Just then, Crane popped out of the desert, dazed and dehydrated. His arms and legs were covered in deep scratches. He had skied across the salt beds and bushwhacked his way across the desert. Because of the shortcut he had taken, Crane was now in second place behind Possert.

I had been in second place but gladly traded it for the refuge of the RV.

When we arrived at our motel, Wish miscalculated the height of an awning over the entranceway and tried to pull our 12-foot 2-inch RV under a 10-foot 4-inch overhang. *Crunch!* The corner of the RV crumbled like tinfoil.

"I'm not paying for that," grumbled Wish.

"Don't worry—we took out extra insurance," said Jane.

"It could have happened to anybody," he said.

"But it happened to you, Wish," I said. "I guess math isn't your strong point."

The first thing I did when I got to the motel was jump in the pool, then I guzzled some Gatorade to rehydrate my system. Jane and Wish collapsed in the room for a few hours, but I was too keyed up to sleep. About 3 hours later, we grabbed some pizza at a restaurant across from the motel. I started talking to a guy dressed in running shorts and a singlet seated in the next booth. "Are you guys runners?" he asked.

"Yeah," I mumbled.

"I'm a runner, too. Where are you from?"

"Pennsylvania."

"Really? I used to live there. Where in Pennsylvania?"

"It's a small town. You've probably never heard of it. Emmaus."

"No way—I graduated from Emmaus High School!"

I peered closer, thinking the guy looked familiar. "Brent Backus?"

Turned out we knew each other through the Lehigh Valley Road Runners, but he didn't recognize me because I had shaved my beard about 6 months earlier. He was thinking about doing the race next year and wanted to see what it was like. For my part, I was happy to see a familiar face. It felt like a positive omen.

At 12:30 a.m. Friday, we drove back to where I'd stopped running. I didn't want to rest too long for fear I would get stiff and lose momentum. During the trip, we passed Possert, and a few miles behind him was Crane, who had taken his first and only break at mile 119.

My plan was to run the next 50 miles without stopping, a feat I could accomplish only by staying positive. I focused on my surroundings, admiring the stark beauty of sagebrush and dunes, so different from the greenery of Pennsylvania and the skyscrapers of New York City.

Thirty miles later, I started to fade, and my pace slowed not so much from the heat as from exhaustion. Wish noticed I was once again weaving, so he joined me on the road. He knew just how to get me worked up, telling me he planned to do a story on a duathlete I knew who had a reputation for cheating.

"That guy's the biggest fraud in the world," I said.

"That's not what I hear," Wish said. "He's the real thing."

"No way," I said. "He's a cheater. He cuts corners."

"That stuff is rumor and innuendo," he said.

We continued this banter for the next several miles until my brain cleared and I was back in the game.

Thirty miles from Mount Whitney, we spotted the twins on the horizon, and it spurred me to try to pass them. They had kept going through the previous night but were now a mess and had camped on the side of the road. When they saw me coming, they tried to move but one sister had such terrible blisters on her feet that she was using cross-country ski poles. The other was crying hysterically. I could see how much it meant to them to stay ahead of me, so I hung back a bit.

I didn't want to be responsible for their demise. They led interesting lives. Born and raised in Austria, they later moved to Mexico, where they had distinguished themselves as models and movie stars. Now they were on their second—or was it third?—career as ultra athletes.

I ended up passing them about 10 miles later, and they slapped me high-fives in a sincere display of encouragement.

At mile 130, my crew and I decided to stop and spend another night in Lone Pine. I was only 5 miles from the Whitney Portal, the trailhead to Mount Whitney, but it was getting dark. From the portal, it was 11 miles to the top, and I knew I wouldn't be able to make it up and back down before sunset. We drove back to the motel we had stayed in the night before, but this time Wish didn't crash the RV. He did insist on sleeping on the room's only cot, however, meaning Jane and I had to share a double bed.

Jane and I joked about the situation. "It's not fair," I said. "I'm in bed with you for the first time, and I just ran 130 miles."

We returned to the 130-mile mark early the next day to begin the ascent of Mount Whitney at sunrise. Jane accompanied me on the climb. It was slow going over rock-strewn switchbacks and narrow trails. It took us 4½ hours to get to the snow-dusted apex, and we arrived around 10:00 a.m., exhausted but elated. We mugged for a few shots on the peak, and then race director David Pompel, who had spent the night on the mountain, congratulated me on my second-place finish. He proceeded to say that I was actually first because Crane cut the course and was going to be disqualified. Then he admitted he didn't have a permit from the Forest Service to hold the race on Mount Whitney, so he had appointed a fake finish line at mile 135 on the portal. Possert had been the first to reach the phony finish but for some reason stopped there, never venturing up the mountain. I was the third one to reach the portal.

That was the last year the Badwater race included a climb up Mount Whitney. Ergo, it is now called the Badwater 135.

So how did I do? I don't know. I never checked the official results. If you have, don't tell me. I like thinking I placed first, second, and third in the same race.

Meanwhile, my career got an unexpected boost from all the post-race publicity. My hometown newspaper, the *Morning Call,* covered my trek in its local pages. When I returned home, I was met at Lehigh Valley International Airport outside Allentown by a cheering crowd and camera crews from Philadelphia TV stations.

Wish followed with a story in *Runner's World* dubbing me Badwater Bart, and my reputation as the magazine's amicable and slightly unhinged ambassador spread. Suddenly, I was fielding invitations around the world from race directors looking to lend some celebrity glitz to their event.

A few years later, one arrived from an unlikely place.

Bart (left) and Jim Crosswhite (right) meet up
with a rhino in Chitwan National Park in Nepal, 1991

Chapter 5

ASIAN RACES

One day in the summer of 1991, an oversized yellow envelope bearing exotic stamps arrived on my desk postmarked by the Indian consulate in New York City. I didn't know anyone in India, so I quickly ripped it open instead of tossing it to the side with the rest of that day's mail.

"Dear Badwater Bart," the letter began. "Please come to India and run our races. We will pay airfare and lodging." It was signed by the tourism director of India.

I suspected that someone had sent the tourism director a copy of the story *Runner's World* had published on my trek through Death Valley. My best guess was Jim Crosswhite, an entrepreneur who organized adventure races for a company called Force 10.

I gave him a call. "Hey Jim," I said. "I just got invited to run some races in India by the tourism director. Do you know anything about this?"

"You bet," he said. "I joined forces with an Indian guy named C. S. Pandey, and we're organizing a new 100-miler in the heart of the Himalayas and two other races. I told Pandey this kind of adventure thing would be right up your alley."

It was. I wanted to visit India, a country that has more than twice the population of the United States but far fewer meat eaters—80 percent of Indians are vegetarians. I had been one since 1982, when my girlfriend, Marty, told me that it took 30 pounds of grain to produce 1 pound of meat. Therefore, if fewer people ate meat, there would be enough food to feed the world. That jibed with my motto, "Live simply so others can simply live."

Then Crosswhite told me a little about Pandey, an ultra-runner in a country where marathons were about as popular as lawn bowling in the Arctic. Growing up, Pandey would run through the jungles, forests, and across the ridges of the mystical mountains for hours. Everyone thought he was crazy, but the man had a dream. He wanted to bring the sport of ultrarunning to India. I was impressed.

"Sure," I told Crosswhite. "I'd love to go to India."

A few months later, I arrived at midnight in India's capital, New Delhi, with Jack Gescheidt, a freelance photographer the tourism industry had hired to document the races. We would be running three events during our visit: the Taj Mahal 5-K, the Himalayan 100 Mile Stage Race, and the Sikkim Half-Marathon.

I had witnessed lots of unusual sites in my international travels so far, but I was unprepared for the mob scene that greeted us at the New Delhi airport. Hundreds of young men clamoring to carry our luggage or hail us a cab, anything to earn a few rupees, clustered outside the terminal. We had to bat them away lest they grab our suitcases and then demand money for their return. I'd been promised by the tourism director's office that we would be picked up at the airport, but no one came to meet us. I scanned the crowd for a sign bearing my name. No dice.

"We better get a cab," I said to Jack.

"I hope the race is better organized," he said.

We flagged down a *tuk-tuk*, a three-wheeled open-air cab pow-
ered by a motorcycle engine, and hopped inside. Two miles into the
trip, the driver stopped when a military officer dressed in a drab
green uniform and beret, with a gun holstered at his side, flagged
us down. He pointed to the driver, then climbed in the front seat
without saying a word. Jack and I were baffled.

"What the hell?" mouthed Jack.

"I don't know," I whispered back, afraid to raise my voice in case
he understood English.

We continued for several miles until the officer pointed again
and then jumped out without a backward glance.

We later learned the military has carte-blanche access to all forms
of transportation, and if an officer flags down a cab, the driver has
to pick him up for free, even if he has a paying fare.

At 1:30 a.m. we arrived at our hotel, the Asian International, and
it was a dump. I guess my celebrity star had not climbed high enough
for luxury accommodations. The paint was peeling off the walls, and
the only light source was a bulb that hung by a frayed wire in the
middle of the room. It was a muggy night, but we couldn't open the
windows because the smell of sewage was overwhelming.

We wanted to tip the porters for carrying our luggage up the
scuffed wooden stairs, but we had given all of our rupees to the tuk-
tuk driver. We reached into our bags and handed them two running
T-shirts instead, and they seemed appreciative.

A few minutes later the manager knocked on our door. "Are
these yours?" he asked, holding up the shirts.

"Yes, but we gave them to the guys who helped us with our suitcases," I said.

"They were not stolen?"

"No, no. We ran out of money to tip them."

He frowned, muttered an apology, and left.

Jack and I decided to stop at the bank the next morning to

exchange currency. We were light packers and didn't want to get into a situation where we were gifting the shirts off our backs.

The Taj Mahal 5-K wouldn't start for a few more days, so Crosswhite invited Jack and me to meet him at Royal Chitwan National Park in Nepal, a popular tourist spot that was a reserve for endangered Bengal tigers and Asian rhinos. Crosswhite thought the park would be the ultimate place to hold an adventure run.

We took a plane to Kathmandu, the colorful capital of Nepal, where I felt immediately at home. The country is filled with old hippies and expats eschewing the materialism of the West. Like them, I never needed a lot of stuff to make me happy. At the time, my wardrobe consisted of two pairs of faded jeans and a few shirts. I owned a 5-year-old Toyota Celica, but I drove it as little as possible, preferring the well-worn seat of my bike.

The animal reserve was more than 125 miles away, near Pokhara, an ethereal city along an old trading route between Tibet and India. Jim arranged for Jack and me to travel there by bus—not an air-conditioned Greyhound but a dinged and dusty tour bus crammed with about 75 people, along with their goats and chickens. The goats would be sacrificed in religious ceremonies and the chickens slaughtered for sale in the markets. Earlier that day in the market, I had seen meat hanging by hooks, covered with flies. I couldn't help but feel bad for my fellow nonhuman passengers, but it was the Nepalese way of life, not mine.

The tight, noisy quarters of the bus made me claustrophobic from the moment I stepped aboard. The Nepalese have a very different relationship with space than Americans do. Here a bench considered large enough for two in the States was occupied by four. There was no way I was going to last 5 hours in the crowded cacophony. After getting permission from the driver, Jack and I reached through a window, grabbed the luggage rack, and hoisted ourselves onto the roof. The view was spectacular, but the bus lurched and wobbled over steep serpentine roads. We were still on top of the bus when we arrived at the reserve—home to monkeys, antelopes, pythons, and rhinos, just a few of the species that live a peaceful existence outside the range of big-game hunters.

Crosswhite was there to meet us, and he laughed at our disheveled appearance. Our hair was bug-infested and plastered against our heads, and our faces were caked with dirt. "I've seen monkeys that look better than you two," he said.

The next day we set out to scout the course Crosswhite had mapped out for a half-marathon. He had hired a guide who would lead us through parts of the reserve via an unorthodox mode of transportation by Western standards—elephants. We mounted the saggy-skinned pachyderms as if we were rajas about to survey our kingdom. In truth, the ride was a bumpy experience, not much better than the bus, but once again the scenery was worth a sore butt.

As we strode through the park, we saw rhinos in the tall grass. Later, we canoed in a hollowed-out tree log along the Narayani River, where crocodiles lounged in the caramel-colored water. After about 4 miles, we docked the canoe on the riverbank so we could test run a 6½ mile dirt path that led to Tiger Tops Jungle Lodge. Crosswhite had his eyes on both this trail and an out-and-back course for the half-marathon.

But before we started running, our guide warned us about fearsome rhinos that would attack if startled. The best defense was to make yourself as tall, thin, and still as possible and hope the rhino missed you during a charge. Rhinos are plant eaters, but they dislike people, especially those on their turf, and they will gore them with their horns.

"Okay, let's practice," the guide said. "I'll be the rhino and you be runners."

This didn't sound good, but I agreed to play along on the chance it could save my life.

"Go!" the guide shouted, and Crosswhite, Jack, and I scattered into the tall grass. I heard the guide before I saw him. I stopped in my tracks and stiffened, barely breathing as I sucked in my gut.

"Excellent," he said, assessing my performance on the rhino test, as it became known. "You did very good."

"That's because I knew you weren't a real rhino!" I said. "I might not have been that relaxed if you were a 2-ton beast with a horn."

And I was right. A little while later, as Crosswhite and I began running, we came face-to-face with a real rhino as we rounded a corner on the trail to Tiger Tops. It was standing as still as a museum exhibit. It squared its shoulders in a display of hostility and dropped its ears.

We forgot all about the rhino test.

"Run!" yelled Crosswhite.

I did. I knew how fast rhinos can go in a short distance, so I sprinted for the jeep, outpacing Crosswhite by several yards. I knew I didn't have to outrun the rhino, just Crosswhite.

As soon as he got in the jeep, he voiced what I had been thinking: "This is no place for a race."

"No kidding," I said. "Adventure running is cool, but no one wants to die."

If only our adventure that day had ended there. When we got back to the river, the canoe was gone. The only way to our lodge was through the water, which was not comforting, as we knew it sheltered snapping crocodiles.

"Move quietly through the water," the guide advised. "And don't move any rocks on the bottom. The crocs will sense us if you do."

We slowly waded into the river, placing our backpacks on our heads so they wouldn't get wet. The water quickly deepened until it swirled around our necks. No one said a word as we tiptoed through the tepid Narayani. The crossing only took a few minutes but felt like hours.

Once on dry land, we had to hike the 4 miles back to camp. It was getting dark, and we didn't want to be caught in the thick jungle without flashlights or lanterns. We also worried about trigger-happy rangers. As a way of preventing poaching, no one was allowed in the reserve after nightfall. Those who violated the curfew risked being shot.

After another run-in with a rhino—we all hid behind trees—we made it to our lodge just as the sun dipped behind the hills. We left for Kathmandu the next morning, boarding another bus. I was grateful to still be in one piece, but other dangers lay ahead. As we crawled around a hairpin turn, I gazed from my rooftop perch to the ravine below. There lay the rusted and twisted carcass of a bus, exactly like the one we were riding, that had fallen off the cliff. I closed my eyes and imagined myself back with the rhinos. At least I had a fighting chance with them.

From Kathmandu we flew to New Delhi, passing over the snow-capped Himalayas, the highest mountains in the world. I was happy for another chance to gaze at the breathtaking view.

This time when we landed at the airport, we were met by someone holding a sign that said "Bart Yasso." We were relieved that we wouldn't have to rely on a tuk-tuk.

The other 18 runners who had signed up for the three races were arriving as well, and we were all staying at the Hotel Kanishka, a towering four-star high-rise in the heart of New Delhi. Our room was opulent compared to the neighboring Asian International, where we had stayed before.

I recognized Dan Ferrara from *Outside* magazine in the hotel lobby. Dan had worked at *Runner's World* and excelled at short-distance races. He was also a city boy who had never seen the inside of a sleeping bag.

"What are you doing here?" I joked. "You know the Himalayan race is 100 miles, and we have to camp for a few nights on the side of a mountain?"

"Yeah, but I couldn't say no to a trip to India," he said. "I'll figure it out."

There was also a guy from *UltraRunning* magazine and Mike Ehlerman, an experienced trail runner from Arizona. Then there were two sisters following the details of Clarence Thomas's confirmation hearing for the US Supreme Court. Anita Hill had testified that week that Thomas had sexually harassed her while she worked for him, and the sisters were of the mind that he was guilty and shouldn't be confirmed.

I didn't know enough about the story to form an opinion about Thomas's conduct, but the women were cute, so I went out and bought a copy of the international edition of *USA Today* so they could have their news fix.

The next day we took a train to Agra, the host city of our first race, the Taj Mahal 5-K. The station was crawling with beggars, many of them children. Some of them, we had been told, had been maimed by their own families to elicit sympathy from tourists. They were missing arms and feet; one child, who suffered from elephantiasis, rested his swollen leg in a wheelbarrow. It was hard to turn down the children as their small fingers pleaded for coins, but charity was discouraged because it was the only way to end the barbaric practice of disfiguring children.

The suffering children were a disturbing contrast to the splendor of the Taj Mahal, the awe-inspiring white marble mausoleum commissioned by Emperor Shah Jahan in memory of his favorite wife. Pandey had planned the race around this Eighth Wonder of the World, designating the dignitary gates as the finish line. We would be the first Americans since President Jimmy Carter to be given permission to pass through these royal portals.

It was a good thing the ending promised to be so magnificent, because the race itself was mayhem. Cars had been banned from the course, but rickshaws were not, and hundreds of them clogged the streets. Just as I started to gain momentum, a rickshaw would cut me off and I'd be forced to navigate around it. It was like trying to run through Times Square at rush hour.

After about the first half-mile, the 19 of us decided it didn't make sense to run competitively when we planned to start a 100-mile race in a few days. So we formed a tight mass and ran as one, passing together through the dignitary gates of the white-domed temple.

Two days later, we arrived in Darjeeling for the start of the Himalayan 100. We would run roughly 20 miles a day for 5 days, a distance made more difficult by high altitude, which made breathing difficult, eating undesirable, and sleeping nearly impossible.

Before the race started, Crosswhite and I visited the home of the region's director of tourism, who bestowed an Indian blessing on us and presented me with a white sash for good luck. No one had ever prayed over me before a run, and I felt as if I were receiving the Catholic sacrament of last rites. Little did I know I would almost need it.

The first day's leg was a 24-mile jaunt that started in the town of Manebhanjang. Every inch of the distance was uphill along a winding cobblestoned ridge that divides India from Nepal. The road was built in 1948 for Aga Khan, a Muslim leader, so he could see the sun rise over some of the highest peaks in the world—Mount Everest, Makalu, and Lhotse. But he never saw the peaks because his emissaries deemed the trip far too dangerous for their Imam.

The day started out warm, so most runners dressed in short sleeves and shorts, not anticipating the drastic climate changes on the mountain. The first few miles we ran through forest, but as we climbed above the tree line, the temperature dropped. The Himalayas appeared in the distant mist, and a few village children stopped to watch and even run with us for a bit. They laughed and tugged at our shirts.

Mike Ehlerman was the first to finish that day, posting a 4:37 time. I arrived at the clearing 11 minutes later and saw him shivering by a fire. "Hey," I said, shaking his hand in congratulations. "Let's get some warm clothes on."

"I'd love to," he said. "But the jeep carrying our luggage and supplies broke an axle climbing the mountain, and it may be hours before it's fixed."

That was a problem. We were both drenched in sweat, and we didn't have anything to keep us warm. It was windy and 40 degrees cooler than when we had started. Mike was a friend, but we were about to become better friends as we had no choice but to draw closer to keep warm.

As each runner arrived at camp cold and hungry, they asked the same question.

"Where's the jeep?"

"It broke down."

"When is it supposed to get here?"

"We don't know."

Then they'd join our tight circle around the fire until the next runner appeared and the questions began again.

Finally, 5 hours later, we heard the rumblings of the jeep.

The group started to cheer and clap their numb hands. Some even hugged the driver. We could finally put on dry clothes and eat. I was starving, but I lost my appetite when I lined up for chow. The only thing on the menu was wheat pasta, and it tasted like tree bark. It was beyond bad. I later learned it was Crosswhite's doing. For some reason, he had a surplus of whole-wheat pasta. He didn't care for it himself and saw the race as an opportunity to unload it. He figured no one would notice how bad it really was since all food tastes funny at 12,000 feet and runners could smother it in sauce. But the airline transporting the race supplies lost the sauce.

"No marinara?" I groaned.

Disgusted, we headed to pitch our tents. I had mine erected in 2 minutes and was about to get inside when I spotted Dan Ferrara of *Outside* fumbling with the stakes and poles.

"Need some help?" I asked.

Embarrassed, he mumbled thanks and then stood back so I could assemble his sleeping quarters. "The last time I camped was in a condo," he said.

By day 3 we were still eating bad pasta, but no one had the energy to complain. The altitude was taking its toll on not only our appetites but also our bodies. On the way down a hill, I twisted my foot on a rock and my ankle swelled like an air bag, immediately turning black and purple. I sat down for a few minutes and then tried to run, but it felt like my Achilles tendon was going to pop. This was serious, and I didn't want to jeopardize my running career. It was clear I couldn't finish the race or even walk to that day's finish line. I would have to catch a jeep back to camp.

As I waited, the sisters paused to see if I needed help. "I'm fine," I said. "I have the best view in the world. The jeep will get me."

But the wild yaks found me first.

"Get out of here," I said flinging rocks at their horned heads, but it only made them more curious and they drew closer for a better whiff of this stinky foreigner. Eventually, they ambled away, but not because they were scared of my aim.

When the jeep finally arrived, I hobbled into the front seat.

"I will save you," said the earnest young driver, who pretty much exhausted his vocabulary of English in that one phrase.

My Gunga Din had arrived.

As we started back to camp on the raddled jungle roads, Gunga Din looked worried. We were inching along, but the steep pitch caused us to pick up speed, so he yanked on the emergency brake. The sudden stop sent the luggage, food, and water in the backseat flying forward, trapping us beneath its weight. The arms of my manservant were flattened against the steering wheel, and mine were pinned at my sides. Neither one of us could move.

Oh, how I wanted to quote Rudyard Kipling, "Din, Din, Din, you lumping lump o' brick dust," but my lips were kissing the windshield. With much contorting I freed a hand and pushed open the side window, allowing just enough space to throw out some gear. Then I liberated Gunga, and we repacked the jeep to make sure the same thing didn't happen again. We still had a ways to go, and my ankle was throbbing.

When we made it back to our hotel in the Sherpa village of Rimbik, we looked at each other, then went our separate ways without saying good-bye. I wasn't going to thank someone who nearly killed me for the ride. Nor would I pen him a poem.

Later that day I was bathing my ankle in a nearby creek because there was no ice in the hotel. That's where the medicine man found me. His creased face was smeared in white and red paint, and his silver hair hung in long strands. He had heard about a group of foreigners staying in the remote village, and he wanted to meet me after someone told him I was injured.

He examined my puffy ankle with his gnarled fingers, then handed me a white capsule the size of a walnut. "If you take this pill, you can run the next day and the swelling will go down," he said in near-perfect English.

I didn't believe him, but I took it anyway. I could barely walk. What other options did I have?

When I woke up on day 4, the first thing I did was check my ankle. "Hey, Jack," I said. "Look at this."

The swelling had gone down, and it didn't hurt when I put pressure on it. Even so, I decided not to run in case I stumbled on a rock and reinjured myself. So I walked the 13 miles from Rimbik to Barahatta, passing tea gardens and emerald jungles.

The villagers who came out to watch us couldn't figure out why I wasn't running, but they encouraged me to do so by smiling and motioning their hands forward. "Yah, yah," they hollered. You could tell they pitied the old guy at the back of the pack who couldn't even sustain a jog.

I made up for it the fifth and final day when I posted the fastest time of the group over 24 miles.

That night we partied at the Planters' Club in Darjeeling by drinking Indian beer and playing Ping-Pong, but I had a heavy heart. Because I had to be transported by jeep for 3 miles at one point, I was branded DNF because I ran only 97 of the 100 miles. But I wasn't alone. Ferrara DNFed, too.

I had one more chance on this Asian journey to redeem myself and reclaim my rightful place in the front of the pack. But the Sikkim Half-Marathon had more surprises than anyone could have predicted.

The least populated state in India, Sikkim, is tucked in the far northeast corner of the country between Tibet, Bhutan, and Nepal. It's clustered with glittering temples, monasteries, and butterflies. But it's so remote that there's no airport or train station, and the only way to get there is by bus or car.

As an incentive for participation in the half-marathon, the prime minister offered the equivalent of 1,000 American dollars to the winner. The enormity of the prize was unheard of at the time, especially when it took the average Sikkimese 6 months to earn that much money. The organizers were convinced someone was going to try to cheat their way across the finish line, so they devised a method they believed was foolproof.

At each of four checkpoints, race officials would jump out from behind a rock or tree and blast the runners with spray paint. Every checkpoint was assigned a different color, and only a few people knew what they were. That way, no one could slap paint on themselves prior to the race and sprint across the finish line. "What do you think of our system?" a race official asked me.

"I think it's the craziest idea I've ever heard," I said. "Why not just record everyone's race numbers at the checkpoints?"

The man shook his head no. There were about 100 people in the race and most of them were local, making it easy for someone to record a friend's number in exchange for half the purse.

I understood his concern at the race's start. Many of the runners were barefoot or in sandals. Others showed up appropriately dressed for a cricket match wearing white polo shirts, pants, and loafers. It was apparent that running wasn't popular in this part of the world, and this crowd's first attempt at a road race wasn't about reaping the health benefits of exercise. It was about cold hard rupees, and the pack began pressing toward the start line and hollering for the race to begin.

"Soon, soon," yelled an exasperated official shaking his clipboard. "I have to explain the rules."

They were worse than I thought. Not only would each runner get tagged, we would have to open our arms in welcome to allow a clear shot of our racing bib. That explained why we were sporting cloth bibs that resembled baby diapers and covered most of our chests. Someone obviously needed a large target. I found out whom at mile 3.

Just as I passed a tree, an official wearing a business suit jumped out and blasted me with red paint. Some of it got in my mouth, and I immediately started choking. Even though I had prepared myself for being sprayed, I was still startled by the swiftness of the attack. I looked in vain for a water station.

I tried not to let the dousing throw off my stride or inhibit me from running full guns, but the anxiety of not knowing when I would get sprayed again replayed in my head like a film reel. If this movie had a name, it would be *Paintball Half-Marathon.*

Turned out not everyone got sprayed, especially those in the back with no hope of winning. The spray zone was reserved for the leading 10 male and 10 female runners, those with at least a fighting chance of carrying home the loot. That included me, although I never would have accepted the money if I had won. I was participating in the race not as a serious competitor but to help promote it. I puffed out my chest with pride anyway because there was paint on it.

I was better prepared for the second checkpoint because a racer in front of me got sprayed first. The official then turned his nozzle on me, hitting the side of my bib. But there were far worse things than being pelted by paint to worry about.

The course was open to traffic, and drivers made a sport of trying to hit us. Twice I nearly got nailed by a passing pickup truck coming around a blind bend. I thought running the Taj Mahal 5-K while dodging rickshaws was bad. In India, cars drive on the left side of the road, the opposite of America, so many runners' instincts for avoiding traffic were discombobulated. The constant honking of horns was a jarring distraction that kept me on edge. I was never able to relax and get in my groove. They did have police at major intersections, and spectators chanted "U-S-A, U-S-A" as the Western runners went by. We were easy to spot. We were all wearing fancy running shoes, but it didn't help us in the end.

The race was won by a lanky 15-year-old local who finished in 1:17, 6 minutes faster than me. I shook his hand after the race. He beamed from ear to ear as they handed him the check. He instantly became a hero in his village. If this was the future of Indian running, it was bright. I decided that when I returned home, I would do something more for the sport in that country than lend my name. I mailed crates of shoes, shirts, and shorts, courtesy of *Runner's World,* to India.

I never heard back, but I drew satisfaction from knowing that next year there would be another 15-year-old boy and maybe even some girls flying down the streets of India in top-notch running shoes. In my mind, they were smiling.

Bart pedals his bike
through Wyoming
during his cross-
country trek, 1992

Chapter 6

CROSS-COUNTRY JOURNEY

No one was happier that I was about to bike across the country than Lenny Vreeland, the former owner of the Broken Spoke Bike Shop in Allentown.

Lenny and I had met 12 years earlier in 1980, soon after he had completed a 3,000-mile bike trek from California to New York City. I had strolled into his shop to trade my 10-speed for a newer model, and we became fast friends. He invited me for a bike ride, then regaled me with stories about every patch of pavement his tires had touched during his continental crossing.

We rode together once a month, and when he wasn't reminiscing about his rolling adventure, he would grow misty-eyed about running the Boston Marathon. When Lenny ran it in the 1960s, runners didn't have to qualify. It was a prestigious race even then, but the only entry requirements were a doctor's note and $3. I was just getting serious about running at the time, and Boston was becoming my goal. Lenny was an athletic pioneer, so I asked him what he did to train. "On the days I didn't run, I rode my bike," he said. "It helped a lot."

So I started to ride regularly as a means to cross-train. I liked being able to cover three to four times the distance in the same amount of time it took me to run. Plus, I could wolf down a sandwich or other real food when I rode, a practice ill-advised when running.

Eventually I started doing duathlons—races that combined running and cycling. By 1992, I had gotten into the habit of commuting by bike the 25 miles to and from the *Runner's World* office in Emmaus. The Broken Spoke was a regular stop, and more than a decade later, Lenny continued to invoke the towns he had passed through on his 3,000-mile ride with the reverence of a dime-store cowboy novel—Tucumcari, Cottonwood, Emporia. At age 63, he couldn't remember what he had eaten for breakfast that day, but he could recall with encyclopedic detail the storefronts, main streets, and people he met along the way during those 15 days on the road.

His fond memories inspired me to draft my own odyssey. I was confident in my fitness and upped my distance to 70 miles a day in preparation for emulating Lenny's travels. I invited my friend, Dan Bensimhon, a triathlete who worked at Rodale's *Prevention* magazine, to come along. He agreed, and we did a 125-mile ride to test the waters of friendship. They were smooth.

With childlike eagerness, Lenny and I pored over maps at the shop, plotting a 20-day route (that's all the vacation I had) that would start in the Pacific waters and end in Asbury Park, New Jersey. An atlas is one of my favorite books, and there's nothing more satisfying than tracing the blue lines with my finger and imagining the adventure each squiggle holds. I decided to travel west to east so each day would be 1 day closer to home, and we'd be able to take advantage of the prevailing tailwinds. To cross the country in 20 days, we'd have to ride roughly 165 miles each day.

Lenny would have loved to have come along with Dan and me, but he had heart problems. Nonetheless, he would live the journey through me, his spirit riding in tandem.

On the day we were to book the flight to Washington state, Dan bailed, saying he had too much to do and couldn't afford the time away. At first I was pissed, but I got over it pretty quickly. I knew he was a good guy who was just way too busy. Everyone figured I'd back out, too, but I firmly believe in finishing what I start. Plus, I had booked 19 motel rooms in advance as incentive to reach each day's destination. I didn't want to have to call each one and cancel.

Two months after first committing to the ride and a day before my departure in August, I took my Fuji Titanium to the Broken Spoke for a last-minute tune-up. "This doesn't look good," said the store's new owner, Randy Bernhard, pointing to a crack in the bottom bracket of the frame.

"I'll ride it with the crack in it," I said.

Randy looked horrified. "You can't do that," he said. "Let's call Lenny."

Lenny, who had retired the year before, lived across the street. Two minutes later, he burst through the door. "Let me see the bike," he said, his wide, Romanesque brow furrowed in concern as he ran his finger across the fissure. "This is serious. You can't use this frame to ride across the country."

"But I'm leaving tomorrow."

"Not on this bike," he said. "How about we put all your components on another frame? You won't notice a difference."

Randy and Lenny worked for hours removing the handlebars, gears, and pedals of my Titanium and attaching them to another model. I fretted, wondering if this last-minute change would derail the trip. But at the same time, I trusted Lenny completely. He was a battle-hardened bike warrior, and if he thought it would work, then it probably would. By this point, he was as vested in the journey, if not more so, as I was.

Besides, what other choice did I have?

When Operation Fuji Fix was complete, I took my bike for a quick spin around the parking lot before we had to take it apart again and box it for the plane. It felt great, like I was reclining on a chaise longue.

I took off from Lehigh Valley International Airport on August 20 with my bike and panniers, or saddlebags, stuffed with three sets of cycling jerseys and shorts, two pairs of underwear, long pants, tights, two short-sleeved shirts, rain gear, socks, a hat, and gloves. I also had extra tubes and tires, as well as a 1-pound wrench that Randy insisted I take. It had enough gadgetry to dismantle the bike, and I called it my MacGyver wrench, after the resourceful 1980s TV character who could make bombs from bedsprings.

Eight hours later, I landed in Seattle and immediately headed to my motel to reconstruct my bike and study maps until the names of the roads were as familiar as my own. Still, I worried. Had I packed enough spare tires and tubes? What if my bike got another crack? Or worse, what if I cracked up? Lenny had biked across the country with a support van and five-member crew, including a mechanic, cook, and masseuse. I would be doing it alone. I slept little that night.

Day 1: Seattle to Wenatchee, Washington, 165 miles

I woke at 5:00 a.m. as a bright orange sun was scaling the sky and rode 30 miles through morning traffic in downtown Seattle to Everett, Washington, where I baptized the back tire of my bike in Pacific waters. The trip had officially started. From there, I headed east to Wenatchee, apple capital of the world. I rode through the green Cascade Mountains, but something about my bike didn't feel right. After a few hours, my butt started to hurt, a discouraging development for the first day of a 3-week ride. By the time I got to my motel in Wenatchee that night, I had clusters of sores on my backside. Turned out my saddle was too high. After adjusting it, I limped to bed.

Day 2: Wenatchee to Spokane, Washington, 60 miles

A plague of biblical proportions greeted me on the road from Wenatchee to Spokane, Washington. Thousands of grasshoppers had descended on this desert byway, and it was impossible to avoid them. My tires smashed their bodies to green goo, and a crunching sound accompanied each death. I felt like the grasshopper reaper on Judgment Day. When I sought refuge at a gas station, the oil-stained attendant seemed unaffected by the invasion.

"Happens every year," he said slowly, especially during hot, dry periods, and it was easily 100°F in the shade that day. I prayed the nearby waters of the Grand Coulee Dam, the largest concrete structure in North America, wouldn't turn red. Little did I know, calamity was just around the next bend.

Day 3: Spokane, Washington, to Thompson Falls, Montana, 160 miles

I was riding through the panhandle of Idaho when I spotted a bunch of police cars ahead. As I drew closer, I saw a checkpoint had been set up across the road.

"Where are you going?" a police officer asked me at the barricade.

"New Jersey," I said.

"All right, wise guy, let's see some ID."

At the time I had no way of knowing that 3 days before, federal agents had ambushed the Ruby Ridge home of Randy Weaver, a survivalist and white separatist. His wife and infant daughter were shot and killed in the confrontation.

I produced my driver's license, but it wasn't enough. Apparently, the agent didn't read *Runner's World*. "Empty your saddlebags," he bellowed.

I complied, tossing clothes, socks, and the MacGyver wrench, which he eyed suspiciously, on the ground. "What do you need this for?" he said, picking up the wrench and slapping it against the palm of his hand like a nightstick.

"It's for my bike," I said, "in case it breaks down. New Jersey is a long way."

Satisfied by my explanation, he deemed me safe to pass and I rode until the town of Thompson Falls, Montana, where signs for LIVE BAIT lit up convenience-store windows, a neon calling card for the town's chief attraction.

Day 4: Thompson Falls to Missoula, Montana, 133 miles

My butt sores were finally feeling better after nightly soaks in a bathtub. After about 133 miles, I crossed into the college town of Missoula, Montana. The LIVE BAIT signs were replaced with COLD BEER, this town's top commodity.

Day 5: Missoula to Butte, Montana, 133 miles

I was on my way from Missoula to Butte, Montana, struggling to get comfortable once again on my bike. Something was wrong, but I couldn't figure out what. My seat was the right height. I had lubricated my butt with Vaseline to avoid chafing. The tires had enough air in them. What could be causing so much irritation? It was my bike shorts—they were inside out. I waited until I hit a deserted patch of road before stopping to correct my wardrobe malfunction. Just as I pulled off my shorts, a pickup truck crammed with three guys in the cab drove by. I'm sure they recounted my predicament with glee when they arrived at the construction site for work.

Day 6: Butte to West Yellowstone, Montana, 160 miles

I was drawing closer to Yellowstone National Park in Wyoming and wanted to shed some weight so I could ride faster. The heaviest item in my pack was the MacGyver wrench, and I hadn't used it since I left Seattle. I decided to get rid of it, but it was such a cool tool that I felt compelled to give it a proper home. Right before the Continental Divide in Montana, I spied the house of an ultimate handyman. There were three pickups parked outside, each one equipped with a shiny built-in toolbox. *This is the home for MacGyver,* I thought. I gently placed the wrench on the driveway and quietly rode away. I hoped whoever owned the trucks would find it later that day and think the tool fairy had paid a visit.

Day 7: West Yellowstone, Montana, to Cody, Wyoming, 152 miles

After paying a $2 admission fee, I passed into Yellowstone through the west side and stopped to watch Old Faithful's dependable eruption. I was awestruck by its prehistoric spew, but a guy standing behind me wasn't impressed. "We drove 200 miles to see this," he said in disgust. I imagined how upset he would have been if he had biked here.

I lodged that night at the Big Bear Motel in Cody, Wyoming. The rodeo was in town, and I went to a nearby pizza joint for dinner. The place was filled with cowboys wearing 10-gallon hats and sporting belt buckles the size of license plates. Then I spotted a guy wearing a baseball cap. He was by himself, so I moseyed over and introduced myself. "It looks like you and I are the only ones here who aren't cowboys," I said.

"No," he said. "I'm a cyclist and I'm biking across the country."

"Me, too," I said.

"When did you start?" he asked.

"Saturday," I said. "In Everett, Washington."

"Me, too," he said.

"That's weird. I wonder why we haven't run into each other before."

It took us a few minutes, but then we figured it out. He had started on Saturday, August 15. I began on Saturday, August 22. His mouth dropped open when he realized how many miles I had been covering a day.

"You're the lucky one," I said. "In 2 weeks I'll be back in my office, and you'll still be out on the road."

Day 8: Cody to Sheridan, Wyoming, 152 miles

After descending Medicine Mountain in Bighorn National Forest in Wyoming, I pulled over in a park to remove some layers of clothes. It was warmer at the bottom of the mountain, and I was sweating. After a few minutes I smelled a familiar odor, ganja, and it reminded me of my former self. I looked around and spotted three teens staring at me from a picnic table.

"Dude, what are you doing?" one asked.

"I'm riding my bike cross-country."

"Dude," he replied in all seriousness. "They have airplanes these days."

Day 9: Sheridan to New Castle, Wyoming, 197 miles

On my way from Sheridan to New Castle, Wyoming, I ran out of water and food at mile 40 but wasn't too concerned. The map showed I would pass through two towns within the next 50 miles, and I figured I could buy supplies there. Except the towns, Spotted Horse and Leiter, no longer existed, or at least no one lived there. The tattered curtains of deserted homes flapped in the breeze. It was eerie, but I had bigger problems than atmospheric anxiety. I was getting dehydrated and hungry, and it was about 90°F. I put my head down and focused on reaching the city of Gillette, Wyoming, at mile 108. When I got there 4 hours later, I stopped at the first store I saw. I was pale and slightly delirious from the heat. The store manager took pity on me and gave me a seat in his air-conditioned office so I could revive. I perked up after an hour, but I still had 90 miles to go until New Castle, where I had booked a room for the night. I stocked up on water and nutrition bars and tried to ignore the nearby motel with a vacancy sign advertising free cable and a pool. I knew if I stopped early, I'd just have to make up the miles in the morning.

Day 10: New Castle, Wyoming, to Kadoka, South Dakota, 187 miles

That afternoon, I entered the Badlands of South Dakota, the one place in the United States I had most wanted to visit. The desolate landscape of the sandstone cliffs and prairie grass fulfilled my fantasies. It began to rain in the distance, and for 20 miles I chased the storm, not once getting wet. As I followed the menacing clouds, I felt as if something or someone was pulling me through the Badlands. I heard voices in the wind. Maybe it was my ancestors. I would have liked to have been a Native American in the 1800s, completely self-sufficient and in communion with nature. I tried to think of a name for myself. Chief Sore Butt! That day's sunset was the prettiest I have ever seen. It stained the sky red with a warm glow.

Day 11: Kadoka to Mitchell, South Dakota, 180 miles

I stopped at a convenience store to buy some PowerBars, when a gang of muscled guys on motorcycles sneered at my wheels. "Get a motor," one of them hissed.

"Oh, yeah? If you were a real man, you wouldn't need a motor," I yelled. In my head.

In reality, I kept my mouth shut and walked away. I wasn't looking for a fight, especially one I couldn't win. Hours later, I passed the world's only Corn Palace, a convention and visitor's center in Mitchell, South Dakota. Its exterior is decorated with murals made from corn, rye, wheat, and other grains. Every year, a local artist designs a different theme; in 1992, the year I rolled by, the palace was celebrating its 100th anniversary with murals depicting the Statue of Liberty, Mount Rushmore, and Native American dancers.

Day 12: Mitchell, South Dakota, to Jackson, Minnesota, 165 miles

The roads from South Dakota to Minnesota were as flat as my prom date, and each small town boasted it was America's friendliest. I realized that from here on out, each night would be spent in a different state. I was halfway home.

Day 13: Jackson, Minnesota, to Charles City, Iowa, 161 miles

Lightning struck precariously close as I headed from Jackson, Minnesota, to Iowa. There was no rain, and I pedaled as fast as I could to avoid the storm. Each time I stopped to buy water and food or to rest, people were curious about my grungy appearance. "What are you doing?" someone would ask.

"I'm biking across the United States."

"Where's your crew?"

"Right here," I'd say, holding up my wallet.

That night I roomed in Charles City, Iowa, known as America's Friendliest Town.

Day 14: Charles City, Iowa, to Lancaster, Wisconsin, 141 miles

As I crossed the mighty Mississippi River into Wisconsin, I felt like I was making progress in my journey home. In Prairie du Chien,

Wisconsin, I stopped at a Pizza Hut. "I'd like a table by the door, two large pies, and a pitcher of soda," I told the waiter.

A few minutes later, the manager paid me a visit. "What did you order?" he asked.

"Two large pies," I said.

"Is someone joining you?"

"No. I'm hungry." Then it hit me—he thought I was going to dine and ditch. "I wanted a table by the door so I can watch my bike," I explained. "I just rode 100 miles, and I'm really hungry."

"Where are you headed?" he asked.

"I'm biking across the United States from Seattle to New York."

He gave me a funny look, but it must have satisfied his suspicion because the waiter brought out my pizza. I scarfed down all but three slices.

"You were hungry," the waiter said as he wrapped my leftovers for the road.

What can I say? I weighed about 140, 20 pounds less than when I had started the trip.

Day 15: Lancaster, Wisconsin, to Harvard, Illinois,
130 miles

As I pedaled toward Harvard, Illinois, the pace of life changed noticeably, replacing small-town hospitality with big-city hurry. I was about an hour outside Chicago, and motorists were impatient with my presence on the side of the road, honking their horns in a display of annoyance. When I stopped at a store to buy supplies, no one asked what I was doing or where I was going. They barely had enough time to fish for exact change before serving the next customer in line. I yearned for Charles City, Iowa, and all the other friendly towns I had pedaled through.

Day 16: Harvard, Illinois, to Rensselaer, Indiana, 159 miles

I was riding through Indiana on roads buttressed by cornfields when I came upon a four-way stop. There was no one around, except a pickup truck behind me, so I slowed at the traffic signal, then sped through.

"Bikes have to stop at stop signs," the driver of the pickup yelled out his window as he pulled up alongside me.

"I did stop," I hollered back. "You're the one who blew through the stop sign."

"Bikes don't belong on these roads," he said. "They were built for cars."

Was this guy for real? I was feeling ornery after battling a terrific headwind all day and wasn't about to take anyone's guff. I got off my bike, thinking he and I should air our differences, but he drove off, leaving me standing in the middle of nowhere, frustrated at being denied a stop-sign intervention.

Later that day I got my first and only flat tire.

Day 17: Rensselaer, Indiana, to Urbana, Ohio, 225 miles

As I neared the Amish farms of Ohio, a bunch of teenagers in a car mistook me for one of the Plain People. I wasn't wearing a straw hat, but my bike pants and shirt were black, as were my panniers. "What's in your pack, Levi?" they asked in a mocking tone.

"Cocaine," I said.

They realized their mistake and drove away. No one has confused me for an Amish person since.

Day 18: Urbana, Ohio, to Wheeling, West Virginia, 180 miles

The rolling hills east of Columbus, Ohio, look a lot like Pennsylvania, and I grew homesick as I passed more Amish farms where wash fluttered on clotheslines and teams of mules plowed the corn-fields. I spent the night in Wheeling, West Virginia, knowing I would be home in 2 days.

Day 19: Wheeling, West Virginia, to Shippensburg, Pennsylvania, 210 miles

This was the hardest day by far. There wasn't a flat stretch in all of western Pennsylvania, and the terrain was more challenging than the Rockies because the roads traversed the tops of tunnels con-structed for the turnpike. I had mailed my panniers home the day before, thinking the lighter load would make me faster, but it was still a struggle. I averaged between 8 and 10 miles an hour going up the hills and 50 miles an hour coming down. I rode 210 miles to Shippensburg, where I stopped for the night.

Day 20: Shippensburg, Pennsylvania, to Asbury Park, New Jersey, 220 miles

Lenny Vreeland, the guy responsible for planting the journey's seed, met me in Fredericksburg, Pennsylvania, and the two of us rode together for the next 10 miles on Hex Highway. He was smiling ear to ear, and his dark eyes twinkled with wistfulness and pride.

"Lenny," I said, embracing him in a sweaty hug. "You'll be happy to know that once I get to Asbury Park, I want to turn around and do it all over again."

"How did the bike work?" he wanted to know.

"Great," I said. "No problems."

"How do you feel? You look tired."

"No, I'm great," I said.

"What did you think about those hills in western Pennsylvania?"

"They were the worst," I assured him, knowing they gave him trouble, too. "It was a hard climb."

"Is it hard not having a crew?"

"Not at all. You know I like being self-sufficient."

For the next hour we swapped stories and impressions. I told him about the grasshoppers, the scads of law enforcement agents at Ruby Ridge, and the other cross-country cyclist whose pace was a bit slower than mine. But then Lenny grew tired and loaded his bike back into a support vehicle that had been following us. Ever since his heart surgery a few years before, Lenny could no longer pedal like the young man who had blazed a path across America on a bicycle.

We said good-bye, and I headed to Asbury Park, where I knew every bump and crook in the roads. I had traveled them hundreds of times on training rides. When I cruised into Frenchtown, New Jersey, a pack of cyclists asked where I was headed. I told them I was just about to wrap up a 3,000-mile excursion. They asked if they could ride with me for a few miles, and I said sure. I had become a rolling novelty, and they escorted me until I was about 20 miles outside the beach resort of Asbury Park, where rocker Bruce Springsteen had gotten his start. A group of teens in a car pulled up next to me at a red light. "How far did you go?" they asked.

"I'm riding my bike across the United States. I left Seattle 20 days ago."

A smile broke out on the driver's face. "Dude," he said. "I think you're going to make it."

And I did. Just as the last glimmerings of the sun tickled the ocean, I dipped my front tire into the Atlantic's chilly surf. I couldn't travel by bike any farther. I thought of Lenny and all the strangers I had met along the way. I may have been by myself, but I was never alone.

The next day I rode to work and hung a map of the United States on my office wall. I stuck a thumbtack into each town where I had stopped for the night. Everyone who came by my office heard about the beauty of the Badlands, the stoned kids in the park, and the kind convenience-store manager who let me cool off in his office. Now I knew why Lenny relished the retelling of each mile and his affinity for America.

Not a day has gone by that I haven't thought about some aspect of that trip. My relationship with maps has changed, too. I no longer see dots and squiggles when I look at the path I traveled. I see cowboys and mountains, cornfields and corner stores, Pizza Huts, swirling rivers, and strangers who became friends. And I see myself, connected by the thread of memory to it all.

The pull of the road was so strong that 2 years later I did the trip again. When I hit the road and crossed the same byways and mountains, my muscle memory and senses kicked into high gear, and I practically floated across the country.

It was the kind of experience that my friend Lenny could appreciate. I got one last chance to share it with him in 2005. Diagnosed with cancer, he called to say he didn't have much time. I hopped on my bike and pedaled to his house. He looked so weak propped up on his couch, but when he saw me his eyes lit up and a smile spread across his face. "What about those hills in western Pennsylvania?" I said.

"Yes, yes," he nodded.

When I left his home that day, I knew his spirit would ride on.

Recovering drug and alcohol addicts, whom Bart trained for the Lehigh River Relay, run in the Lehigh Parkway in Allentown, Pennsylvania, 1995

Chapter 7

CLEAN STREAKS

The security guard with bulging arms stood near the edge of the grassy field and watched in silence as I introduced myself to the six guys who had signed up to run the Red Cross Lehigh Valley River Relay, a 22-mile footrace from Allentown to Easton, Pennsylvania.

He was there to protect me in case these out-of-shape convicts from Keenan House, an inpatient drug and alcohol rehabilitation center in Allentown, became unruly during the twice-weekly workouts I'd be conducting. I was pretty sure that wouldn't happen, but Aaron Blake, senior counselor of the center, wasn't so sure. "Addicts can't be trusted," he'd said. "They're unreliable."

I understood his concerns, but I still wanted to give it a shot. When I founded the relay race 2 years earlier in 1990, I'd wanted to pick an unlikely group of candidates each year to train for the relay as an introduction to running. I had been too busy getting the race off the ground to train anyone until now, so the Keenan House residents were my inaugural bunch. I chose them because I had experienced the redemptive powers of running in my own recovery from drugs and alcohol and hoped the sport would do the same for them.

Although Aaron liked the idea, he said participation in my program had to be voluntary, and he couldn't guarantee that anyone would sign on. I showed up at the Keenan House a few days later and made my sales pitch. "The race is a relay, so we need at least five runners who are each willing to run a 4½-mile leg," I said. "We'll train 2 days a week, 1 hour a day, for the next 8 weeks."

The group let out a collective groan, but their eyes widened when they realized that the training would take place off-site. As inpatients, they weren't allowed to leave the premises, and the promise of a few hours of freedom was tantalizing.

"So, you're saying all we have to do is run?" asked one resident with a shaved head and tattoos. "That don't seem like much."

"You're going to have to work hard," I warned them. "No goofing off. This won't be a playdate. In return, you'll get the benefits of exercise and the satisfaction of knowing you did something positive."

Aaron asked me to leave the room so they could discuss my offer. When I was allowed back in 15 minutes later, I had six new tough-talking recruits. There was James, a 29-year-old African American from Philadelphia who had been commuted to Keenan House 2 months earlier after being released from state prison on drug charges. He was built like an NFL linebacker, and his body was chiseled from lifting weights.

At 25, Michael was the youngest of the group, a former high school wrestler released from county prison 4 months before. Daryl, 36, was short and stocky but long on enthusiasm. He didn't say much, but he was always the first on the field, and I could tell he was into it. At 44, Joey and Eric were the old men of the group, and Joseph, 29, had the physique of a runner—long and lean. He was

Latino, and his body was sheathed in tattoos, but he had a soft side that he later revealed.

They looked like a tough bunch, and I knew I was going to have to win them over first and gain their respect later. On the first day of practice, I showed up with a carload of free running shoes and T-shirts courtesy of *Runner's World*. "Who wears a size 10?" I said, popping open one cardboard shoebox after another. "How about a 13?"

They couldn't believe it. Not only were they off the Keenan House grounds, but they were getting free stuff. "Dude, you're all right," James said.

That's when I told the security guard to go home. I knew I wasn't going to have to worry about these guys. If anything, my new posse would protect me.

"All right, guys," I said. "We're going to start slow. We'll work up to running a mile without stopping and gradually build up to five."

"We can run a mile, man," said James. "That's no problem. The question is, can you keep up?"

Years of alcohol and drug abuse had taken its toll on these guys, but what they lacked in stamina they more than made up for in confidence. They all believed they could run at least 10 miles without much effort.

"Let's go," I said, leading the group around a 600-meter loop in Trout Creek Park in Allentown. By the second lap, they had all fallen behind.

"I got a cramp, bro," one said, clutching his side.

Another fell on his knees and ralphed in the weeds.

"No breaks, guy," I said to the vomiting runner. "Keep going. Walk if you have to."

Suddenly they weren't so cocky, but they all showed up for

practice a few days later. Cramps and sore muscles were not going to stop this crew from a few hours of sunshine.

After 3 weeks, I noticed a change. They could run two laps without stopping, then a mile, then two. Their newfound endurance was a source of pride, and they stopped taking cigarette breaks between workouts. I felt a kinship with them. I had once walked in their shoes, and now they could run in the ones I had given them.

For all their problems and brushes with the law, I could tell they were good people. It was their misfortune to be under the spell of drugs and trapped in addiction's seductive embrace.

But I never revealed my past to them. It was still a source of shame, and I didn't want to shatter their respect for me as a coach and marathon runner. I also didn't want to tarnish my reputation at *Runner's World.* In retrospect, I wish I had told them about my troubled past. I had proven addiction could be overcome, and it was a lesson they could have carried with them in times of self-doubt.

They were running a continuous 3 miles by week 5, but they still had a ways to go. During one practice, Joey hit a wall and couldn't run. "I ain't doing this no more," he said, slowing to a trot.

James caught up with him. "Come on, brother," he said. "You've got a lot more in you."

It was a transcending moment. These men, who for most of their lives had focused only on scoring drugs and getting high, were looking out for one another. They started to see themselves as a team, part of something bigger than their immediate needs, although they still complained of physical woes. Michael, the former wrestler, suffered hamstring problems. James developed a stomach ulcer, Joseph had back pain, and a few of them experienced asthma attacks from the exertion.

Yet, they were willing to put it all on the line and even named themselves the Clean Streaks, a shout-out to their recent sobriety and perceived speed. In the beginning they would have been satisfied with finishing the race, but now they bragged about winning it and fought among themselves over who would accept the trophy during the awards ceremony. There's nothing wrong with feeling confident about a race, but their expectations were now inflated, and I only hoped they wouldn't be discouraged if they fell short of their goal.

Two days before the race, a Lehigh County judge who had sentenced a few of the runners to prison on drug-related charges called me. A local newspaper had run a story about the team, and he had recognized some of the men. "I just wanted to thank you for helping these guys improve their lives," he said. The judge said he planned to run the race, too, but didn't want the men to know in case they sought retribution on the trail. I told him I didn't think that was likely, considering the men's strong desire to win, but I agreed it probably wasn't a good idea to reveal that the man who had sent them to the slammer would be on the course.

On July 26, 1992, roughly 750 runners gathered at Lehigh Canal Park in Allentown for the start of the race. Most of them were experienced runners who logged 40 miles a week. They wore brightly hued singlets and shorts, sunglasses, and white ankle socks with Nike and Adidas logos. My guys showed up in cutoffs and white tanks that revealed colorful body art.

"Where are the running clothes I gave you?" I asked.

"They ain't cool," said Joseph.

But when a volunteer handed them their race bibs, they were only too happy to conform. This wasn't a prison number but one they could wear with pride, and they helped each other attach their bibs as if they were boutonnieres on prom night.

They stuck out like teenagers at a bingo game, but everyone knew who they were anyway from the newspaper article. The other runners welcomed them with hearty handshakes and calls of "Good luck." The men were stunned by the warm reception. No one cared where they had come from or what they had done. They were runners here, same as everyone else.

I couldn't have scripted it better, but one thing worried me: They still thought they could win. They really believed it. I didn't think they had a chance, but who knew? The fact that they hadn't bailed after 8 weeks was testament enough to their determination.

I gathered them for one last pep talk. "Okay, guys, this is it," I said. "You're part of a team. Others are counting on you. If you do this, you can do anything. Now get out there and kick some butt."

"Clean Streaks!" they cheered.

The relay was 22 miles, meaning each member of the team would run a little over 4 miles. Eric was the alternate.

Daryl was the first runner, but he made the same mistake I had during that first race with my brother, George. He went out way too fast and had to slow about a mile into the charge to catch his breath.

Joey was next. He knew he wasn't the strongest athlete and was worried about disappointing the team. So when Daryl handed him the baton, he took off. "I will do this if I have to crawl across the finish line," he muttered under his breath. "Don't be the weak link in this chain."

Four miles later, huffing and red in the face, Joey passed the baton to Michael, who later handed it to James for the longest leg. "Go, go!" shouted Michael. "We can do this."

James dug deep, remembering his high school days on the gridiron. If only he had stayed clean, he thought, but at least his stomach ulcer wasn't bothering him. James was tearing it up, but the team was being outpaced by the other runners.

Then it was Joseph's turn. The fastest of the group, he was the anchor. The other runners and I had gathered at the finish line to welcome him home. Everyone was cheering for him now. "Clean Streaks, Clean Streaks," the crowd chanted.

A few yards from the finish, Joseph spotted me and smiled. His pace quickened and he sprinted to the end, then raised his arms in celebration. His team hugged him as tears rolled down his face.

"You guys did awesome," I said. "This was worth all your hard work and meeting you guys out on the trail. I'm proud of you. Stick around. The other runners want to meet you. You're the talk of the town."

Those men didn't seem to care that they hadn't won. They were caught up in the excitement of finishing their first race. For once they were receiving recognition for doing something positive and not being punished for screwing up, and they relished the acceptance of the other runners.

Joey asked if he could borrow a quarter from me to call his mother. "She's not going to believe this," he said, his voice choked with emotion. "I did it. I never gave up."

The other runners congratulated them, and they accepted their kudos with grace and humility. Out of 150 teams, the Clean Streaks placed 110th, not as high as they would have liked, but it was a start.

"Running is about patience," I said. "These other teams have been running for years. You guys just started. So what's next?"

"Boston, bro," cried Daryl.

After the race, we headed back to the Keenan House to celebrate over bowls of ice cream and cake. There was even a trophy engraved with their names. The other residents appeared jealous of all the attention bestowed on the Clean Streaks and a bit remorseful they hadn't trained, too.

James came up to me after the party. "Thank you for trusting me, man," he said. "No one's ever done that before."

"You keep running," I said. "Maybe one day you'll beat me."

"You watch out because I'm going to do it," he said. "Even if it takes me until I'm 65."

I couldn't stop smiling. I felt their achievement was my own. For 8 long weeks I had pushed them out of a lethargy brought on by poor choices. They got a taste of a better world, but now it was up to them to stay sober.

I wished them resolve. Luck wouldn't be enough.

A few months later I returned to the Keenan House, but my posse was gone. Some had been released, and others had returned to prison. It's a transient place, Aaron explained, and residents come and go. The population is rarely static. "It's amazing that those six guys stuck with you for as long as they did," he said.

I felt sad. My team had scattered, but about 6 years later I ran into Daryl at a high school basketball game. I shook his hand. "How's it going?" I asked.

"Good, good, but I'm not doing too much running anymore."

"So you didn't do Boston?"

"No, man," he said, staring at his feet. "I got busy."

"Hey, that's okay, you do what you can."

"That's my son," he said, pointing to a long-legged youth on the court. The boy looked strong and powerful, a less developed version of his father. "I told him about the race and how you trained us," he said. "He was impressed. He wants to run. Maybe we'll run together."

"That's cool," I said.

I could tell he was uncomfortable, my presence invoking painful memories of his past. "Well, take care," I said.

I never saw him or anyone else from my posse again. I wish I could say that they stayed clean and found jobs and went on to be productive members of society, but I just don't know. I only hope the experience has been etched in their minds as a shining moment of possibility.

BARE BUNS FUN RUN — FINISH LINE

Bart crosses finish line at
Bare Buns Fun Run,
winning the textile-free
masters division, 1997

Chapter 8

BARE BUNS FUN RUN

I had run a lot of races by 1997, but the Bare Buns Fun Run at a nudist camp in Washington State would be my first au naturel. Bare Buns wasn't the only nude race in the country, but it was the largest—the Super Bowl for racing "buffs."

It took place every July at Kaniksu Ranch, a 240-acre family nudist resort 40 miles north of Spokane, in a valley between two rugged mountain passes. The race started in 1984 as a way to change the public's perception about social nudity and dispel misconceptions that nudist colonies are hotbeds of sexual activity, said Steve Anson, director of Bare Buns. Social nudity is about liberation, not copulation, he explained, a belief shared by some famous guys. Benjamin Franklin and Henry David Thoreau were big proponents of walking around naked, calling the practice "air baths," and former president John Quincy Adams enjoyed skinny-dipping in the Potomac.

Twelve people ran the first race, and by the late 1990s, the field had grown to between 700 and 800 runners. It's one of the few clothing-optional races open to the public, and it draws people from all 50 states. Some are runners, but most just want a glimpse into the lives of nudists, Steve said.

The American Association for Nude Recreation boasts a membership of 50,000, which means there are a lot of people out there who enjoy taking off their clothes and hanging out in a social setting. I just never thought I was one of them.

Yet here I was, inviting the female director of a Colorado marathon to accompany me to the Bare Buns Fun Run. As you can imagine, this is not an activity one enters into lightly, and she had her reservations.

"Our first date can't be at a nude race," she told me over the phone. I guess she feared that if things worked out between us, we'd have to tell our children that their parents hooked up at a nudist ranch—not exactly a romantic or wholesome family history to be repeated through the generations.

"How about you fly out for the weekend and we go hiking instead?" she suggested. "That way we can get to know each other a bit better before we, you know . . ."

"Take our clothes off?"

"It will just be more comfortable."

"Okay," I said. "I'll see you soon."

A week before the race, I flew from Pennsylvania to Colorado for 2 days of fully clothed dinners and trail running. I suggested we take off our shirts to get a taste for nude running, but she wasn't buying it. "Let's save it for the race," she said.

That Sunday she took me to the airport, and we said good-bye.

Five days after I returned home from Colorado, the Date and I met again at Spokane International Airport, where we rented a car and drove together to the Kaniksu campground, a few miles from Deer Lake and Kaniksu National Forest. We were still wearing our clothes, or textiles, as professional nudists refer to them, when we pulled up to the ranch gates.

"Should we take off our clothes?" the Date asked.

"I don't know," I said.

It was a dilemma. I didn't want to take off my pants prematurely, but I didn't want to violate any rules by keeping them on. Eventually, two nude camp greeters approached the car. I breathed a sigh of relief. The woman was about 50 pounds overweight, and the man . . . How should I put this? Let's just say that I wasn't going to be the smallest in my division.

Now, if I had been met by a 20-year-old Adonis, I might have peeled away in despair like most men, but the organizers of the race probably had that figured out. I suspected these people were carefully chosen to instill confidence in those of us who had brought along our insecurities.

"Welcome to Kaniksu," the man said.

"Hi, I'm Bart Yasso. I'm the guest speaker at the race."

"We've been waiting for you, Bart," he said.

I introduced them to my date. "We're nudies—I mean, newbies," I said, laughing at my slip.

"You have the best spot in the whole campground," the woman said. "Your tent is at the finish line, and we have it all set up."

"Great," I said.

"A bunch of runners have already shown up," the man said. "Why don't you slip out of your clothes and get comfortable? There's some great hiking trails, volleyball, and a pool if you want to take a dip."

Anson somehow heard that I had arrived and came out to say hello. "You finally made it, Bart," he said. "How do you like my running uniform?"

He turned around to show me his bare bottom.

"It could use some ironing," I joked.

"Your tent is down there," he said. "I'll see you at dinner."

Steve had been bugging me for years to run the 5-K and be the guest speaker at the pasta dinner, but I kept putting him off, unwilling to expose myself to unnecessary ridicule. I finally agreed to do it to get him off my back, and now I was about to run his race with nothing on mine.

The Date and I drove to our tent and parked the car. Unpacking was easy. I had only brought an extra pair of running shoes, socks, and a fleece jacket in case it got cold. Our tent was nothing more than a nylon bubble with a zipper, but for the next 3 days, it was home. We ducked inside to disrobe.

"You first," she said.

"Maybe we should play strip poker?" I suggested.

"Let's just get this over with."

We peeled off our clothes and laughed at our nervousness, hoping it was only temporary. Then we walked outside wearing only bug spray and sunscreen.

It felt weird at first, but everyone was naked—the young, old, skinny, and rotund. They were munching on nachos at the snack bar, spiking volleyballs on the sand court, and lounging by the pool.

"Hey, look at that guy," the Date said. "He's reading the newspaper upside down."

The display of flesh was like passing a car wreck on the highway. You didn't want to look, but you had to look. You couldn't help it. My eyes were drawn to boobs, butts, and, um, other things. But after a few minutes I had seen my fill. I couldn't handle any more nudity. It was like eating too much chocolate chip cookie dough. I felt a bit queasy. "Let's go for a hike," I suggested.

"Sounds good to me," said the Date.

We grabbed two bottles of water and walked toward the trail, which was marked by a wooden sign.

"So, do you think you'll be able to run faster without clothes?" my Date asked.

"I don't know. I think I might get distracted. Is this what you expected?"

"I'm not sure. Everyone seems so completely unself-conscious of their nakedness," she said.

We exchanged small talk for the next hour or so, until we passed a group of nude hikers from the ranch. They were wearing running shoes, so we figured they were there for the race.

"Hi guys," the one said. "Having a good time?"

"So far so good," I said.

"Aren't you Bart Yasso from *Runner's World*?"

"That's me."

"Hey, we're going to do a training run around the course tonight. Want to join us?"

"I'd love to. See you tonight."

We parted ways, and the Date and I continued on our hike. "So how are we going to do this?" I asked.

"Do what?"

"This. Us. You're in Colorado, and I'm in Pennsylvania."

"I don't know. I guess we'll figure something out."

"Hey, did you hear that?" I asked.

"What?"

"Sh-h-h, listen."

"It sounds like a car," she said.

"I know. I don't think we should be hearing cars."

The campground wasn't that big, but somehow we had missed the trail marker and ended up on the side of a highway in no-no land, property off-limits to the clothing-challenged. We could see houses not too far in the distance. "We should head back," I said. "I don't think this is part of the camp."

We turned around and started walking toward what we hoped was the Kaniksu clubhouse. "Can you imagine if we would have gotten arrested?" the Date said.

"I'm not sure how I would have explained that one to George," I said, referring to my publisher, George Hirsch.

But then, George was not a man of convention, so maybe he would have understood. Actually, he encouraged my crazy stunts; plus, running in the nude wasn't so far-fetched. The early Greek Olympians ran relays, threw javelins, and wrestled sans loincloths. Legend has it that competing nude in the Olympics began after one contestant took off his pants so he could run faster. I didn't think they had pants back then, but competing nude had its practical side. For one thing, there was no place to hide a dagger; also, it was stinking hot in Greece.

On an aesthetic level, the athletic male body was considered an object of beauty, a gift to the gods, which explains all those statues made in exacting detail. And it wasn't just eye candy for married women; they were barred from watching the naked male athletes compete in the Olympics.

I'm not saying I looked like one of those marble statues, but I was having fun. Public nudity felt incredibly liberating. Plus, it was a good way to save money on clothes. However, I was planning on wearing some during my speech the next night.

"You mean I have to give the speech naked?" I asked Steve, incredulous at this newly discovered detail.

"Bart, you're at a nudist ranch. No one wears clothes."

"But it's a pasta dinner," I argued. "What if I drip spaghetti sauce?

"That's why there are napkins," he said.

Roughly 200 naked, hungry runners showed up at the dining hall Saturday night to carbo-load. They were all buck naked, including me, the inspirational speaker, who would have to stand at the front of the room. I prayed for a podium, but there wasn't one.

My Date, on the other hand, had become perfectly comfortable wearing nothing but her birthday suit after spending hours on the volleyball court. For reasons I don't understand, volleyball is big at nudist camps. There was a line of people waiting to get in on the game, and they played from morning until night. Our tent was near the court, so I got an eyeful, and I'm here to tell you that there's a reason the sports-bra industry is so profitable. There was more jiggling on that volleyball court than on the Dow Jones on a volatile day.

As I climbed on the stage at dinner, I thought about how, when I'd first started giving speeches, I'd envision the audience in the buff to quiet my knocking knees. Now everyone was really naked, including me. If anyone heckled, I'd need therapy.

"I've done a lot of public speaking, but this will be my first time naked," I told the audience, most of whom would not be running the next day's race but had shown up to be entertained by a slide show of my running adventures. Normally, I try to get runners excited for a race, but this gig called for a different approach. Instead of inspiring running stories, I fed them travel stories, which was more their speed.

The next day was the race, and at 5:30 a.m. the air temperature was a chilly 50°F. I put on shorts and a fleece jacket, but I was still freezing my butt off. The weather warmed up once the sun came out, and everyone disrobed, including me.

The Bare Buns 5-K is clothing optional, but few people wear it. There's something voyeuristic about being the only runner wearing clothes in a group of 800. Allowances, however, are made for those who need some support. Large-breasted women can wear sports bras and well-endowed men jockstraps, up until they reach the "drop zone," a distance of 200 yards before the finish line. There they have to remove the items to qualify for a textile-free finish.

For the record, I wasn't going to stop at the drop zone, but there was plenty of swaggering at the start by a few delusional souls who feared they would suffer an injury without the confines of heavy equipment.

My Date, who decided not to run because she was still nursing a knee injury, was given permission to snap photographs. Normally, photographs aren't allowed because of privacy issues, but Steve allowed her to take a few long-range shots for my slide show. Close-ups, however, were taboo.

Steve had given out bib numbers at the pasta dinner, and when I reached inside my race packet, I noticed there were safety pins. "Hey Steve," I said. "What am I supposed to do with these?'

He gestured toward another runner, who had attached his race bib to a nipple piercing. "He's done this before, hasn't he?" I said. I opted to secure my bib to my arm with yarn.

Actually, it was easy to distinguish the professional nudists from the amateurs by their tan lines. The pros didn't have any.

With 10 minutes to go before the race, I did some strides and then joined the other runners at the starting line.

"Hey, Bart," a runner said. "How's it hanging?"

He must recognize me from the pasta dinner, I thought.

"Good luck, Bart," another one hollered.

"Hey Bart, don't run too hard."

Everyone it seemed knew my name. Steve was on the sidelines laughing, so I ran over to find out what was going on. He immediately fessed up. "I put a note in everyone's race bag saying Bart Yasso from *Runner's World* magazine would be wearing bib No. 1," he said. "You're a celebrity!"

I was suddenly very thankful for the no-photos policy.

When the starting gun fired, a ribbon of flesh surged forward along a dirt path that looped around the camp past Pacific redwoods and pine trees. This was not a denuded forest.

The course marshals were naked. Most of the volunteers at the two water stops were naked, the spectators were naked, and the one lone wheelchair athlete was naked. When I hit the turnaround point, I was momentarily distracted by the wave of naked people running toward me. I tried to stay focused, but it wasn't easy. This was better than the girlie magazines I used to stow under my bed as a teen.

But then my competitive side kicked in as another runner caught up to me, and I started sprinting. I thought it might feel weird or uncomfortable to run without shorts, but I was wrong. From an anatomical standpoint, running in the buff felt no different than running fully clothed, an observation not likely popular with the multibillion-dollar running apparel industry.

When I saw the finish line, I poured on the heat, beating my competition by, er, a nose and winning the master's division.

The Date greeted me with a hug. "You did great," she gushed. "How was it?"

"Interesting," I said. "Especially the water stops. Guys had orange vests on and no pants."

Then it was time to pick up my T-shirt and medal. Unlike other races, where your T-shirt is included in the race packet, Bare Buns hands them out at the end to keep people honest. There are two versions, one for nude finishers and a less desirable one for clothed runners. Mine read "I ran nude at the Bare Buns Fun Run."

The awards ceremony was also conducted in the flesh, and I received a medal for winning my age division from a woman in a white robe who reminded me of Grace Slick, the lead singer of Jefferson Starship. At the time I thought it was odd that she was semiclothed, but I later learned naturists wear robes when they're menstruating.

Steve asked me to help hand out the finishing medals. "Congratulations," I said to each runner as I put some Bare Buns bling around their necks.

"You going to do one of these again?" a woman asked.

"You bet," I said. "This was the best."

When all the finishers had received a medal, the Date and I headed back to our tent to dress and pack. For the first time in 3 days I put on underwear and stepped into cotton shorts. I slowly buttoned my shirt. It felt scratchy against my sunburned chest. The Date reluctantly pulled a dress over her head. We laughed at our former modesty.

"It's time to go back to the real world," she said.

"Where it's illegal to take off our clothes," I added.

"Only in public," she said coyly.

"All of our friends are going to want to do this, you know."

"Yeah, but I don't want to see them naked."

Steve came to say good-bye. "See ya, Bart," he said. "You were a good sport."

I thanked him for the experience, and the Date and I got in our car and drove through the gates of Kaniksu Ranch to no-no land. She and I never did get married, but we continued to see each other for several months after Bare Buns.

I never did a nude race again, but it wasn't because I felt uncomfortable or squeamish. There just aren't a lot of opportunities to run naked.

The weekend after I returned from Bare Buns, I did a local 5-K race. After taking off my sweatpants I started to remove my shorts but caught myself in time.

Oops. Wrong race.

REWARD

PAID BY THE
DEER LAKE PROPERTY OWNERS ASSOCIATION

FOR INFORMATION LEADING
TO THE ARREST AND CONVICTION
OF PERSONS INVOLVED IN
THEFT OR VANDALISM OF
ASSOCIATION MEMBERS PROPERTY
SHERIFF'S OFFICE: 1-800-572-0947

KANIKS
Ranch
8 mi

Bart enters Kaniksu
Nudist Ranch where the
Bare Buns Fun Run took
place in July, 1997

Taco Bell drags Bart to the
start of the race in Westcliffe,
Colorado, in May, 1998

Chapter 9

BURRO RACING

Taco Bell was the meanest, fastest, most stubborn burro I've ever met, and he despised me from the moment we crossed paths. He snorted in protest when I tried to scratch him behind the ears and bared his teeth at the sounds of my sweet talk.

"This one's a little temperamental," said Bill Lee, better known as Red Tail Mountain Man, describing my running partner for a 10-K burro race in Westcliffe, Colorado.

"I don't think he likes me," I said, slowly backing away from Taco Bell as he shook his head and pawed the ground.

"Nonsense," said Red Tail Mountain Man, who raised and trained burros at his ranch in Idaho Springs, Colorado. He resembled an old prospector, with his long white beard, weathered face, and wiry frame. "He just has to get to know you."

There wasn't much time. The race began in an hour, and Taco Bell was in no mood to bond. This wasn't an encouraging beginning to a relationship expected to last for 6.2 miles.

"Now remember," said Red Tail, "you're in charge. If he gives you any trouble, just press your elbow into his neck."

I hoped I wouldn't have to do that. I love animals, but this one was pushing my patience, and I knew getting him to the finish line was going to be a battle of wills.

Burro racing is the only sport indigenous to Colorado. It was started as a way to infuse the local economy with tourist dollars at its Gold Days celebration and pay homage to the area's mining heritage. Legend has it that in the 1880s, two competing miners discovered gold in the same place and raced to the courthouse to file their claim first. Because burros carried supplies, the miners were forced to run, leading the animals with a rope.

The first burro race in 1949 was 22 miles from Leadville, a dusty one-stoplight town 10,430 feet high in the Rocky Mountains, to Fairplay, an old mining outpost. The *Rocky Mountain News* offered $500 to the winner, enough to buy a car in those days. A bartender at a hotel in Fairplay upped the ante, saying he'd give a case of beer to every finisher. Twenty-one men showed up with their animals, but two were disqualified because they brought mules, not burros.

What's the difference? Mules are the domesticated offspring of a female horse and a donkey, and a burro is a small donkey. A jackass is a wild donkey or someone who runs a race with a burro.

The burro race continued the next year, but the people of Leadville started to grumble because the finish line was in Fairplay, and that's where everyone waited out the results, ate lunch, and shopped. On race day, Leadville was a ghost town once the starting gun fired. The next year, race organizers reversed the route, but that angered the shop owners in Fairplay. So after that, each town held its own burro race.

As the sport gained popularity, other towns got in on the action. Today there are about six burro races in Colorado, as well as others in New Mexico, Arizona, and Nevada.

I agreed to do a burro race not for the promise of a case of beer but at the suggestion of my friend Nancy Hobbs, executive director of the American Trail Running Association. She thought I'd enjoy the challenge and novelty of running with a burro. As I stood nose to nose with Taco Bell, I wasn't so sure, but if there's a theme to my life, it's this: I don't seek out adventure, but it usually finds me through well-meaning friends.

In June 1998, I flew to Colorado Springs, where Nancy lives, and the two of us drove to Westcliffe, home of Hal and Mary Walter, burro racers extraordinaire. Hal is a two-time world champion, author of *Pack Burro Stories,* and an ultra-runner. Nancy wanted me to meet Hal so he could give me some tips. I wasn't sure this was necessary. How hard could it be to pull a burro by a rope? Nancy assured me it wasn't that simple.

Hal warned me not to underestimate the amount of athleticism needed for the sport. "A burro is fast," he said. "It can easily run a 3-minute mile. People think burros are these slow, putzy animals, and they have no clue. But the truth is they can run as fast as a horse, and they can accelerate quickly from nothing."

Still, I considered myself in good shape. No donkey was going to make an ass of me. "How do you train?" I asked.

"You have to spend time with your burro so you know its moods and what buttons not to push," Hal said. "The best racers have an almost marital relationship with their burros."

"Do you run with them?" I asked.

"Sure, about three times a week. But there's more to the sport than being fit," he said. "You have to be part strongman, part animal whisperer, and a little bit nuts."

At least I had the nuts part down. Maybe that's why Taco Bell resisted my efforts to establish a relationship.

"Come on, boy," I said, taking the reins from Red Tail before the race. "Let's go for a little practice jog and get to know each other better." But he wouldn't budge. "Come on," I said, pulling on the rope. "Let's do this."

He turned his head and started running in the other direction. "Stop, stop," I shouted, clinging to the rope.

"Hit him in the neck with your elbow," Red Tail yelled, but I wasn't anywhere near Taco Bell's head. I was at his rear end, so to speak.

So much for showing him who's boss. Both Taco Bell and I knew who that was: him.

There were about 30 of us at the start line that year, including Danelle Ballengee, a professional endurance athlete. Eight years later she would almost die after falling 60 feet to the floor of a canyon in Moab, Utah. Her 3-year-old dog, a German shepherd/golden retriever mix, led rescuers to her broken body, saving her life and demonstrating the strong bond between people and animals.

Unfortunately, there was no human-animal connection between Danelle and her burro, Nestor. Like me, she struggled to hold on to the rope. I later discovered why Danelle and I had been given the most cantankerous burros in the bunch. Red Tail, who owned the burros, figured the two of us had the strength and athleticism to control the animals or at least keep up with them.

He was wrong on both counts.

There are just a few rules in burro racing, and they're goofy. First, the burro must carry 33 pounds of gear, including a pick, a shovel, and a gold pan to symbolize Colorado's mining past. Second, the runner and burro must stay connected at all times by a 15-foot rope. Third, the runner may "push, pull, drag, or carry" the burro, but the burro can't carry the runner. Last, the athlete must keep his burro under control at all times. Other than that, anything goes.

"Good luck," Nancy said as Taco Bell and I ambled toward the start line.

"I'm going to need it," I said.

A bearded guy who looked like the cartoon character Yosemite Sam fired the starting gun. The noise startled Taco Bell, and he took off with the speed of a bullet train. I could barely hang on to the rope.

From the corner of my eye, I noticed another runner, Tom Sobel, a seasoned burro racer, had tied the rope between his legs and would jump into the air so that at times his feet weren't touching the ground. I was impressed but not enough to imitate his strategy. I was not going to risk losing my manhood over a burro race, especially since Taco Bell still had his intact. He was an uncut male, or a jack, meaning he hadn't been castrated. That's what made him so aggressive and horny. He had to be muzzled during mating because he would try and seduce the jill, a female burro, with love bites, and not of the tender persuasion.

For the next 2 miles, Taco Bell set a blistering pace, running under a 6-minute mile. Ordinarily, I can run that fast, but the thin air made it difficult to breathe, so I yanked the rope to slow him down. I wanted to give him a neck butt, as Red Tail had advised, but I was so far behind him that I couldn't even reach his tail. Taco Bell must have sensed my distress because he ran faster, ripping the rope from my hands.

"You bastard," I cursed, now burro-less and embarrassed. "Get back here!"

There was nothing to do but chase after him. I wasn't the only runner in hot pursuit of a fleeing burro. Danelle's had broken free, too.

There are no water stops along the racecourse; instead, there are catch points where volunteers retrieve errant burros. That's where Taco Bell and Nestor had been snagged.

"Which one's which?" Danelle asked. The burros looked the same with shaggy manes and brown hides, but it didn't take me long to pick out Taco Bell. He was the nasty one trying to get away. Nestor was nuzzling and kissing his captor while Taco Bell was rearing his head in a hissy fit.

"Thank you," I said, retrieving his rope from a panicked-looking volunteer.

"Man, he's ornery," the guy said.

A few people in the crowd chuckled.

"Is this your first time?" one asked.

"Can you tell? Guess I'm not any better with burros than I am with women."

Taco Bell brayed in agreement and took off running until the halfway point at mile 3.

Then he stopped.

"Come on, Taco Bell," I said. "Let's go." But he wouldn't move an inch. He was as stubborn as a mule.

I recalled what Hal had said about burros—the best racers are married to their animals. I was still a single guy, but at one time I had a live-in girlfriend and was somewhat indoctrinated into the ways of women. I could be smooth on occasion.

"Come on, Taco Bell," I said. "You can do it."

"We've only got 3 miles to go, baby."

"You're the fastest and cutest burro in the race."

I looked around and noticed three or four other runners couldn't get their burros to move, either.

"Don't these burros know this is a 10-K?" I joked. "Someone should teach them how to do negative splits."

Even good old Nestor was holding firm in the middle of the course.

By now the experienced runners, like Sobel, were out of sight. Positive affirmation was clearly not working on Taco Bell, so I dug deeper into my courtship bag of verbiage. "That saddle is slimming," I told him. "What? No, your ass isn't big!"

"I can't wait for your mother to visit."

"You're a great cook. Honest."

But he wouldn't budge. He was clearly resistant to my charms. I had to figure out something else.

"All right," I said. "If I can't flatter your butt into gear, then I'll have to drag it."

And that's what I did, hoof by hoof, bellow by bray, all the way to the finish line. By the time we got there, Taco Bell was too worn out to try to bite me anymore. For the first time, we stood side by side, teammates at last. I had tamed the wild beast, but at a price. I was utterly exhausted, having been whipsawed by a burro. The divorce proceedings could now begin.

I never tried my hand at burro racing again after posting a dismal finish at my first race. Then, not too long ago, Red Tail Mountain Man told me that Taco Bell had to be put down after injuring his foot in a fight with another jack. The wound wouldn't heal, and everyone who knew Taco Bell said he wouldn't have wanted to go on that way.

He had been irritable to the end, and I was sad to hear of his demise, if only because I had now been denied the pleasure of killing him myself!

Dr. Y: Bart explains his marathon training equation

Chapter 10

INVENTING THE YASSO 800s

I had just finished running a trail race in New Zealand when a guy standing next to me started raving about a new speed workout that can predict marathon time.

"It's so simple," he said. "The time it takes you to run 800-meter repeats in minutes and seconds works out to be your marathon finish time in hours and minutes. I tested it, and it's really true."

I knew all about the workout and tried to interject. "Really, I . . ."

"They were invented by this guy named Yasso . . ."

"I . . ."

"He's a Russian scientist."

"I . . ."

"He's a genius. He developed a mathematical equation that calculates . . ."

Just then the race director called my name. "Third place overall goes to Bart Yasso," he announced.

The guy next to me finally stopped talking. "You? You're Yasso?"

I shrugged and walked to the podium.

I understood how he could have become confused. I was befuddled myself. Here I was at a trail race in a remote part of New Zealand halfway around the world, and a stranger had invoked my name. How could I, Bart Yasso, former troublemaker extraordinaire, a small-town boy from Fountain Hill, Pennsylvania, have developed something embraced by runners around the globe?

The training system sprang from my determination in 1981 (I was 25 at the time) to run a 2:50 marathon so I could qualify for the fabled Boston Marathon, a feat that required me to knock 17 minutes off my best time. So I came up with a training regimen to increase speed. Once a week, in addition to my regular workout, I ran 800 meters, and then jogged 400 meters. Eventually I worked up to a continuous 10 repetitions and recorded the time for each set in my running log.

And there the numbers sat, the penciled scrawls remaining unnoticed among the long runs and tempo workouts, notations that chronicled my training journey toward Boston. The 800–400 meter repetitions became my standard speed workout for every marathon—Chicago, Marine Corps, Twin Cities—the numbers were dutifully noted.

I didn't crack their code until 3 years later, when I was reviewing my old logs for training inspiration and noticed a correlation between the average time it took me to run 800 meters 10 times and my corresponding marathon finishing time. Here's how the numbers worked out: If I ran each 800 meters in 2 minutes and 40 seconds, then I was in shape to run a 2:40 marathon. If I did 800 in 2 minutes and 50 seconds, then it was likely I would run a 2:50

marathon. Out of 15 marathons, the formula failed only once, making the 800s a good predictor for a race finish. I wondered if it was just a fluke or grounded in some physiological happenstance, like an internal GPS without a satellite.

I never put the numbers to a Fibonacci test, like in *The Da Vinci Code*, but they worked for me, and that was good enough.

I told a few people along the way, including Rodale's director of fitness and health, Budd Coates, about my workout, but for the most part it stayed under the radar—that is, until 1993, when I roomed with Amby Burfoot, then executive editor of *Runner's World*, at the Portland Marathon. I wasn't there to run the marathon. I was doing my job as race and promotions director for the magazine, but I was training for the Marine Corps Marathon in Washington, DC, later that fall.

Early every morning I got up for a run. One day, as I was lacing up my shoes, Amby sat up in bed and asked if I had a goal for the marathon.

"I'm going to run a 2:47," I said.

"You're certain about that?"

"Absolutely." Then I explained the system I had devised, hoping Amby wouldn't think I was crazy and call the marathon police. Rather, he was intrigued; a bit skeptical, too. "I wonder if it would work for other runners?" he asked.

"I don't know, but you're welcome to look at my training logs."

For the next few weeks, Amby crunched numbers, posting formulas on the walls of his office like John Forbes Nash Jr., the mathematical genius portrayed in the movie *A Beautiful Mind*. If anyone had the smarts to figure it out, it would be Amby, who has a deep interest in the physiology of training. He never did discover an equation to explain it, but the correlation held for the marathoners of all abilities that Amby personally interviewed.

One day he called me into his office. "I think you're on to something," he said.

"On to what?" I had forgotten that he was still investigating my hypothesis.

"The 800s," he said. "They work."

"I know they do. I told you that."

"But this is significant," he said. "This could change the way people train for marathons."

Until then, training methods could be quite complex, and predicting how someone would do in a marathon often required a calculus degree with a chemistry minor. It always sounded something like this: Do tempo runs at 80 percent of your max VO_2, minus your age, plus your resting heart rate, divided by your shoe size. Then mile repeats should be done at 15 seconds slower than your 10-K race pace, minus your anaerobic threshold, plus your lactic-acid buildup.

I'm kidding, but you get the point.

Amby admired the 800s for their simplicity and wrote about the exercise in the October 1994 issue of *Runner's World*. The morning it came out, I immediately flipped to my photo and laughed. I was posed as a professor wearing a mortarboard, bifocals sitting low on my nose. I held a pointer, and behind me was a chalkboard full of mathematical squiggles. The caption read: "Dr. Y.: Bart Yasso explains his marathon training equation." It was a spoof, but I guess not everyone understood that, including the runner I'd met in New Zealand. I put it aside to read later.

After lunch, Amby came into my office and asked what I thought.

"Looks great," I said.

"Did you read the story?"

"I was going to do it later."

"You should read it."

"Why?"

"You just should."

I opened the magazine and there in paragraph four, Amby officially christened the workout the "Yasso 800s." In early drafts of the story, the workout had been labeled "TK 800s"—"TK" is a magazine abbreviation for "to come," meaning the name would be filled in later. Amby knew all along the workout would be called the Yasso 800s, but he wanted to surprise me.

He told me that when physicists discover a new subatomic particle, they claim the right to name it. Same goes with astronomers: Locate a new star and you can call it anything you want. Amby reasoned that even skaters and gymnasts get moves named in their honor, so why not runners?

I thought it was really cool that he thought enough of me to do that, but I was secretly terrified. What if the Yasso 800s didn't hold true for all runners? I pictured the bags of hate mail I'd receive from angry marathoners who'd thought they would qualify for Boston based on their Yasso 800 times but then fell short during the race. I thought about moving to Russia but figured that within a month or two, no one would remember the exercise that bore my name, and the Yasso 800s would disappear off the face of the earth, a mere blip in a running world that's seen its share of fads.

Except they didn't. They became more and more popular, and soon I couldn't go to a race without someone coming up to me and saying, "Hey, you're the guy who invented the 800s."

I didn't really invent 800 meters. That distance, twice around the track, existed long before I showed up. But the Yasso 800s have become as much a part of the marathon lexicon as mile repeats.

Having a workout that bears your name is both a blessing and a curse. The Yasso 800s aren't a perfect prognosticator of marathon time; adjustments need to be made for a hot day or hilly course, but that's just common sense. For the most part, adjustments depend on how extreme the temperature and terrain are. As a rule of thumb, runners who have done only three or four marathons should add about 10 minutes to their projected finish time, and more experienced runners should add 4 or 5 minutes. But again, it really depends on the individual runner and his or her ability to handle heat or steep hills.

Regardless, the Yasso 800s are a good barometer of fitness. Case in point: A runner I once met at the New York City Marathon told me he figured he could do no better than a 2:28 marathon. But a few weeks before the race, he did 10 Yasso 800s and averaged 2:21. So he ran a faster pace and qualified for the Olympic marathon trials, posting a 2:21 finish. His experience and that of countless other runners shows that the Yasso 800s could be less about science and more about confidence.

But they don't work miracles. You still have to do long runs, hill workouts, and tempo runs. And you have to do more than one 800 to predict your marathon time. One guy found that out the hard way. He based his pace at the Chicago Marathon on running one 800-meter repeat instead of 10, went out too fast, and crashed and burned. He blamed me for his poor finish. "They should be called the asshole 800s," he told me, red-faced.

"You have to do 10 of them in one workout five to six weeks before the race!" I said.

Other than that guy, I heard from a staggering number of runners who loved Yasso 800s. I was blown away that a two-time winner of the New York City Marathon had incorporated them into his Winning Training School in Italy. In 1995, Orlando Pizzolato told me at a *Runner's World* party before the New York City Marathon that he had been using the Yasso 800s, which he calls the Yasso test, to train runners ever since reading Amby's article. "It is wonderful," he said, moving his hands as fast as he ran. He had brought hundreds of runners from Italy to that year's race, and all of them expected to do as well as their Yasso tests had predicted.

"Will you come to Columbus Circle tomorrow to take a photo with my runners?" he asked. "They would love to meet you. You're all they talk about. You are a superstar."

How could I say no to my fans?

At 9:00 a.m. the day before the race, I made my way to the Upper West Side, wearing my best running clothes for the group photo op. As I approached the circle, Pizzolato gestured toward me: "There is Yasso."

The runners started cheering. "*Bellisimo,* Yasso!" they called out in a chorus. "*Bellisimo,* Yasso!"

I was embarrassed. I had never been called beautiful by a group of men in shorts. Not even my mother had used that endearment. "No, no," I protested. "Pizzolato is the famous one. He won New York twice."

But they didn't understand what I was saying. "*Prego, prego,*" they replied.

They planted me in the middle, and we all smiled brightly for the first of what would become an annual photo event.

"Say 'Yasso,'" ordered the photographer. I hoped that wouldn't replace *cheese* as the obligatory phrase before a photograph is snapped at Italian marathons. Everyone's mouth would be puckered into an O.

A few years later, I got a call from the race director of the Napa Valley Marathon, who told me that the popularity of the Yasso 800s had extended south of the border but with a twist. The winner that year was a 44-year-old native of Mexico who was living in California. He won the race, beating his best time from the year before by a significant amount.

"I asked him what he did differently," race director Rich Benyo told me. "You know what he said? 'The Yahoo 800s.' Guess that means Yasso's out and Yahoo's in."

I don't think the guy was talking about the search engine, but ever since personal computers became a way of life, the workout has spread like kudzu. Google "Yasso 800s" and at least 20,000 matches appear, ranging from testimonials on personal blogs to fodder for chat rooms to mentions in articles.

In the almost 14 years since the article first appeared in *Runner's World,* there's been heated debate over the efficacy of Yasso 800s. Some people get too hung up on the science, debunking the entire exercise if it doesn't correspond within seconds of their finish time. I'm the first to admit they're not perfect; they were—and are—simply a way for me to measure athletic ability.

But they're not easy, especially after the ninth or tenth one. Runners come up to me at races and apologize for cursing my name during training.

"That's okay," I say. "They're named after my wife."

Finish line of the Taj Mahal 5-K in Agra, India, 1991

1998 Men's US Mountain Running Team on Reunion Island before the race.
Jeremy Wright, who died in Afghanistan in 2005, is second from left, wearing a hat.

Chapter 11

REUNION ISLAND

I was on a tiny island in the Indian Ocean about to run my first race as a member of the US Mountain Running Team. I wasn't actually on the team, but one of the regular guys got sick, and my friend Nancy Hobbs, who was manager of the women's team, asked me to take his place.

She told me it was on Reunion Island, off the coast of Madagascar. I thought it sounded like fun.

But then I met the mountain—or, rather, spied it from the windshield of a helicopter. "That's what we're going to have to run up?" I asked the race director, who had singled me out for a tour of the course after learning I worked at *Runner's World*.

"That's Piton des Neiges," he said. "It's an extinct volcano. There's an active volcano on the island, too, but it's probably not the best spot for a race. It's erupted more than 100 times since 1640."

Piton des Neiges was 10,069 feet above sea level, the highest point on the island, but I didn't know that when he had invited me to view the course the day before. I'd thought he wanted to show me the route by foot, so I appeared at his home that morning in my running clothes. He took one look at my attire and burst out laughing. "Are you in for a surprise," he said.

Surprise wasn't the word I'd use as I gazed at the craggy red cliffs zigzagging through the green forests of the island. *Dread, horror,* and *fear* were more like it.

"I told you I couldn't run it," he said, as we flew over the volcano's yawning mouth. "It's too steep. It would take 3 days to get up the thing. You can't drive a car to the top, either, so we have to fly in the water and other supplies." He also pointed out a small church at the crest of the mountain, a sanctuary for the Christian villagers who made their homes on the volcano's ledge.

The course appeared more grueling than the Pikes Peak Marathon in Colorado, an up-and-back race billed as the toughest marathon in the world. I had done that race in 1991, and by the time I got to the bottom, I was a bloodied mess from falling five times. I had deep gashes in my face, legs, and arms, as well as scraped elbows and knees. I was embarrassed as I limped to the medical tent, certain I was the only runner who had tumbled down the hill. But I had to stand in line at the triage center to have the pebbles removed from my wounds, which can get infected if they're not cleaned out right away.

"This is going to hurt," said the first nurse, using what looked like a soft toothbrush to remove debris from my elbow.

"Nothing can hurt more than running up and down that mountain for 4½ hours," I said. "You could use a wire brush, and I'd still be in less pain."

She laughed and pointed me toward the next nurse, who was applying Mercurochrome to runners' abrasions.

"So tell me," I said, "am I the bloodiest finisher so far?"

"You may not be the bloodiest, but you're in the top three," she said. "Congratulations."

"Do they give out awards for being the most beat up?"

"Sure," she said, directing me toward the bandaging station. "You get extra gauze pads."

I loved it. I was surrounded by blood brothers and sisters, runners who relished the pain of battle as much as I did.

But now, as I snapped out of my Pikes Peak reverie and gazed at the inactive volcano below my feet, I hoped there was not only a church but a hospital at the peak of this knee-busting mountain.

The first World Mountain Running Championship was held in Switzerland in 1985, but the United States didn't field a men's team until 2 years later. The women's squad was formed in 1995, and Nancy was on the team. At that year's championships in Edinburgh, Scotland, she placed 67th overall and was the third US finisher. Now Nancy was the women's manager. There are six men and four women on each team, but only the scores of the top four men and three women count in competition.

Because I was the sixth man and the oldest to boot, it was doubtful my efforts would make a difference, but you never know what kind of day your teammates are going to have. On race day, I would still have to give it my all.

Teams from 29 countries were competing for the championship, held each year on a fabled vertical ascent in a different country. In 1997, the Italian men's team and the French women's team had won the championship in the Czech Republic, a better-known landmass than Reunion Island. Every time I told someone where I was headed, they'd ask, "Whose reunion is it?"

Reunion Island is about 30 miles wide, roughly the size of Hawaii, and one of the most beautiful places in the world. There are sandy beaches, waterfalls, lush green forests, and ancient crumbling craters. Adventure sports abound. You can scuba dive in the clear waters, hike, and surf.

Getting there was quite an ordeal, though. A few days before, we had flown 8 hours from JFK International Airport to Paris, where we had a layover. From Paris, it was another 12-hour flight. We were all exhausted and cranky when we arrived at Reunion, and our accommodations didn't improve our outlook. They were little more than tents on wooden platforms with a communal bathroom down the road.

The grumbling stopped, at least among the men, when we went for a walk. There were about 50 topless women sunning themselves on the beach, and they were some of the most beautiful women in the world, with dark skin, almond eyes, and high cheekbones.

"Hey, Jeremy," I said to my bunkmate, a 23-year-old from Wyoming. "This is better than a five-star hotel with turndown service."

Jeremy was speechless. At first I chalked it up to silent appreciation, but I later realized it was a permanent condition. Jeremy didn't talk to anybody. But it didn't stop me from trying. I lobbed one-liners, monologues on my travels, and a verbal dissertation of my training methods, but Jeremy remained stoic.

Until I insulted his home state of Wyoming. I hadn't meant to— I didn't even know I had said anything wrong—but Jeremy was apparently sensitive about the Equality State. I was talking about my experience at Pikes Peak, a race Jeremy had won a few months before, and I innocently noted the beauty of Colorado.

"Colorado?" he said, vehemently. "Wyoming is so much nicer. The mountains are amazing; it's peaceful. I don't know why everyone prefers Colorado."

Whoa! I must have hit a sore spot, but it broke the ice. Or maybe he just got tired of my chatter and figured that if he didn't respond, I'd never shut up.

"Sorry, dude," I said. "You're right, Wyoming is really nice."

The next day was the traditional World Running Championship parade, similar to the Olympic parade of athletes but on a much smaller and less grand scale. We were all required to wear our team uniforms, but Nancy had forgotten to bring me a spare. "Don't worry," she said. "I think the women have an extra jersey."

"It doesn't have a built-in bra, does it?" I asked, worried that I wouldn't be able to fill it out.

"No, it's just like the men's, except it's cut a bit smaller."

For the record, I have never worn women's clothing since.

But the uniform snafu was only the start of my day of emasculation. The teams were lined up alphabetically, so the US contingent was near the end. Maybe it was because I was the oldest on my team or because I was the slowest or because I was a man in a woman's jersey, but Nancy handed me a rope tethered to a cow. I would be its escort for the duration of the parade. I don't know why they chose a cow to be in the parade, other than we were on a remote island and there weren't a lot of choices—no llamas or Arabian horses to be had; just cows. But Miles, as we nicknamed her, was a pretty cow, and she was decked out in fresh-cut flowers and a silky sash like the type beauty-pageant contestants wear. Only one thing detracted from her good looks: She had bad breath.

The villagers, many of whom were barefoot and smoking weed, lined up along the parade route to cheer the athletes and throw flower petals at our feet. I garnered additional applause for leading the doe-eyed Miles.

The race started the next day at the base of the volcano. The first 400 meters was a circular jaunt through a small village of thatch-roofed huts. There was so much natural beauty in this place, it was easy to forget it was a Third World colony. The people lived in paradise, but most of them didn't have indoor plumbing or electricity. From there we started the ascent up the volcano. It wasn't only steep, the trail was riddled with tree roots and rocks. I was amazed how quickly my teammates navigated the terrain—almost like billy goats—and I soon lost sight of Jeremy's blond head. Apparently, he had reserved his energies for the race, while I had expended most of mine trying to entice him into conversation.

My goal was to run every single step by shortening my stride and never looking more than 3 feet in front of me so I wouldn't be able to see the full climb. I knew if I did, I'd be psychologically doomed. The muddy trail became more slippery with the passing of each runner, and I was way in the back, a first in my running career. My calves soon ached from trying to keep my balance, and I knew I had to pace myself to reserve some energy for the top.

The only relief came in the form of comic relief. Volunteers at water stations passed the time by smoking ganja, and its sweet fumes wafted through the air. They were the happiest volunteers I've ever seen. "You are looking fantastic," they'd yell with bright smiles. "Keep going."

One hour and 51 minutes later, I finished and felt good about my performance. I had done as well as I could, and I turned to one of my teammates to talk about the race. "No one passed me," I said, "and I caught a few runners at the end."

"Of course no one passed you," he said. "There were only a few runners behind you."

He brought me down pretty fast. Out of 124 runners, I had placed 106th, but at least I didn't DNF. As a team, the US men placed 8th, its best finish at the time. Because four other guys on the team had run faster than me, my time didn't count, thank goodness. The women's team came in 12th place.

Later that day, we posed on the beach for a team photo. I tried to convince the women to take off their shirts like the other female sunbathers, but they rejected my idea resoundingly.

That night, Jeremy and I exchanged e-mail addresses and promised to stay in touch. Maybe he would be more talkative in writing.

Once in a while Jeremy and I would shoot each other a note to say hello or share our results at a race, but that was about it. Then, in 2005, I learned he had died in Afghanistan, where he was a communications sergeant and Green Beret in the army's Special Forces. The news hit me hard, and I called Nancy. "Did you hear about Jeremy?" I asked.

"Yes," she said. "It's a shock. He had been stationed in a communications tower, and I thought he'd be safe. But I guess no one is over there."

"How did it happen?"

"He was on routine patrol when his Humvee hit a homemade bomb," she said. "I talked to some of his buddies. They said every day he would run up and down this huge mountain by his base in Kabul. He really loved mountain running."

Two years later, I helped organize a half-marathon for US soldiers in Afghanistan. It was scheduled for the same April day as the Lehigh Valley Half-Marathon in Allentown, to give the soldiers abroad and Lehigh Valley participants a chance to feel connected to one another even though they would be running half a world apart.

I worked with Sergeant John Cristiano of the 82nd Airborne at Bagram Air Force Base in Afghanistan, and he was enthusiastic about the race. I sent over Lehigh Valley Half-Marathon bib numbers so the soldiers' results would appear in the local newspaper and race Web site. They also got T-shirts and goody bags. Cristiano and his crew mapped out a 13.1-mile course near the base, and 40 soldiers participated, many of whom had never before run a race, much less a half-marathon. Afterward, he e-mailed me saying it had been a success because for a few hours, the men and women who ran were able to feel like civilians again, the stress of combat eased by the freedom and simplicity of running.

Jeremy would have been pleased; speechless, but pleased.

Penguins pose on King George Island with *Akademik Ioffe* in background

Chapter 12

ANTARCTICA MARATHON

Julia Jones was obsessed with puking. It's all the former beauty queen talked about. "I know I'm going to throw up, Bart," she said. "I always get seasick."

She had good reason to be concerned. We were about to cross the dreaded Drake Passage, where ocean swells can rise up to 50 feet. The Drake, a waterway between South America and Antarctica, contains some of the roughest seas in the world and inspired the old mariner saying about latitude: "Below 40 degrees, there is no law. Below 50 degrees, there is no God." Our ship, the *Akademik Ioffe*, would pass between 56 and 60 degrees south latitude on its way to the bottom of the planet for a marathon.

"I'm worried about getting sick, too," I told Julia, a former Miss Italy and now a columnist for the Italian running magazine *Correre*. "But you can't dwell on it or you'll talk yourself into it."

"I can't help it," she said. "I'm scared to death."

We were all a bit frightened after taking careful note that the seasoned crew of this Russian vessel were all wearing antinausea patches behind their ears.

"I'm going to die," I told my buddy Steve Dodson, an anesthesiologist from Macungie, Pennsylvania, who was traveling with his wife, Loretta. "I only brought two Dramamine."

"Don't worry," he said. "If it gets really bad, I have enough drugs to put everyone on the ship to sleep for 2 days."

We wouldn't be arriving at King George Island, a glaciated outpost off the northern tip of Antarctica where the race would be held, for another 3 days, so Steve's plan had potential.

It was 1999, and I had been invited by Thom Gilligan, president of Marathon Tours, to run a race in Antarctica called the Last Marathon. Gilligan started the biyearly race in 1995 as a way to give adventure runners a chance to run a marathon on all seven continents, an accomplishment that grants induction into the exclusive Seven Continents Club. At last count, membership included 125 men and 44 women. But that's not the only reason why the Dodsons were along. They were in hot pursuit of their own side goal, having sex on all seven continents.

There were about 170 runners on the trip, and we met up on February 7 in Buenos Aires, then flew to Ushuaia, capital of the Argentine province of Tierra del Fuego, and the world's southernmost city. Ushuaia looks like it's at the end of the earth, too. It's a ramshackle town where the sun rarely shines. It's also populated by prostitutes who are no longer welcome in the country's glitzy capital of Buenos Aires.

We spent a night in Ushuaia before boarding the ship, and a couple of guys on the trip were bummed to learn hookers don't accept traveler's checks. "Hey Bart," one said. "Do you have any cash? We'll pay you back."

"Sure, what do you need it for?" I asked.

"Um, me and my buddies want to go into town tonight," he said.

"How much do you need?"

"How much do you have?"

"I have a couple hundred bucks."

"Can you spare $200?"

"Whatever you need, man," I said forking over a wad of bills. "Have fun tonight."

I didn't learn what my hard-earned greenbacks had paid for until we got on the boat, and by that time the specter of seasickness made the nocturnal exploits of my fellow marathoners seem less interesting. "Who do you think will throw up first?" I asked Steve.

"Greg, or at least I hope so," he said.

Greg had come along as a member of Fred's Team, a group of runners that raises money for cancer research. The charity was started in 1991 by Fred Lebow, the founder of the New York City Marathon, who died in 1994 of brain cancer.

Each member of Fred's team was supposed to raise a couple of thousand dollars for free passage on the trip, but Greg hadn't raised the full amount. Steve wasn't coming along as a member of Fred's team, but he didn't think it was fair that Greg was freeloading.

"I think it's going to be Julia," I said.

"Care to make a wager?" Steve asked.

"I'll bet you $5."

"Deal."

Then we opened the pool to some other runners, and the pot grew to $30.

"My money's on Lisa," said Bill Serues, a former naval officer and employee of Marathon Tours, referring to Julia's dark-haired roommate.

"I'm going with Margaret," said Gilligan, betting against the oldest member of our group, who was 70 at the time.

It didn't take long for the wager to be decided. As soon as the captain announced we had entered the Drake Passage around midnight, Julia was feeding the fishes over the deck's rail.

"Pay up, men," I said at breakfast the next morning. "Can I call them or what?"

That day the seas were rough and most of us, myself included, passed the time in the fetal position in our cabins. There wasn't much to do anyway. After all, this was a freighter, not a cruise ship, so there were no shuffleboard courts, swimming pools, or casinos. The exercise room had a few free weights and a stationary bike, but it was broken.

A few of us made it to dinner that night, but not Julia. "She's still retching," Lisa said.

"Maybe I should help her?" I offered out of a sense of chivalry that had absolutely nothing to do with her stunning good looks.

"I think she'll be okay," she said.

I managed to gulp down a few spoonfuls of soup and called it a day. I started feeling better the next morning and decided to go for a run on the deck. We were still in the Drake Passage, but I badly needed air. The deck was small, and it only took about 35 seconds to complete a loop. I had run about 10 loops when the ship climbed a 20-foot swell, then dropped, leaving me suspended in midair like Michael Jordan going up for a jump shot. But what goes up 20 feet lands hard, and when I was reunited with the deck, it felt like my ankles were being rammed through my hips. Black water sloshed over the railing and doused me in a cold spray. It was the last time I ran at sea.

The next day we dropped anchor about a mile off the coast of King George Island, and the crew handed out certificates saying we were "In Continent." "My 100-year-old grandmother never got one of these when she lost control of her bladder," I joked to Bill, my cabinmate. "We all just acted like it didn't happen."

The marathon was in 2 days, and Bill, Thom, and I had to mark the course for the February 13 race. We boarded a Zodiac and headed for land carrying 1,000 red flags, a GPS device, a case of beer, and two bottles of vodka. We made separate trips back to the boat in the Zodiac for two four-wheelers, which we needed for travel across the tundra.

The beer and vodka were for the Russian scientists at Bellings-hausen Station, one of four international research posts on the island. The scientists study weather, geography, and wildlife during the summer months, which it was now, although a few stay for the winter, when temperatures can dip to −40°F.

From the Zodiac we could see the rocky shoreline, a few huts in the distance, and eight or nine Russians in orange one-piece ski suits who had gathered to greet us. Or so we thought.

"Welcome to Bellingshausen," called out the station's doctor, the only one of the group who spoke good English. The rest grabbed the beer and vodka and disappeared into their huts. I couldn't blame them. Ours was the first boat to arrive on the island bearing alcohol in over a year.

Left alone, the doctor offered to run the marathon.

"Not in those shoes you won't," I replied, eyeing his fur-lined rubber boots. "But we can get you some running shoes."

"No, no," he said. "I make joke."

"May we stay with you tonight?" Thom asked him. "We need to mark the racecourse tomorrow."

"But of course," he said. "It is nice and warm inside our station."

And it was. The station was heated, and they had added a *banya*, or wet sauna, by hooking up a car engine to the water tank, which in turn pumped steam into the sauna through a series of pipes. It was 200°F in there, and I literally couldn't breathe in the steam. But the high temperatures didn't faze the Russians, who swilled their newly acquired vodka and beat each other with tree branches they had brought along from home to improve circulation. "Good, good," one said, raising his shot glass in a toast. "You drink vodka?"

"No, no thank you," I said, bailing for fresh air. Thom and Bill lasted a bit longer but soon followed my lead.

Dinner that night was penguin stew cooked in a huge vat. I didn't want to be rude and not eat their food, but clearly this was not vegetarian fare.

"Bart, have some stew," said the doctor.

"Thank you," I said accepting a small bowl. Then I ducked into a corner and downed a PowerBar. Explaining vegetarianism to this group didn't seem worth the effort, considering this would be our only evening with them. They understood the language of vodka, and that was enough.

After dinner, the Russians watched MTV until the wee hours of the morning. "I don't think there's a whole lot of research going on here," I said to Bill.

"Are you sure they're even scientists?" he asked.

"Maybe they got in trouble at home and were sent here for punishment," I whispered.

The doctor must have overheard us because he led us to a room where the computer took up half the wall. He flipped a switch that looked like something out of a Frankenstein movie, and purple volts of electricity fizzled and danced in two 9-foot glass tubes.

"Whoa," I said, hoping he wasn't going to hook me up to the machine and steal my brain. "That's one impressive machine."

Then he showed us our sleeping quarters, which were raised wooden slabs.

"I'll sleep here," said Thom, opening his sleeping bag on what looked like an autopsy table, although I had no idea what they needed it for on King George Island. Penguins?

The three of us got up early the next day to mark the course. The plan was to insert red flags every 200 meters. There was no existing trail, so runners would rely on these markers to find their way up and over a glacier, across streams, and along the beach to the finish line.

As we started out, a German ornithologist warned us of nesting skuas, fiercely predatory birds that attack intruders by slapping them upside the head with their webbed feet. I wasn't too concerned. I had banded birds of prey at Hawk Mountain Sanctuary along the Appalachian Trail in eastern Pennsylvania, and figured I could handle some scrawny-looking gull.

But as I was drilling a hole in the frozen ground to insert a flagpole, out of the corner of my eye, I saw a dark shape bearing down on me. I dove to the ground, but the skua flew low and hit me on the head with its feet. "Ouch, that hurt," I yelled. Before I could even get to my feet, another one attacked from behind, knocking my hat off.

Bill and Thom were about 400 meters behind me, close enough to see the drama unfold but too far away to help.

"I come in peace!" I yelled. "I just want to put up these flags."

But the skuas weren't messing around. They had rallied the troops, and I could see three or four of them coming toward me with their wings outstretched like a squadron of fighter planes. Resistance was futile, and I covered my head with my arms. *Whack, thump, bam,* they landed stinging blows to my skull and arms.

Then I had an idea. I grabbed a pole from the four-wheeler and taped a flag and my hat to the top. I held it above my head with one hand to distract the skuas, which are drawn to the highest point, while drilling holes and inserting flags with the other.

It took us 8 hours to mark the course, an out-and-back loop that started and ended at the Uruguayan station near Collins Glacier. When we were done, we decided to invite the scientists at the other research posts to run the marathon. Unlike the Russian base, the Chileans had modern equipment and lived in a sort of commune with their families. There was a school, houses, and a church. "If we can get away from work, we will come," one scientist said.

Scientists from the Chinese and Uruguayan bases were intrigued but declined the invitation.

Only three Russians took us up on our offer, but they didn't have appropriate shoes. A few runners had brought extra pairs, so we promised to try to get them their sizes for the race.

When we got back to the boat, all the runners wanted to know the challenges of the course, but Thom asked me to remain tight-lipped until dinner, then update everyone on the terrain at one time.

"The mud is incredible," I said. "It nearly sucked off my shoes. The glacier is in good shape. It's a climb, but at least it's dry. If you're in shape to run a 3-hour marathon, add about 30 minutes to your time. If you're in shape to run a 4-hour marathon, it will take you about 45 minutes longer."

Now I had to break the news about the psycho birds. "Okay, the mud, the glacier, and the 26 miles—that's the easy part. Let me tell you about my friend Sammy Skua, who kills people. They're like hit men out there. I don't think they'll be as aggressive during the race because there will be a lot of us running. They weren't after me as much when I was with Bill. They're territorial, and they're letting you know we're on their turf." I ended on what I thought was a positive note. "We survived the Drake, right?" I said, glancing at Julia. "This will be only slightly worse."

After dinner, a bunch of us sat around and drank wine. "So what did you guys do?" I asked the Dodsons.

"We sailed through the Antarctic Sound to Paulette Island," said Loretta. "The water was so blue it looked like someone had poured Ty-D-Bol cleaner into it."

Antarctic Sound is better known as iceberg alley for the glaciers that rise from the serene waters surrounding Paulette Island, home to penguin rookeries, seals, and albatross.

"Loretta got propositioned by a penguin," Steve said.

"What?"

"Yeah, two Adélie penguins put pebbles at Loretta's feet," he said.

We had heard about this mating ritual during an onboard lecture. Adélie penguins use stones to build nests, and females will prostitute themselves in exchange for this scarce commodity. By depositing a stone in front of Loretta, the penguins had indicated a desire to mate.

"I was wearing black pants and a black jacket," Loretta said. "They must have gotten confused."

"You were the best-looking penguin on the island," Steve said.

Race day was clear and cold, about 20°F, and we boarded the Zodiacs to the peninsula, which was shrouded in mist. Because there were no manned aid stations, runners were responsible for bringing their own water, Gatorade, and nutrition bars. My job was to deposit their supplies in boxes along the course so they could grab them as they ran past. I set up two drop-off points, and since it was an up-and-back course, they had access to their food and water roughly every 3 miles.

When I rejoined the group, Thom announced I would be lead runner. "We don't have a lead vehicle," he said. "So everyone follow Bart."

This meant, of course, that I would have to run faster than everyone else, but I wasn't sure I could. In Buenos Aires, a guy named Fred Zolker beat me during a 4-mile run. Not only was he faster than me, he hadn't spent the last 2 days slogging through mud while fighting off the devil's winged warriors.

Thom fired the starter pistol, and Fred and I took off, sharing the lead in friendly silence. All was going well until we neared the Russian base at mile 4, and we saw that everyone's food, water, and soda had been strewn across the tundra by the skuas. Using their beaks, the birds had punched holes in the Coke cans and plastic bottles and ripped open the foil wrappers of the PowerBars, which was a feat unto itself. I have trouble opening PowerBars with pliers. There was some grumbling from behind, but there wasn't anything anyone could do. I refused to go one-on-one with a skua for anyone's water, even Miss Italy's, because I already knew who would win.

Skuas: 1; Bart: 0.

The ground wasn't as muddy as the day before, and the black ocean was visible from the course.

As I turned around to complete the second loop of the course, I was surprised more runners weren't behind me. There were a few, but then no one—just an expanse of space. Where was everyone? I started to get worried and decided to go find them. Leaving Fred in charge, I sprinted toward the Uruguayan base, where I grabbed a four-wheeler and headed off across the tundra. After a few minutes, I spotted a group of them near the Chilean base. Turned out researchers there had turned the course arrows to point to their station because they thought it would be fun to watch the runners go by. They didn't think they had done anything wrong. Fortunately, the runners weren't too far off course, and Bill Serues and I got them back on track.

By the time I returned to the halfway point, where I had stopped, I decided not to run anymore. I was cold, and my muscles were getting stiff. Plus, Margaret, the 70-year-old, was out somewhere on the icy course, and I wanted to be available if she needed help. "Hey Margaret," I said when I found her. "How are you doing?"

"I'm great," she replied, waving me on. "Couldn't be better."

Then I headed to the finish line to watch Fred and Steve go stride for stride to an exciting tundra finish. Steve had been in the lead since mile 21, but with less than 100 feet to go, Fred outkicked him to win. The men shook hands, and the few of us at the finish line cheered.

The awards ceremony was held that night on the boat, but the question on my mind was whether Steve and Loretta had sneaked off behind a glacier to gain membership into the Sex on Seven Continents Club. "It doesn't count if you did it on the boat," I told them.

"Maybe in your book," said Steve.

Everyone slept soundly that night as we began our return voyage to Ushuaia. At breakfast the next day, the captain announced that in honor of Valentine's Day, we were going to have a special party. "Everyone needs to bring a date," he said.

A date? Seventy percent of the ship's population was men, which meant everyone and their brother would be knocking on Miss Italy's cabin door. I had to act quickly. I grabbed my coffee and hightailed it to Julia's room. "Will you be my date?" I asked. "For the Valentine's Day dinner."

"Sure," she said. "See you tonight."

I have a date with Miss Italy! I have a date with Miss Italy! I felt like Rudolph the Red-Nosed Reindeer when Clarisse told him he was cute: "I'm cute, I'm cute. She said I was cu-u-u-ute."

I ran to tell Bill, who was writing his wife, Jane, a love letter. "I don't think they have postal service here," I said.

"I'm going to fax it to her," he said. "The captain said I could use the ship's machine. Want to come with me?"

Use of the fax machine wasn't free. It cost $7 a minute, but Bill figured the Valentine would go through quickly. It didn't. It moved slower than the glaciers in the Antarctic Sound. "Come on," said Bill, as the fax scanned each character of the letter line by line.

"There goes another $7," I said.

"Bart, you're not helping."

But how could I? The male code of friendship called for teasing, if not outright derision. "It will probably come out blank on the other side," I said.

Five minutes later the fax went through.

"Hey, it's the thought that counts, not the $35 you just threw overboard."

"It's still cheaper than a dozen roses," he said.

I picked up Julia at her cabin at 6:00 p.m., and we proceeded to the dining room, which was decorated with red hearts and cupids. As we ate dinner, the ship once again entered the Drake.

"How do you feel?" I asked Julia.

"Fine," she said. "I don't feel sick at all."

It must be my calming presence, I thought.

Just then the captain interrupted my fantasy world by announcing he'd never seen the waters so smooth.

"It's the Drake Lake," he said over the ship's intercom. "This only happens one or twice a year."

Dining with an Italian beauty queen is even rarer.

Two years later, I would get married in Italy.

**Runners of Antarctica Marathon
run on Collins Glacier, 1999**

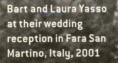

Bart and Laura Yasso at their wedding reception in Fara San Martino, Italy, 2001

Chapter 13

ROMA-THERAPY

I was on my honeymoon in Italy in 2001 when the joint pain struck again during the Rome Marathon.

It was my wife's idea to get married in Casoli, the village where her maternal grandparents were from, and then run 26.2 miles the next day. That sounded great until my knees starting aching just after I took a short break to have my photo taken with my mother and sister, Anne Marie, at Trevi Fountain. They were among 12 of our family and friends who had made the trip to see Laura and me get married.

Everyone, including myself, had believed that at age 45 I was a confirmed bachelor, but then I met Laura Kulsik in 1993 at a Road Runners Club of America convention in Portland, Oregon. She was receiving an award for outstanding editor of her club's newsletter. I couldn't take my eyes off this cute California girl wearing torn jeans with holes the size of grapefruits in her knees. I was intrigued, especially when I learned that her first priority as a runner was helping others succeed in the sport. That's why she had gotten involved with RRCA, eventually becoming a California state representative and then RRCA's Western Director.

I was representing *Runner's World* and tried to talk to her after my presentation. "Hey, congratulations on your award," I said. She pretended she hadn't heard me and walked away.

What a snob, I thought, but then someone told me she was painfully shy. We would run into each other at Road Runners' conventions and marathons. Gradually she warmed up to me, but it wasn't until the advent of e-mail that our relationship became a solid friendship. Then, in 2000, I asked her to go on vacation with me to Borneo. When you're 44, you don't ask a woman to dinner on the first date. The hour had come to be bold.

Turned out Laura couldn't get away for an entire week, so we agreed to have our first date at the New York City Marathon. It was a good one, and 3 months later we decided to get married in Italy that March.

But when spring came around, I knew something was wrong. I was feeling run-down, achy, and out of breath. I knew in my heart it was Lyme disease. My doctor had told me there was a chance it could return, but I didn't want to believe it. I had beaten it once, and I never wanted to go through the long days of recovery again.

Casoli is a small town in the province of Abruzzo, 100 kilometers northeast of Rome, near the Adriatic Sea. Before we could be married, we had to obtain permission from the Italian consulate, hire an interpreter, and rent the town hall for the ceremony, which would be conducted by the village's mayor, who happened to be a woman. That made her the mayoress.

Word got out that the granddaughter of one of their own was going to be married in their small community, and people would smile, point at Laura, and say "Di Lauro," the last name of her grandparents.

We would be the first foreigners to be married in this region, and we felt like celebrities. Everyone greeted us with the familiarity of an old friend—the meter maid, bank teller, barista at the espresso bar, and clerk at the hosiery store where I had to buy dress socks for the wedding because I forgot to bring my own. I had packed plenty of running socks, though.

There were no hotels or bed-and-breakfasts in Casoli, so we stayed one village over in Fara San Martino, known as the pasta capital of the world. The day before the wedding, we went for a run with some of our friends and got caught in a 60-mile-per-hour windstorm. I tried to shield Laura from the flying gravel, but it pummeled our faces and bodies until we got back to the hotel. Laura's face was red and swollen from the stones, but she told me there was no place on earth she would rather be than in Italy with our families and friends, about to get married. Despite the pummeling, she looked lovely the next day.

For the wedding ceremony, Laura wore a simple white dress, and I put on a Donna Karan Italian-made suit.

The mayoress spoke perfect English, but by law we had to hire an interpreter to translate the ceremony. His name was Tony, but he must not have known a lot of English, because the mayoress would deliver a 2- to 3-minute sermon in Italian, and his summation took 15 seconds. There were a lot of hard looks between the two, with the mayoress knowing full well Tony hadn't repeated the entire text of her message. Finally she pronounced us husband and wife—*uomo e moglie*—and everyone cheered.

A few minutes later, my cell phone rang. It was my older brother George, calling from Pennsylvania to congratulate us on our nuptials. His timing, as always, was impeccable. The reception was held at La Taverna, a small restaurant that sits near the crystal blue waters of Lake Casoli. Dinner was a seven-course meal, not your typical pasta feed before a marathon, but neither Laura nor I was looking to set a personal record. We sat back and enjoyed the antipasto, *maccheroni alla chitarra* (the local "guitar pasta"), and lots of vegetarian dishes—all made with fresh local ingredients and accompanied after each *piatti* (plate) with local wines including Montepulciano d'Abruzzo, Trebbiano d'Abruzzo, and grappa.

But it wasn't indigestion that dogged me the next day—it was a recurrence of Lyme disease.

Now, on the steps of Trevi Fountain, I couldn't hide my discomfort from my mother. "What's wrong?" she asked.

"Nothing," I said.

"But you look like you're in pain."

"I'm fine. I'll see you at the finish line. I love you, Mom."

I was in agony for the rest of the race, but I vowed to finish. It was part of the prenuptial agreement, and no one wants to DNF on their honeymoon. Besides, I was in one of the world's most cosmopolitan cities, a far cry from the rugged rooftops of Africa. If anything happened, I could easily hail a cab to a local hospital.

Laura and I met up at the end of the race at the Arch of Constantine, where Ethiopian Abebe Bikila won the marathon in the 1960 Olympics and was the first African to bring home a gold medal. He had been a last-minute replacement for his team, and when he arrived in Italy, Adidas, the shoe sponsor, didn't have any shoes left that fit him. No problem. He ran barefoot and set an Olympic marathon record time of 2:15:16. Later, asked why he ran barefoot, Bikila replied, "I wanted the world to know that my country, Ethiopia, has always won with determination and heroism."

I ran the race a bit slower, 3:46, but it's easy to get distracted during the Rome Marathon. The course takes you past some of the most amazing sights: the formidable columns of Saint Peter's Basilica, the imposing ruins of the Colosseum, the elegant Spanish Steps, and almost 100 piazzas, or town squares, popular hangouts for tourists and residents. Plus, I'd stuffed myself the night before at the reception and then, well, it was my wedding night! To top it off, I'd gotten pegged in the head by a water bottle someone threw off an overpass, and I was feeling a bit woozy.

We returned home a few days later, but to opposite coasts. We lived apart for the first 10 months of marriage trying to figure out who should uproot whose career. We met regularly, never being apart for more than 2 weeks at a time; but in the end, Laura decided to leave her job as a graphic artist for the state of California and move to Center Valley, Pennsylvania, to be with me.

In June 2001, 3 months after we got married, I flew to California to visit Laura, an ultrarunner in her own right who was preparing for a 100-mile run. The month before she had won the Quicksilver 50-K in San Jose, California, the Silver State 50-K in Reno, Nevada, and the Dam Run 50-K in Auburn, California. We were hooking up with some friends for a 15-mile trail run. It would be Laura's last long run before the Western States 100-miler, where she would place third female overall, setting a course record for the masters women.

I stayed behind the pack knowing I was only going to go 6 to 8 miles, but I had to stop after mile 2. I couldn't breathe, and my joints ached so badly, I couldn't take another step. I knew I was in trouble again.

When Laura returned from the 15-miler, she could tell I was hurting. "Stop fooling around and go see a Lyme specialist," she said.

Normally, I ignore people's good advice about my health because I'm stubborn and don't like doctors, but this time I did what she said when I returned home. The specialist ordered a DNA test, and the results weren't good. "Bart, you've got chronic Lyme disease," he said.

"What does that mean?"

"It doesn't go away."

"Ever?"

"It's going to take you a lot longer to recover this time," he said. "We're going to have to treat it really aggressively."

He inserted a PICC line in my vein and a shunt in my forearm so I could attach an intravenous drip. I would have to administer antibiotics twice a day for the next 4 months. I continued to go to work, hanging my IV bag on the fire sprinkler head in my office, which coworkers took to calling a MASH unit. "Hello, Hotlips," Wish would say when he walked past my door.

The drugs restored my energy, and I started running again, but the movement jostled the shunt, which stung my arm. So I began wrapping an Ace bandage around the shunt to secure it. The throbbing would subside after 4 miles.

The whole episode felt like a bad case of déjà vu. It was only a few years before that I had been pace captain at the Chicago Marathon while battling Lyme disease, and now it was happening again at the Portland Marathon. I would be leading the 3:20 pace team, and I figured I could handle that. Plus, Amby wouldn't be there, so no one would have reason to question my health, as happened in Chicago. I would be the one introducing the pace leaders to the runners, and I had no intention of spilling my guts about the recurrence of Lyme Disease.

The race took place in October 2001, a few weeks after terrorists attacked the World Trade Center and Pentagon and downed a plane in Shanksville, Pennsylvania. I spent the plane ride to Portland wondering not if the guy next to me had a box cutter in his shoe but whether my bags of antibiotics were okay in the cargo hold. Prior to 9/11, I could carry my IV drip bags on planes without being hassled, but now it was a whole new world. I had to pack my meds in dry ice and check them before boarding, then hope they would arrive still intact. I needn't have worried. All 12 pouches made it to Portland in one piece.

Things went well at the pace seminar, but as I removed my bandage so I could rewrap it before the race the next day, one of the runners saw the shunt. "What's that, man?" he asked.

"I'm taking intravenous meds, and I need this in my arm."

"You're not taking steroids, are you?"

"No, man. This stuff doesn't make you faster."

He seemed satisfied by my explanation.

The race wasn't a problem, and I easily kept my runners on track. This time, no one doubted my abilities or pace like they did in Chicago.

At mile 25, a middle-aged runner on my pace team told me he had tried to qualify for Boston 22 times. "I'm going to make it this time," he said.

"You got it in the bag," I told him.

He started crying.

"Dude, what are you doing?" I said.

"I can't believe it. Boston's my dream."

"No crying in pace teams. We still have a mile to go. You can cry at the finish line."

He sniffled away his emotion and dropped a fraction behind me. I saw him again at the finish, bawling and hugging a friend. I clapped him on the back. "See you in Boston," I said.

Unlike Chicago, where I felt depleted after leading the 3-hour group, I walked away with a smile on my face. Helping others reach their goal was once again a rewarding reason to run, and it energized me. If Chicago had led me to learn the importance of running for myself, Portland restored my belief in my own invincibility. For the second time, the meds had worked.

In March 2002, Laura and I returned to Casoli to run two marathons. We had pledged to not only honor and cherish each other but also run all of Italy's 50 marathons. On this trip, we planned to do the Naples and Vigarano Marathons. We were staying in nearby Modena with Julia Jones—Miss Italy from the Antarctica marathon—and her boyfriend, Piero, the coach of the Italian Olympic marathon team.

The day before the Vigarano Marathon, Piero took me to a park saying he wanted to critique my running style. "Were you injured as a child?" he asked after we had done a few laps.

"Just the usual stuff. You know, a broken arm, sprained wrist, bumps and bruises. Why?"

"You have terrible form!" he said. "You carry your arms too far from your body, you're bowlegged, and you have bad posture. You do everything wrong."

"Really? But my shoes are tied and my hair is in place."

"I don't get how you're able to run so fast," he said.

I laughed at his assessment. The fact that I was still running with chronic Lyme disease outweighed any form issues he may have thought I had. So I would never run in the Olympics. I had Italy.

I knew I would have to post a fast time at the Naples Marathon because Avis closed at 12:30 p.m. that day, and we needed to pick up our rental car to drive to Casoli for dinner with Laura's relatives. The race was supposed to start at 9:00 a.m., meaning if I finished at noon, I'd still have 30 minutes to run the 3 miles to Avis near the train station. But the race director got a talker on. He blabbed in Italian, a language I don't speak, until 9:20 a.m. Every minute was 60 seconds I'd have to make up in my run to the finish. "What could he possibly be talking about?" I asked Laura.

"I don't know, but let's get on with it, folks," she said.

Every now and then we'd get a blurb of translation. "Make sure your bib is on the front of your shirt." "Attach your chip to your shoe."

I started to sweat. If we didn't pick up that rental car, we'd have to take several trains to Casoli and be late for dinner.

Finally, the gun went off. I focused on maintaining a 7-minute-per-mile pace with the intensity of a tourist's first gaze at the *Pietà*, Michelangelo's famous sculpture of the Virgin Mary holding the fallen Christ, but it wasn't easy. The Naples Marathon was complete chaos. Vespas, in-line skaters, and bikers clogged the course. Cops were supposed to stop traffic at intersections for the runners, but they were too busy flirting with girls in bikinis to take their official duties seriously. That meant runners had to clear their own paths. "*Attencione, attencione!* Get the hell out of my way," I yelled in pidgin Italian at the cell-phone-talking, cigarette-smoking tourists who had strayed onto the marathon route.

The aid stations were stocked with sugar cubes and apple and pear slices, and runners had to specify whether they wanted water with or without "gas," meaning carbonation. I asked for water without gas because I had enough of my own.

I crossed the finish line at 12:23 p.m., with 7 minutes to spare. I knew I'd never make it to Avis on foot in time, so I hailed a cab, promising the driver 30 euros if he could get me to the train station in 5 minutes.

Italian taxi drivers don't need incentive to drive crazy. They do that on their own, running red lights, dodging pedestrians, and cutting off bicyclists for sport. As he veered wildly through the crowded streets of Naples, I feared for my life, but we made it just in time. "*Grazie,*" I told him, handing over the promised bills.

An Avis employee was awaiting my arrival, keys in hand. I signed for the car and sped off, picking up Laura, who was the 10th female finisher and the recipient of a cash prize. When all was said and done, I'd run the Naples marathon in 3:02. Laura did it in 3:31.

The next weekend we headed to Ferrara for the Vigarano Marathon, where we ran the first few miles on top of a wide stone wall built to fortify the city in the 15th and 16th centuries. The wall has since been converted to a grassy walking path, and it afforded a spectacular view of the Byzantine architecture of the ancient city and the turrets of a castle where the race's pasta dinner had been held the night before. From there we headed to the countryside, past farms and vineyards, where men working in the fields paused to cheer us on. Old women in villas threw open the shutters of their second-story windows and yelled *"Bellisimo!"*

But the best part was the two bottles of Pinot Grigio we each got at the end for finishing the race. I ran a 2:58 and Laura did a 3:25, both of us posting faster times than the week before in Naples. That night we uncorked a bottle of our race schwag and toasted our success. To hell with those finishers' medals.

I continued to feel good and do well at races, despite the analysis of my running style that I had received from Miss Italy's boyfriend.

As my health continued to improve, George called one day with bad news. "I have prostate cancer," he said.

I was stunned. At age 51, George was still my invincible big brother. After 4 years of football in college, he had played rugby for another 16 and had never once gotten hurt. He never stopped running, either. Now he was sick, and there was nothing I could do. "You're going to beat this," I told him.

But he didn't. On November 13, 2003, George died at home. Our immediate family gathered at his bedside as he took his last breath. I couldn't believe my brother was gone. My thoughts turned to that day when he had challenged me to a road race, then kicked my butt. Who knows how I would have turned out without George's steady affection and guidance. I wanted to curl up and cry, but George needed me to care for his wife, two daughters, and son. Just as George had nurtured me, I vowed to be there for his family.

In November 2004, my brothers Gerry and Spud helped start the George B. Yasso Memorial Christmas City Tip-Off Challenge, a high school basketball tournament. Spud and I helped organize the George B. Yasso 5-K Run in Fountain Hill. Both charities raise money for college scholarships in our brother's name.

Two and a half years later in 2006, my Lyme disease returned with a vengeance, inflating my knees like basketballs. I went to see my doctor again, and he did an MRI. The scan showed degenerative joint damage in the right knee and ample evidence of arthritis. "Your running days are over," my doc told me.

"I can't run marathons anymore?"

"No, you can't run."

I left the office in a fog. What was I going to do? Running was a big part of my life. It was what I did. I toyed with the idea of resigning from *Runner's World*. You don't have to be a runner to work there, but it was an important part of my job. In a moment of levity, I thought about applying to a basket-weaving magazine. My Spanish teacher used to say I'd better take up basket weaving because I was never going to make it as an interpreter, but I couldn't craft baskets from straw, either.

In the end, I didn't quit. I decided that however many miles were left in my body, I would use them judiciously, waiting for a glorious morning when it would be neither too hot nor cold, and then only running on a scenic trail. I still consider myself a lifetime runner, but I only go 2 or 3 miles at a time. I made peace with it after recognizing that running isn't about how far you go but how far you've come. Looking back at my checkered youth, I knew I'd traveled very far indeed.

Bart and Sarah Reinertsen at the
Runner's World Heroes Gala in New York City
November, 2004. Sarah had just received
a Hero of Running Award from the magazine.

Chapter 14

INSPIRING RUNNERS

Legendary runner Frank Shorter once told me that even though he had won silver and gold medals in the Olympics, no one has gotten more out of the sport than I have. That's because in my 20-year career at *Runner's World,* I have been lucky to meet and mingle with tens of thousands of runners from around the world, from elite athletes such as Carl Lewis, Michael Johnson, and Joan Benoit Samuelson to diehards who sweep their age divisions in local races to newbies testing the running waters at their first 5-Ks. It's been an honor to meet every one of them, and I love hearing about the circumstances that drew them to the sport. These people seek me out, not to gain publicity in *Runner's World,* but simply to share their stories and be validated.

There was the woman who was so overweight that she ran in the dark so no one would see her. After losing 200 pounds, she started running during the light of day. Abused women have told me that they didn't find the courage to leave their husbands until after they gained self-confidence through running. Then there are the people who have overcome illness and run to affirm their lives.

Everyone's stories have had an impact on me, but a few runners have truly been an inspiration, not only to me, but to the sport by overcoming adversity and leading by an example. These are runners I consider my personal heroes.

Sarah Reinertsen

Things were going according to plan for Sarah Reinertsen. She was in New Zealand, where 2,000 runners from 45 countries had gathered at sunrise on January 1, 2000, to become the first group to run a marathon in the new millennium. But at mile 3, Sarah noticed that her prosthetic leg was literally falling apart. Nuts and bolts were popping out of the artificial knee joint. Rather than miss the chance to finish the race 19 hours before the ball dropped in Times Square, Sarah kept going, not even stopping to screw the pieces back in.

I was awed by Sarah's indomitable spirit and fortunate enough to have gotten to know her.

It's hard enough running a marathon on two good legs, but Sarah does it with an above-the-knee prosthetic leg. She has been running since age 11, 4 years after her left leg was amputated because of a birth defect. She started running because she figured no one thought she could.

At age 13, she broke the 100-meter world record for female above-the-knee amputees. Her record of 17.99 seconds still stands.

Since then, Sarah, who is 32, has never stopped pushing herself. She's completed the Boston, New York, and Los Angeles Marathons. In 2004, she took her first stab at completing the Ironman Triathlon World Championship in Kona, Hawaii, which includes a 2.4-mile swim, 112-mile bike ride, and 26.2-mile run. But Sarah was disqualified when she missed the bicycle cutoff time by 15 minutes. She came back the next year with a mission she called "Unfinished Business" and completed the race in 15:05 hours, becoming the first female amputee to finish one of the most challenging events on the planet.

I was so taken by Sarah's grit that I twice invited her to speak at the Lehigh Valley Half-Marathon prerace dinner. She has an infectious personality and never fails to inspire everyone, the able-bodied, disabled, young, and old.

Sarah was at the start of the 1-mile *Runner's World* kids' race one year when the gun went off and a little girl, no more than 6 or 7, fell down and got stepped on by the other children. Sarah immediately came to her rescue, helping her up and then running hand in hand with her to the finish. As a child, Sarah had experienced frustration in gym class, and the memories of being the last one picked for a team still rankle her. She knows how empowering running can be, and she didn't want this little girl to feel discouraged and have a bad experience at her first race. The next day, when Sarah ran the half-marathon, the girl and her family showed up with signs to encourage Sarah and thank her for her kindness.

In many ways, Sarah is just like every other runner, including myself. Running gave her something to strive for. The only difference is that she's had to work a lot harder to achieve its rewards. If you base your concept of an athlete on tenacity and determination, she is the greatest one on the planet.

Ryan Hall

I was watching this 24-year-old superstar about to smash the American record by more than a minute at the Houston Half-Marathon in January 2007, and he was pumping his arms into the air and high-fiving spectators. He still had a half mile to go, but he was whooping it up like he was already on the winner's podium. *Why doesn't this kid just put his head down and finish fast?* I thought.

But that's not Ryan Hall. Later, at the press conference, he explained. He wasn't celebrating his anticipated win but honoring all the hard work that had taken him this far. He was having the run of his life, he said, and all the sacrifices he had made along the way were about to pay off. It was worth losing 2 or 3 seconds to acknowledge his family and the fans cheering him. Even with the lost time, he was the first American to run a half-marathon in under an hour.

I was impressed that someone so young could have such a mature outlook on the sport—look how long it took *me* to celebrate running for its own sake.

It's all the more amazing considering Ryan never considered himself a marathon runner. He was a high school prodigy and a three-time cross-country all-American who made a name for himself in the 5,000 meters in college. Houston was his first official half-marathon, and he blazed onto the marathon scene 4 months later in April 2007 by breaking the US debut record in London. Seven months later, he earned a spot on the US Olympic marathon team by winning the trials in 2:09:02, an Olympic trials record. This time, when he slowed at the finish to honor his achievement, I understood his motive, and the crowd ate it up. He's not only a great runner but also a fantastic human being.

I got a chance to know him better when I invited him to be a guest speaker at the Lehigh Valley Half-Marathon in Allentown the week after he ran London in April 2007. I wasn't sure what he was going to talk about, but I was glad when he spoke about his philosophy of applauding oneself for working hard. "It's not all about what you do in the race tomorrow," he said. "It's about what you've done to get here."

"Be bold yet wise. Race by effort not by pace."

I could tell people responded to his message. Here was the baby-faced future of American running delivering a message so humble and heartfelt, it was hard not to be moved by his sincerity. I knew people would carry his words with them through Allentown the next day and run a better race because of them.

What was even more mind-blowing was when Ryan said he wanted to be me when he grew up. He told me this after watching my amusing slide show featuring photos from the exotic locales of the races I've run.

"No, you wouldn't," I told him. "The Olympics beats any crazy marathon I've ever done. If I had your talent, I wouldn't waste it on a burro."

Even though running had led us down different paths, this kid, who was half my age, and I held a mutual respect for one another. He's even hoping to replace me at *Runner's World* when I retire. I can't think of anyone better for the job.

Billy Mills

I had heard Billy Mills's story of unlikely Olympic gold long before I had met him, but now I had a chance to find out firsthand what it was like for him to have crossed the finish line in Tokyo in 1964.

No one had expected Mills, a Native American born on a South Dakota reservation, to qualify for the Olympics, let alone win the 10,000 meters. No Native American ever had, and Billy Mills, a college All-American in cross-country, had spent the last several years in the Marines. He had even stopped running for a brief time.

But none of that mattered in October 1964. With two laps to go in the race, Mills sprinted past 10,000-meter world-record holder Ron Clark of Australia and Mohammad Gammoudi of Tunisia to take the gold.

"How did you do it?" I asked, as we ate dinner 2 nights before he was scheduled to speak at the Lehigh Valley Half-Marathon in April 2004.

He beamed. "It was just my day to shine," he said. "That's the beauty of life and our sport. If you work really hard and have big dreams, it can happen."

Mills said at first he didn't think he'd won because the judges and race officials looked so confused. "I thought maybe I had run a lap short," he said.

But that wasn't the source of their puzzlement. "Nobody knew who I was," he said. "They were all scratching their heads."

Mills is a natural-born storyteller, no doubt a trait he inherited from his ancestors. But what I like about him is the way he manages to work a message about diversity into his tales—how people of all races, colors, and abilities should be accepted and celebrated.

Sister Andrena Mulligan

I had never before asked a nun if she would model a bathing suit for a photo shoot, so I waited until she had finished her glass of wine. "Sister Andrena," I said, "did you pack a bathing suit?"

She gave me a withering look. "Why?"

"I thought it would be cool to get a picture of you on the beach holding a surfboard with Diamond Head in the background. It will make every other runner in the world jealous."

Not that they weren't jealous already. Sister Andrena was one of 10 runners chosen from 1,800 entries who won an all-expenses paid trip to Hawaii in March 2004 for the Honolulu Marathon courtesy of *Runner's World*. The winners were chosen from entrants in an essay contest explaining why running the Honolulu Marathon would be a dream come true.

For Sister Andrena, it was a matter of economics. As a Catholic nun living in the border town of Eagle Pass, Texas, she would never have been able to afford an airline ticket to Honolulu, let alone accommodations at a beachfront hotel. She was a volunteer at two nonprofits, distributing food and medicine to migrant populations and helping orphaned children who were mentally and physically impaired. Oh yeah, she was also a runner, logging 51 marathons in 18 years.

Naturally, she was one of the winners. So now it was my job to coax her into showing some skin at a *Runner's World* photo shoot, and my Catholic upbringing was making it difficult, to say the least. Lucky for me, if there was ever a nun game enough to pose with a surfboard, it was Sister Andrena.

She met the photographer and me the next afternoon wearing the modest black racing-back tank she had brought along for the trip. "It will only take about 30 minutes," I told her. "You're a trouper."

But the photographer kept delaying the shot, complaining about the light. Sister Andrena never said a word, but she kept looking at her watch and fidgeting. "I'm so sorry, Sister," I said. "Just a little longer. Don't worry; we'll get you off this beach in no time."

Finally, the sunset met with the photographer's approval, and he snapped some pictures. But it was too late for Sister Andrena to get to Mass. She had planned to go Saturday night because she was running the marathon early Sunday. I knew right there I had punched my ticket to hell. I had not only talked a nun into wearing a bathing suit but also made her miss Mass.

Hopefully, I'll receive some redemption from the subsequent good deeds performed by my wife. Laura organized Run for a Reason, doing three marathons in 2 days on two continents. First, she ran the London Marathon on Sunday, April 17, 2005, then got on a plane to Boston, where she ran the course twice. She raised $7,000 for Sister Andrena's clinic, Casa Bethesda, which treats homeless people with mental and physical disabilities in Mexico.

In grade school, nuns beat me up; but in Sister Andrena I found a kindred soul, a runner who drinks a glass of wine before a race and can tell a joke with the finesse of a late-night television host. She is as devoted to running as she is to saving the world, and that makes her a hero in my book.

George Hirsch

In was October 2003, and George Hirsch had retired the year before as publisher of *Runner's World*, but that didn't mean he was slowing down. In terms of running, he was faster than the competition, winning his age group at a host of races across the country. But in Chicago that year, he was suffering some back pain and didn't feel well. That wasn't enough reason for him to sit out the race, but he struggled through the 26.2 miles until the end, when he collapsed from dehydration about 50 yards from the finish. I saw him go down, while watching from the sidelines. I tried to help him but security wouldn't let me onto the course. "But he's my dad," I said. "You have to let me help my dad."

In a way, George was like a father to me and to many people at *Runner's World*, a larger-than-life patriarch who led by example, tenacity, and sheer exuberance. He was also the most mentally tough runner I have ever met.

Security finally let me through, and I picked George off the ground. He had chipped a few teeth, and his nose, lip, and knees were bleeding profusely. Despite his injuries, he insisted on finishing the race on his own. Afterward, I helped him to his hotel. "Come on, George," I said. "Let's get you to your room and clean you up."

But when we walked into the lobby, the race press conference was in full swing, and George wanted to listen to it.

"George, you're bleeding," I said. "You look like an accident victim."

He waved me aside and strode before the cameras, flashing a gap-toothed smile that spoke volumes about his commitment and love for the sport.

That was the thing about George. Even though he held the job as publisher of *Runner's World* from 1987 to 2002, he was never reluctant to get his hands dirty or embrace the athletes and fans who cherished the sport as much as he did.

Mike Huckabee

In September 2007 I was sitting in a lounge chair on a white sandy beach in Hawaii watching the blue water sparkle in the sunshine when I decided to e-mail my new friend and devoted runner, Republican presidential candidate Mike Huckabee. "I just ran the Front Street Mile in Maui," I wrote, "and now I'm drinking a rum runner with an umbrella in it. How are you?"

A few minutes later he replied: "I just did a 3-mile run in the cornfields of Muscatine, Iowa. Where did I go wrong?"

I had met Huckabee the year before at the Little Rock Marathon in Arkansas, where he had invited runners and other dignitaries to the governor's columned mansion for an American Running Association Conference. At one point, Huckabee had been the most famous fat man in the state, weighing in at 280 pounds, his girth fueled by a diet of southern fried chicken, deep-fried pickles, and pecan pie. His nickname was Governor Wide Body. But a diagnosis of type 2 diabetes in 2003, 2 years before he hit 50, scared him into losing what turned out to be 110 pounds. He credits running with helping him get in shape and drop the weight. Leading an active lifestyle became so important to him that he wrote a book called *Quit Digging Your Grave with a Knife and Fork* and launched an initiative in Arkansas to promote the benefits of exercise and eating right. It was a crusade worth pursuing: Arkansas had the sixth highest level of adult obesity in a nation where 65 percent of the population is either overweight or obese.

The 2006 Little Rock Marathon would be Huckabee's third marathon and his second in Arkansas. I was invited to the prerace gathering because he was a big fan of *Runner's World* magazine. After lunch, I figured Huckabee would excuse himself to go deal with important matters, but he pulled me aside to talk about running. "What's it like to work at *Runner's World*?" he asked.

"It's the greatest job in the world," I said. "They pay me to run all over the globe."

"I wish I could get a gig like that," Huckabee said.

"I'll see what I can do," I said.

He laughed, then turned serious. "Do you have any advice for tomorrow's race?"

I figured he already knew all about the importance of drinking enough fluid and not going out too fast, so I counseled him on the one thing that would only apply to a politician. "Don't run too fast. That way, you'll look good when you cross the finish line," I said.

"What do you mean?" he asked.

"Everyone will be taking your photo, so you don't want to look like you're about to collapse and be unfit for office."

Huckabee said he didn't care about his personal appearance. He was looking to set a personal record. And he did, running the marathon in 4:26:05.

I greeted him at the finish line. We posed for a photo, and he looked good despite setting a PR. Good thing he hadn't listened to me.

Huckabee is one of my heroes, not only because he understands the benefits of running but also because he uses his influence to spread the word. He not only walks the walk, he runs the run.

Bart and 2008 Republican presidential candidate Mike Huckabee at the Little Rock Marathon, 2006

An Inukshuck, an Inuit marking, near the start of the Arctic Cruise Marathon

Chapter 15

ARCTIC MARATHON

In a remote outpost in Quebec's Arctic, a young Inuit had just won a kicking contest, extending his right leg higher than I thought possible and touching a leather ball tethered to a rope that was steadily raised in increments, like a high-jump bar.

I wonder if he's a fast runner, I thought, sitting in the bleachers of the village's new gymnasium, a gift from the Canadian government. My curiosity wasn't innocent. I was in Kangiqsujuaq, population 572, with the rest of the passengers from the Russian vessel the *Lyubov Orlova* for the First Arctic Cruise Marathon. It was August 1, 2006, and the race was being held the next day on a rocky strip of mining land. We anchored in Wakeham Bay to recruit Inuit runners and volunteers for the aid stations.

Jay Glassman, who organizes the Toronto Marathon, designed the race as a way to introduce the benefits of exercise to the indigenous people of the Arctic. Despite the physical exertion required to survive in the wild, the Inuit are not particularly healthy. Alcoholism is rampant, and most adults smoke.

I approached the kicking champion of the Inuit Games, 23-year-old Charlie Alaku, who had arms as big as firewood and a chest that bulged with the girth of a beer keg. "You're quite the athlete," I said. "How about running with us tomorrow?"

"How far?" he wanted to know.

"Well, the marathon is 26.2 miles, but you can run a half-marathon or even be part of a relay team."

"I will do the marathon," he said.

"Do you run?"

"No, but I'm in shape."

"Do you work out?" I asked.

"No," he said.

"What do you do?"

"I harpoon whales to feed my family."

That took far more effort than running a marathon. First he speared the animal from a kayak, then dragged its body to a nearby shore, where he cut up the meat. Then he rowed the whale meat home, an exhausting trip that sometimes took up to 6 days.

The practice sounded primitive, but hunting whales is still a way of life for the Inuit. Canadian law allows it only for these Arctic people; the blubbery meat is a significant source of protein in a land short on food options.

Charlie was strong but not aerobically fit, so I finally convinced him that the half-marathon would be a more manageable distance than the marathon. The race, after all, was the next day.

"Oh, all right," said Charlie. Then he lit a cigarette.

In this land of polar bears, walruses, and midnight sun, the Inuit maintain strong ties to their heritage. The kicking contest was just the start of that day's entertainment in Kangiqsujuaq. The villagers receive few guests, so they were excited to demonstrate traditional dancing, drumming, and throat singing, a wacky competition practiced by women. The object is to imitate an animal sound from the Arctic and see who can hold it the longest without laughing.

By the time the ceremony ended, we had recruited one Inuit to run the marathon; two, including Charlie, to do the half; and a five-member marathon relay team. Three Inuit agreed to hand out water at the aid stations.

The race was the next day, but our adventure had started 5 days earlier, when 60 of us boarded the *Lyubov Orlova* in Churchill, Manitoba, a remote village on the southwestern shore of Hudson Bay. Some days polar bears outnumber people in Churchill, and the bus driver who picked us up at the airport carried a shotgun to ward off attacking bears.

We weren't all runners; some were just tourists looking to immerse themselves in the beauty of the Arctic and the Inuit culture, but we invited them to do the race anyway. A few, like Claudette, a 70-year-old grandmother who had never run before, immediately agreed.

The Russian crew was a harder sell. They kept to themselves for the first 2 days of the cruise, rebuffing our advances of friendship with stony faces and cold eyes. It was light for 20 hours a day on the Hudson Bay, so the crew would play basketball on the deck beneath the glow of an orange and pink sky after they got off their shift at 1:00 a.m. One night I elbowed my way into a game.

"Are you one of those runners?" a Russian crew member asked during a break.

"Yes," I said. "But we're looking for more. How about joining us?"

"We are not runners."

"Everyone's a runner," I said. "You've just got to get out there and train."

"But the race is only a few days away."

"You don't have to do the marathon—you can run as a five-member team," I said. "It would be fun to have teams from Russia, the United States, and an Inuit village."

"I love the idea of representing our homeland," he said. "We miss it very much. Let me talk to some of the other crew members. But how would we train?"

"Well, there's no crash course in running," I said. "It's a game of patience, but you can start by running laps around the ship. Don't push yourself, though."

They took my advice to heart, and the next night, after they finished washing dishes and mopping the cafeteria floor, they ran around the deck wearing army boots because they didn't have running shoes. Some ran in bare feet, and one woman wore pink ballet slippers. You had to admire their determination.

Charlie didn't have any running shoes, either; luckily, he wore the same size as me, and I had an extra pair.

The night before the race, the 11 Inuit who were going to either run the race or volunteer boarded the ship with us. We were cruising early the next day into the fjord of Douglas Harbor, where we would be transported to shore by Zodiacs, motorized rubber rafts.

As usual, the pre-race meal was pasta, but the Inuit took a pass. They had brought their own food—raw caribou. "Bart, would you like to try?" a woman named Mary asked, blood from the raw meat dripping down her face.

"No thanks," I said. "I'll stick with pasta."

I didn't have the heart to tell her I'm a vegetarian. I'm not sure she would even be able to comprehend why someone would give up eating meat in a place that depended on it for survival.

A slide show of my running adventures was the night's entertainment. I told them about the time I ran the Mount Kilimanjaro Marathon and a bunch of barefoot village children lined the course to cheer us on. They spoke Swahili, so I couldn't understand a thing they were yelling, but they all said the same thing: "*Pole* (pronounced POH-lee) *pole muzunga.*"

After I crossed the finish line, I asked the race director what "pole pole muzunga" meant.

"It means you are a very slow white man."

My humor must have translated in Inuit because everyone laughed. It was the icebreaker this crowd needed to bond. Running is a sport rich in camaraderie, and I wanted the Inuit to have the best possible experience so they would continue running and inspire others to do so once they returned to their village.

After dinner, several Inuit invited me to play a game of Texas hold 'em. "Sure," I said, hoping I remembered the rules. "I'll be right back. I need to find a deck of cards."

"I have cards," said Jacko, pulling a deck of Nevada Style 1860s from his jacket pocket. "But what about poker chips?"

"How about we use sugar packets?" I suggested. Everyone liked the idea, so we assigned different values to blue Equal, pink Sweet'N Low, yellow Splenda, white granulated sugar, and brown raw sugar. "Okay, here's how you play," I said.

Jacko waved me off. "We know how to play," he said, pulling out a pair of sunglasses to hide his expression.

Turned out Jacko and the Inuit boys were hustlers. There's not much to do indoors in Kangiqsujuaq during the dark days of winter, but thanks to the marvels of satellite television, the Inuit had learned the fine art of playing cards by watching the World Series of Poker. It was one of their favorite shows, so we all adopted the character of a player. There was the Unabomber, Jesus, and Devil Fish.

I was Scotty Nguyen, baby. (For those who don't know: "Baby" and "yeah, baby" are this famous poker player's trademark sayings.)

Despite our unusual chips, it was a serious game backed by real money, but our banter must have sounded odd to anyone who strolled by.

"I'll see your Sweet'N Low and raise you two Equal."

"Raw sugar is too rich for my blood."

We played in the ship's bar until 12:30 in the morning. I lost $20, the monetary equivalent of a cup of sugar, but I didn't mind. The Inuit were having fun, and any uneasiness between our cultures had dissolved.

A few hours later, the alarm clock went off, rousing me from sleep at 5:00 a.m. I didn't want to eat a big breakfast because I was going to be running the marathon relay with my partner, Jason Annahatak, so I ate only a few slices of toast. Jason was an Inuit and a lecturer on the ship who had graduated from college in Montreal the year before. He was a local hero, proof positive that an Inuit from Kangirsuk, a small Arctic village, could get a college degree, and his photograph was plastered on billboards in towns throughout the Arctic to inspire others. On the ship he received an e-mail saying he had been accepted to Columbia University's graduate school in New York City to study educational psychology, and he shared the good news with the rest of the passengers, many of whom began sending e-mails to friends in search of housing for Jason.

Later that morning we were on the Zodiacs motoring toward the racecourse and saw caribou grazing on the moss-covered hills. There were about 40 of us from seven countries, and we ranged in age from fresh-faced teens to the aforementioned 70-year-old. Race organizer Jay Glassman and the Inuit volunteers had set up mile markers along the course and tents for the water stations, but it was still a 5-mile hike up a rocky expanse to the start line. A road had washed out the night before, making it impassable for the truck Jay had planned to to use to transport the runners.

When we all reached the start, the relay runners were then taken by ATV to their stations.

I was dropped off a little past mile 13, the halfway point, where I would wait for Jason, the first runner of our two-man team. After a while, my stomach started to growl. "Man, I'm hungry," I said to the three female Inuit volunteers assigned to that spot. "I could eat a horse."

"No horse," one said, "but you are fast enough to run down a caribou. If you catch it, we will cut it up for you."

I was flattered. No woman had ever offered to kill a caribou for me before, but raw meat wasn't what I had in mind. I didn't want to hurt their feelings, so I politely declined. "I need to conserve my energy for the race," I said.

I forgot about my stomach when the first runner, Fiona Savage, ran by. We high-fived, and she slowed to drink some water. "It's really desolate out here," she said.

A little while later my wife, Laura, arrived. "This is so beautiful," she said. "See you when you pass me."

Then came Jason. He slapped my hand, and I took off across the mining road, past commanding rock formations, caribou, and an occasional waterfall. The Inuit volunteers had also built small Inukshuks along the course, stone markers symbolizing safety, hope, and friendship. Who knew the Arctic was such an inviting place?

This was a race worth doing. Earlier that year, when I had been diagnosed with chronic Lyme disease, I had vowed to conserve the miles left in my body for memorable runs. My knees ached with every footfall, but I was able to disassociate myself from the pain by focusing on the stunning landscape. I had never been to the Arctic, and I enjoyed every stride.

But the real reward came about a mile from the finish, when I crested a hill after passing through a vast region of isolation. There, a group of Russian women had gathered to cheer on their crewmates. They had fashioned pom-poms from orange garbage bags and shook them and yelled when any runner approached the finish line. To think only days ago we couldn't get them to crack a smile! The ending of the race and journey could not have been scripted any better. The Russians were cheering; Laura, Claudette, and the other female runners had built a fire from moss and were singing "Frère Jacques," the only song everyone knew all the words to; and round-faced Inuit children were passing out freshly caught char, an arctic fish. It was the ultimate sushi bar.

We had started the journey as Russians, Germans, Canadians, French, Americans, Irish, and Inuit, but we ended as athletes. Running does that to people. It brings unlikely folks together and fosters a fellowship like no other sport.

When I crossed the finish line, the Inuit runners all chanted the same thing, "Qal-luu-naaq suk-kai-tua-luk."

"What did they say?" I asked Jason.

"You are a very slow white man."

Later that night, the awards were handed out at dinner on the ship. Fiona Savage of Canada won the marathon in 4:01 and received a handmade soapstone sculpture of a nesting falcon. A very excited Russian crew won the five-member relay race with a finishing time of 3:45:45, despite 3 days of training and improper footwear. They embraced the other runners.

Charlie had finished the half and announced he was now hooked on running. We hoped his enthusiasm would encourage other Inuit to follow in his footsteps.

The next morning, when our Inuit friends disembarked, it felt like we were losing a part of our family.

"Keep running," I told Charlie as we shook hands. "Maybe next time you'll win."

"It was an honor to compete," he said. "In my culture, what matters is doing your best, not winning. I did my best."

"Yes, you did, Charlie."

It was the perfect lesson for this far-flung trip.

**Bart and Inuit running partner
Jason Annahatak near the start of the race**

Karl Glassman,
aka Hanukkah Harry,
carrying a torch to his temple

Chapter 16

STUNT RUNNERS

Everyone in the running world knows them. They're the equivalent of a family's eccentric uncle or batty aunt. They've latched on to a gimmick that gives them a way to stand out among the sea of singlets and shorts for reasons they are at a loss to explain. Some juggle balls or run an entire course backward. Others, like Roger Jensen, carry yo-yos, working in tricks like "walk the dog" at each mile mark. It's not unusual to see a group of Santas running in a December marathon, women running in bunny ears and cottontails at Easter, or Blues Brothers competing in Chicago.

My friend Karl Glassman made a name for himself commemorating the Festival of Lights. In 1982, his photo appeared on the front page of the *Morning Call* newspaper on the first day of Hanukkah for carrying a torch from Lehigh Valley International Airport to his synagogue 7 miles away in Allentown. The torch had been flown in from Israel, where it had been blessed by a Tel Aviv rabbi and used to light a menorah at his temple, Congregation Keneseth Israel.

From a news standpoint, Hanukkah gets overshadowed by the madness of Christmas, but the story of a bald, energetic dentist running through the streets of Allentown with a flaming torch was an irresistible tale. The newspaper covered the event for the next 10 years, dutifully reporting every December from a temple press release that a new torch had come from Israel.

Then, in 1993, reporter Margie Peterson accompanied Karl to the airport, where he pulled the original torch from the trunk of his car and dusted it off.

"I thought it came from Israel," she said.

"It did," said Karl.

"But the press release says it was flown in this year."

"It does?" said Karl. "I don't know. I haven't seen the release." Unbeknownst to Karl, the temple had sent out the same press release year after year, changing only the date of the run.

The next day, Peterson blasted Karl and his Hanukkah parade in the newspaper, all but calling him a fraud. A controversy ensued, and the temple board members called a meeting. "What are we going to do?" one asked.

Karl thought that the best way to minimize criticism was to have a new torch blessed by a rabbi in Israel and then flown to JFK International Airport.

"And then what?" a board member asked.

"I'll run it back to Allentown," he said.

"But that's 90 miles away," another elder said. "You can't run that far."

"I'll think of something," Karl said. "I'll call Bart."

Karl was not only a friend and fellow runner but also my dentist. I fondly referred to him as Hanukkah Harry because Hanukkah Karl doesn't have the same ring. He called me the next day. "Hey Bart, I want to run a torch from JFK to Allentown," he said. "That newspaper article gave our temple a black eye, and I want to generate some positive press. I can't run the entire 90 miles, but maybe we can get some guys together and take turns running."

It sounded like a crazy running adventure, and I'm always up for one of those. He recruited four other Gentiles—Bill Ruth, Neal Novak, Tony Heinz, and Leslie Korscmaros.

We picked up the torch the following year at Israel's El Al baggage terminal at JFK. I had mapped a course to Allentown that started on a narrow path near the Belt Parkway. Karl would be the first runner. But the torch was damaged during the flight, so as soon as we lit it, fuel started dripping down Karl's arm and onto the ground. Karl was afraid his arm was going to catch on fire, so he dropped the torch, which ignited the spilled fuel on the road. Soon 3-foot-high flames were racing across the entrance of the El Al terminal. We tried to put out the fire with towels from our van, but not before it caught the attention of a cop.

"We're going to jail tonight," I told the boys. "We'll get out because we didn't do anything wrong, but we're definitely going to be spending some time in the big house."

"What the hell is going on here?" screamed the police officer. "The freaking road is on fire."

"I know this doesn't look good, officer, but this is Hanukkah Harry, and he's running this torch from JFK to his temple," I said, looking contrite and gesturing toward Karl. "The torch was blessed in Israel and we just picked it up, but it had a fuel leak."

"I don't care what it had," he said. "Put out the freaking fire and get your asses out of here. I don't ever want to see you again."

"Yes, officer," I said. "Thank you."

We were able to fix the torch, and Karl resumed running until we hit the Verrazano-Narrows Bridge. There weren't any pedestrian paths on the bridge, so we drove Karl the 2 miles to the other side. From there we took turns running through the night until we arrived at a sobriety checkpoint near Rutgers University in New Jersey at 2:30 a.m. A cop shined a flashlight into the van, revealing our sweaty and bleary-eyed faces. "What are you guys doing?" he asked.

Once again we explained the epic journey of the Hanukkah torch.

"Are they drunk?" a police officer at the checkpoint yelled.

"No, they're just crazy," the cop replied.

At around 7:00 a.m. we arrived in Allentown, where a group of people from Karl's temple waited to run the final 2 miles with him. A police escort was also waiting for him, along with a *Morning Call* photographer.

The boys and I drove to the temple steps to wait for Karl's triumphant arrival. But as he neared, only the torch was visible. The crowd had engulfed Karl, so the photographer couldn't get a clear shot of him climbing the steps of the temple for the next day's paper. "The biggest photo op is coming up, and Karl is stuck in a pack of congregants," I said to Neal.

"You watch. He's going to break through like Walter Payton," he said, referring to the NFL Hall of Fame running back.

And that's just what happened. Even though he had run 45 miles, the last 20 continuously, Karl somehow managed to find a last burst of energy to outkick his fellow congregants.

The photo in the next day's paper was Karl's exuberant face thrusting the torch into the air, the flame flickering in the gray sky.

Karl's torch run brought him some attention on this one occasion, but there are plenty of others out there who consistently go to great lengths to distinguish themselves from the crowd. Take Coat Man. In 1995, he spotted me manning the *Runner's World* booth at the New York City Marathon. Dressed in black wing tips and a heavy denim coat, Coat Man—real name Dennis Marsella—tried to capture my attention with a quick wave. I knew what he wanted. Unfortunately, there was no way to avoid him.

After much pleading, Coat Man had finally convinced *Runner's World* to do an article on his unusual running attire: He does marathons, even prestigious ones like New York, in a dress shirt and tie, bright yellow socks, and the same coat and dress shoes he had on that day in the expo room. He also carries a pizza box with a wine bottle on top, holding it steady like a Papa John's delivery man for the entire 26.2 miles.

Coat Man considers himself a stunt runner, an Evel Knievel of running. He has spent hours perfecting his skills and believes that his theatrics prove he is as tough as any elite athlete, but he felt he had come out as some sort of loon in the *Runner's World* story. He never lost an opportunity to remind me about how he had been maligned, writing me letters on the backs of envelopes to make sure I read them, and tracking me down at marathons: "Bart, that just wasn't right. Tell the editors they have to do another story."

"Dennis, we've gone over this before. You know that's not going to happen, so I'm not going to bother to ask," I replied.

"I know, I know," he said, shaking his head.

I kind of felt sorry for Coat Man as I watched him walk away. In many ways, he was right. What he did was really hard. I can't imagine putting on a pair of wing tips, let alone running in them, for an entire marathon. That's got to kill your feet. And a heavy coat—I tried piling on the clothes to train for the extreme heat of Badwater and barely made it a few yards before stripping down to my running shorts.

Coat Man had done it time and time again, logging more than 100 marathons, including 23 in New York. But instead of making a name for himself as an elite athlete, he is known as a crazy runner.

In most cases, these stunt runners are normal in all other aspects, considering their pursuits as nothing more than harmless fun, a chance to cut loose. Another familiar face at races is Keith Straw, a 55-year-old Brit who is reserved by nature, typically wears a pink tutu when he runs the Lehigh Valley Half-Marathon. I've also seen him run in a woman's red hat and pearls. Not that there's anything wrong with that.

Another friend, Jeannie Wokasch, ends every marathon with a signature cartwheel. Her gymnastic feat is so well known that spectators make sure they head for the finish line when they see her nearing it. But her stunt has been known to catch people off guard. At the Honolulu Marathon one year, she was running next to the prince of Norway when she realized he would be in her way. "You got to move over," she told him, eyeing the finish line.

"What do you mean?" the puzzled prince asked.

"I need room."

The next thing the prince saw were Wokasch's legs lifting into the air.

Then there's my buddy Bob Babbitt, who works for *Competitor* magazine. In 1998, as part of the Rock 'n' Roll Marathon in San Diego, he and some friends thought that, in keeping with the race's theme, it would be fun to dress up in Elvis costumes. After all, there would be musicians performing along the route. Bob and his friends liked running as Elvises—or is it Elvi?—so much, they've been doing it ever since, though not at every race. (I plan to join them this June in San Diego.)

In many ways, the running world invites these sideshow antics. Unlike other sports, there are no hard-and-fast rules about what you wear. While professional football players wouldn't be allowed on the field without a helmet, marathoners don't even have to wear running shoes. They can run in high heels, combat boots, or fuzzy pink slippers. Heck, people have won notable marathons in bare feet. But even in this carnival atmosphere, there are crazy runners such as Coat Man who defy belief and are truly in a class unto themselves.

You hear Geta-man before you see him. My wife, Laura, experienced this firsthand a few years ago at the Honolulu Marathon. She was around mile 9 when she heard a muffled clip-clopping sound. As she ran farther and got closer to him, it became louder and louder, like a thunderous sound of hooves. *"Horses,"* she thought, *"on a marathon course in the middle of a race?"*

Rounding a bend, she saw the source of the clatter: a man dressed in a traditional Japanese kimono and running in wooden sandals known as getas. As she strode by, Laura couldn't believe anyone could run in such footwear. But what was especially surprising was that the man was quite fast. Later, at the finish line, there were more than a few bruised egos as runners confessed to being overtaken by Geta-man.

"He passed me at mile six," said one man.

"When I saw him ahead of me at the finish line, I almost died," commiserated another.

"Who is he?" Laura asked.

Nobody knew a thing about him, even his name. "He only shows up at Honolulu," said one runner.

Geta-man may be a mystery, but Cowman, another costumed runner, is a well-known figure on the Hawaiian Islands, where he makes his home in Kona—and everywhere else in the running world, for that matter. Real name Kevin Shirk, Cowman has run everything from the Hawaii Ironman and Ironman Brazil to the Western States 100-miler and the Boston Marathon. He was fast enough to qualify for Boston back when the cut off time was 2:50.

But running fast obviously doesn't interest him. Cowman competes in a grass skirt and a heavy helmet adorned with bull horns. He enters each race under the moniker Cowman A-Moo-Ha. I'm not sure who is he trying to be—a witch doctor from *Gilligan's*

Island, maybe? But he's certainly not the type of athlete who needs a goofy getup to gain notoriety. I've seen him run. He can do it on brawn alone.

Cowman, now in his sixties, has always been a free spirit. He was living in Tahoe on July 4, 1976, when the town held a Bicentennial parade. He chose to streak through the festivities wearing the bull horns and nothing else.

Probably the craziest of the bunch, though, is Pennyman, who hails from Tucson and in everyday life uses the name Steven Baker. Pennyman runs marathons in a suit made entirely of pennies. He made it himself, spending 800 hours painstakingly fashioning 3,568 copper coins into a wearable form. His zealous effort earned him a spot in *The Guinness World Records* book in 1990.

I wince every time I see him in it. The darn thing weighs 32 pounds, meaning he has all that extra weight stressing his knees and joints at every step. I'd like to say he is penny-wise and pound-foolish, but despite wearing the suit he somehow manages a 3:50 marathon every time.

Pennies are Baker's obsession. He covered an entire 1969 Ford van with pennies. At every marathon, he sets up a booth where he hawks jewelry, shirts, and bathing suits, all made from pennies with his very hands.

Baker thinks pennies are the key to solving the world's problems. If everyone gave someone a penny, he says, we'd all be in a much better place. He tried to take his message of hope to the hallowed halls of Congress, running as a write-in candidate for the US Senate in Arizona in 2006. I'm sad to report he didn't win.

I've talked to Baker a number of times, and he seems like a nice enough guy, the kind of doughy-faced neighbor who will clear the snow from your driveway just because he loves his snowblower that much. I always thought of him as some kind of vigilante trying to better the world one penny at a time. But then I Googled him and found out why the very coin that most people would just as soon have disappear has become so much a part of who he is. In an interview for the University of Arizona's newswire, he made this confession: Nobody ever noticed him when he went to bars—that is, until he started donning his coin suit and transformed himself into Pennyman.

I burst out laughing when I read it. Pennyman was looking for attention.

That's the way it is with stunt runners. They think they need some shtick to make it in the running world; that nobody will accept them for who they really are. And I end up being a crazy magnet. Sooner or later at races, they all make their way to me, hoping that I can get them some well-deserved mention in *Runner's World*. As far as they're concerned, what they are doing is truly amazing. "Bart, don't you think there should be a special category for stunt runners?" they ask. "You know, like age categories."

I feel for them. I really do. It's hard to stand out in a crowd that includes elite athletes. It's pretty easy to feel like a nameless face, especially when there are thousands of runners in town for a big race. Wearing a pink bunny costume is a surefire way to get someone to take notice. It may even get them on television.

But, as with every sport, there are only a few superstars in road racing. Plus, runners are among the friendliest, most nonjudgmental people in the world. That's probably why there hasn't been some movement to come up with official rules that would dictate what can and can't be worn in a race. Everyone is welcomed at the marathon table. All you need is a desire to run.

Bart finishes his first marathon, the *Prevention* Marathon, in Bethlehem, Pennsylvania, March, 1981

Chapter 17

THE FINISH LINE

It was February 2007 and I was sitting at a table in a ballroom at a San Diego convention center with my friends from *Runner's World*. We were waiting to hear who would be inducted into the Running USA Hall of Champions.

"This next person was integral in implementing programs to help race directors from all over the country," said Basil Honikman, president and CEO of the Running USA Hall of Champions, whose past members include race directors, Olympic coaches, and other running luminaries. "He is America's running ambassador. He has brought the joy of our sport to countless people and has met more runners than anyone in the industry."

I turned to Amby Burfoot, who was next to me. "I have to meet this person," I said. "It sounds like he does what I do."

Amby smiled.

"He's run a few races, too," said Honikman. "Like Badwater . . ."

I looked around the room and realized I was the only one there who had run across Death Valley. I looked at Amby with disbelief. "Me?"

"Our next inductee into the Running USA Hall of Champions is Bart Yasso."

I was so stunned I could barely get out of my chair, and the room erupted into a standing ovation as I made my way to the podium. For once I was speechless, but thankfully the shock eased as Honikman invited me to say a few words. "I've crossed over 1,000 finish lines in my running career, but nothing can compare to the honor I feel by being inducted into the Running USA Hall of Champions," I said. "To receive this award in front of the most influential people in the running industry is something I will cherish for the rest of my life."

I looked out into the audience and saw the faces of the people I respected most: Amby; Khalid Khannouchi, former world marathon record holder; Ryan Hall, American half-marathon record holder; David McGillivray, race director of the Boston Marathon; and Mary Wittenberg, race director of the New York City Marathon. I only wished my father, who died in 2006, and my brother George, who died in 2003, could have been there.

I couldn't believe the sport was giving me one of its highest honors. It should have been the other way around; I should have been the one paying homage to running. After all, it saved me from a life of substance abuse and set me on a course where I got to run on all seven continents and meet the most dynamic people, including Charlie, the whale-hunting Inuit; Jeremy Wright, my roommate at Reunion Island, who died in Afghanistan in 2005; and *Today* show host Natalie Morales, whom I trained for the 2006 New York City Marathon.

My 30-year running career flashed before my eyes, and I thought of how much not only I, but the very sport itself, had changed and grown in 3 decades.

When I first started racing in the late 1970s, it was an all-boys club. Only about 10 percent of race participants were women, but

Kathrine Switzer was working to change that. In 1967, she was the first woman to run the Boston Marathon with a race number after registering as K. V. Switzer. There was no rule against women entering the race, but it was widely believed that female athletes weren't capable of running 26.2 miles, and if they did, their uteruses would fall out. Switzer, who was 20 at the time, knew it was hogwash. She had been training with the men's track team at Syracuse, where she was a student, and had run 31 miles a few weeks before.

The Boston Marathon race director, Jock Semple, had no idea there was a dame in the pack until a group of journalists in the press truck he was riding in pointed her out. He became so enraged that he jumped off the truck and tried to rip Switzer's number off her sweatshirt.

Lucky for Switzer, her boyfriend, who was also running the race, was an all-American football player. He didn't appreciate Jock roughing up his girl, so he body slammed him to the ground. Switzer finished the race in 4:24 and paved the way for the inclusion of women in marathons and long-distance races.

Switzer made it her mission to open opportunities for women by helping to organize races and successfully lobbied for a women's Olympic marathon event. Joan Benoit Samuelson won that first Olympic gold in 1984, displaying such grace and strength when she entered the stadium in Los Angeles that millions of women and girls around the world slipped into running shoes for the first time. The stirrings of a revolution had started, and today 40 percent of marathon participants are women. At half-marathons, they represent 55 percent of runners, a statistic I always point out to single men.

For many women, running is as much about socializing with girlfriends as it is about exercise. That's why Kristin Armstrong's

Runner's World column and blog resonate so strongly with female readers. Her amusing and poignant tales of friendship, kids, and other "badass mommy athletes" first appeared in August 2004 in response to the changing demographic.

Not only are there as many women as men runners these days, but they're proving they're almost as fast. Consider Paula Radcliffe, who smashed the women's marathon time by 2 minutes in 2003, running a 2:15:25 at London. In 2007 she won the New York City Marathon in 2:23:09, while the winning man, Martin Lel, finished in 2:09:04. When Radcliffe crossed the finish line in Central Park, her husband handed her their 9-month-old daughter, Isla, proving uteruses are impervious to running.

My sister Anne Marie started running at the age of 55 as a way to work through her grief after her husband died of leukemia. She joined a women's running group called First Strides in Allentown, started by my Badwater buddy Jane Serues. She quickly felt at home among so many supportive and encouraging women and soon started placing in her age group at races. Now she coaches other women. Anne Marie then convinced our younger sister, Mimi, to join First Strides to lose weight. Mimi's gotten hooked on running, too. They're no longer just siblings, but running buds.

Not only has the gender line blurred since I went for that first run with Brandy the dog, but the running apparel and equipment industry has exploded into a $6 billion business. In the old days, we put on a pair of gym shorts, running shoes with soles as thin as Silly Putty, and a $10 watch. These days, 10 bucks'll barely buy you socks. A good pair of running shoes typically costs around $100. Add to that a shirt and shorts made from fabric that not only wicks away sweat but has built-in UV sun protector and a GPS device that tracks pace, distance, and monitors your heart rate, as well as a fuel belt to carry energy gels and drinks, and you're dropping $600 just to go out your front door.

Those must-have products make the sport easier and more comfortable, but it still comes down to putting one foot in front of the other, an exercise now practiced by people of all ages and abilities. The National Sporting Goods Association estimates that 29 million Americans consider themselves active runners.

In the early 1980s, only serious athletes competed in marathons, with the average finishing time being 3:32:17 for men and 4:03:39 for women. Participants of half-marathons were also zealous athletes.

Out of 416 finishers at the *Prevention* magazine's half-marathon in Allentown in 1986, 404 posted times faster than 2 hours, meaning only 12 ran a slower time. Compare that to the 2007 Lehigh Valley Half-Marathon, where less than half of the 3,000 runners finished in under 2 hours.

But no race was more stringent in the 1980s about who could and couldn't run in its marathon than Boston, demanding a 2:50 qualifying time for men under 40. That was a hard time to post for me even as a 25-year-old. In 1982, the year I ran Boston, the official results booklet only published the times of the runners who finished under 3 hours 35 minutes. Seventy-five percent of the field accomplished that on a warm day.

Boston eventually relaxed its qualifying standards by 20 minutes in 1990 after participation started to drop, despite the sport's exploding popularity, because fewer runners were able to qualify.

Today, the average marathon finishing time is 4:15:34 for men and 4:46:40 for women, but it's not uncommon for some people to take 6 hours to complete the race. They're as committed and enthusiastic about the sport as the 3-hour marathoners.

This acceptance of all abilities is what differentiates running from every other sport. In football, there are 22 people on the field and 60,000 in the stands. It's the opposite in running. Everyone's on the field and in the fold.

In the New York City Marathon, everyone runs the same course over the Verrazano-Narrows Bridge, through Harlem and Central Park. It just takes most runners a bit longer than the elite athletes who may have blazed a world record on the same streets that their feet now touch.

That's because running is egalitarian, and you're never too young or too old. Consider 80-year-old Helen Klein, who set an age-group world record at the California International Marathon by running a 4:31. From the back, Klein looks like a schoolgirl, her muscular legs and trim waist a testament to her athletic prowess. When I first started in the sport, 50-year-olds were considered over-the-hill.

In the early 1980s, my 46-year-old friend Carmen Hagelgans and I drove together to a 10-K race in Nazareth, Pennsylvania. I doubted he would do well because in my 24-year-old-mind he was old; he competed in the masters division. But he kicked my 20-something butt and beat me by 3 minutes. Then there's Ed Whitlock, who ran a 2:54 at the Toronto Waterfront Marathon at age 73 in 2005. These people are changing our perceptions about age and life expectancy.

When I saw Ed at the finish line that year, I told him I didn't care if I could run a sub-3-hour marathon when I was his age. I just wanted a full head of hair like his, but it's already too late for that.

That's the beauty of the sport. Everyone is welcome to participate. All you have to do is put on a pair of running shoes. At some races, you don't even have to wear clothes.

Through all of this, *Runner's World* has evolved with the times under the leadership of editor in chief David Willey and publisher Andy Hersam, who oversaw a redesign of the magazine in 2004. Later that year, it was rated No. 1 on *Adweek* magazine's Hot List, and circulation has grown from 425,000 in the late 1980s to

640,000 in 2008. That's in no small part thanks to Rodale, a company whose visionary spirit has allowed me to make a living doing what I love most—inspiring runners.

There were about 300 of them in the room the February night in 2007 as I was being feted by my peers. I hoped it wasn't the precursor to a retirement party. When I returned to my seat, Hersam walked over to me and eased my fears. "In a lot of sports, when they induct someone into the Hall of Champions, it means their career is over," he said. "But we're going to work together for many more years. We have a lot more to accomplish in this sport."

His words were exactly what I wanted to hear. The sport is still evolving and attracting new acolytes every day, and I would like to be around to welcome them to our nomadic country club. Roughly 20 new marathons are launched every year in this country, as well as in exotic destinations that not only provide new challenges but also appeal to a runner's sense of adventure.

The sport is on an uptick, and who knows how high its popularity will climb? I just know I want to be there. I may not be able to run fast or far anymore, but I can still make every runner feel like a hero. If you don't feel welcomed in a sport or a job or a family, you don't stick around. Running is about acceptance—of yourself and others. When you're out on the trail sweating, it doesn't matter if the guy or gal next to you works at a fast-food joint or is CEO of Kellogg's. It doesn't matter what color they are, or how old they are, or what religion they practice, if any at all.

Running celebrates our commonality. Are we human because we can run on two feet, or does running make us human? I know I feel more like myself when I run, even if it's only a few miles, or at least I feel like the self I like best. Running inspires creativity, relieves stress, and gives us insight into ourselves and the world, making the human condition more tolerable.

But it is not enough to confine these benefits to ourselves. As runners, we each have a duty to accept the role as mentor to a slower runner or a new runner or someone who doesn't think he or she can walk around the block, let alone finish a 5-K. Remember, we're not some members of a snooty, noses-in-the-air fraternity. We are runners! So let's spread the message. Can you imagine how grand this planet would be if everyone were a runner? Obesity? Not a problem. Depression? Never heard of it. Sluggishness? Get the hell out.

On the plane ride home from San Diego the day after my induction, I thought again about this unexpected life I never dreamed I would lead.

But maybe I did dream it in the thousands of miles I ran over the years, first to beat my dependance on booze, butts, and drugs; then to earn my father's praise by proving I was good at something; and, finally, to enjoy the ride. Shakespeare got it wrong when he wrote "To sleep: perchance to dream." We run to dream, with our subconscious thoughts shaping the path of our lives.

I thought about regrets as well. Did I have any? I was sad that I wouldn't be able to train with my niece Victoria in cross-country. I had wanted to run with her through wooded trails, offering tips to improve her performance in easy companionship. But my knees weren't up to it anymore. "That's okay, Uncle Bart," she said after I had to stop 3 miles into a run.

I thought I had exorcised the last race demon from my system, but now, as I reviewed my past, I knew there was one race I still had left—Comrades, known as the greatest footrace on the planet and the world's oldest and largest ultra marathon. It takes place in South Africa between the cities of Pietermaritzburg and Durban and covers five major hills. The race was started by Vic Clapham, a soldier in the 8th South African Infantry during the Great War of 1914. The pain, death, and hardship he witnessed left a lasting impression on him. So when peace was declared in 1918, Clapham wanted to create a unique way in which human frailties could be put to the test and overcome, honoring those who had lost their lives. Remembering the searing heat and tough conditions he and his fellow soldiers had endured, he decided to host a 56-mile race and call it the Comrades Marathon as a living memorial to the spirit of those who had fought in the Great War. The first Comrades took place on May 21, 1921.

It is the one race that still haunts my dreams. So I wonder, can this 52-year-old man with bum knees go 56 miles through the hills of South Africa? Is there another epic race left in me? Or will it go down as my greatest regret?

The starting line beckons.

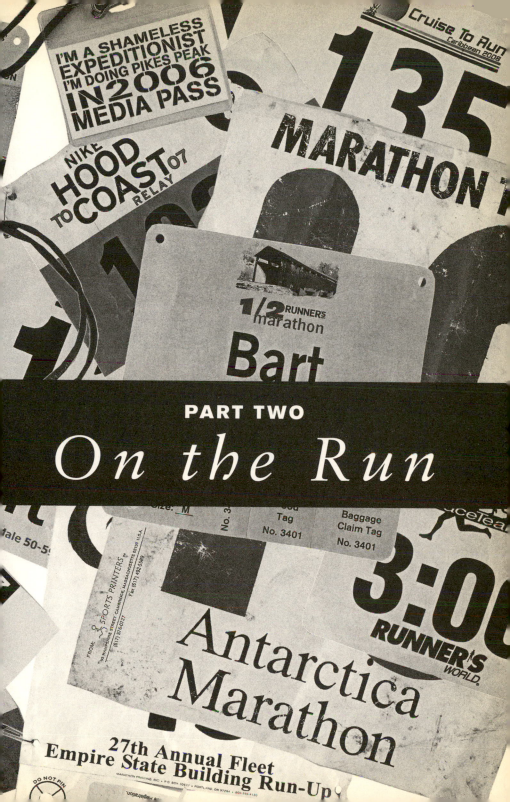

PART TWO

On the Run

Bart about to
cross the finish
line at the 2001
Rome Marathon

Chapter 18

THE PERFECT 10

I used this program to train for the Smoky Mountain Marathon, which is the only marathon I won, in 1998 at the age of 43. In the past I had focused on strenuous workouts, rarely taking a day off to rest. But this schedule allowed for several easy and rest days, so I gained more from my quality workouts.

Recovery is the most important part of a training program. Runners try to accomplish everything in a calendar week. As a masters runner (age 40 and up), I needed to allow more time for recovery. However, getting in quality workouts with subsequent easy days and rest days usually cannot be accomplished in a 7-day cycle. And why should it? Clinical studies have shown that because running utilizes the same motions over and over, excessive workout intensity and duration does not allow for proper physiological adaptation. Muscles and tendons fatigue easily, and as a result, overuse injuries occur. Failure to allow for easy days and rest days between quality workouts is the most common training mistake and leads to injury.

The Perfect 10 program I designed has more emphasis on rest and recovery, so the quality workouts become more beneficial. If you follow a 10-day cycle instead of a 7-day cycle, not only will you run faster, chances are you will also stay injury free.

In my dream job at *Runner's World* the only tough part is hearing from injured runners. I hate to see someone train 6 months for a race and then get injured in the training phase. The most common injuries are from overuse. I always hear runners say they got injured on one of their tempo workouts, speed sessions, or long runs. With the Perfect 10 technique, you'll avoid injuries by resting more and going slower on the easy days to recover fully and gain strength for the quality days. One of the many lessons I learned from several trips to East Africa is that the Kenyans go very easy on their easy days and very fast on their quality days. The easy days can be anywhere from 5 to 8 miles, depending on how you feel. Your easy days should be done at a conversation pace, or approximately 2 minutes per mile slower than your 10-K race pace.

Rest days and easy days are interchangeable for more flexibility. However, the quality days should stay where they are in the program.

If you run marathons, don't always train as a marathoner. You can do lower mileage at a faster pace on timed and tempo runs.

Cross-training: Cross-training will strengthen your heart and other muscles you don't use in running. It will enhance your fitness level, build muscle, reduce body fat, and increase flexibility. Cross-training should involve sustained aerobic activity like cycling or an elliptical trainer; rest-day cross-training should be a nonimpact activity such as stretching, a core-strength class, yoga, pool running, weight training, or swimming.

Hill workout: Find a hill that will take you a few minutes to climb, and mark off a "short" repeat (about 250 meters) and a "long" repeat (1,000 meters). Do a set of short hills: three or four sprints up the short repeat, then a jog back down. Then do a set of long hills: three or four loops of a hard run to the top, a jog back to the top of the short segment, and a sprint to the bottom, followed by another three or four short hills. Adjust the repeats depending on the miles you need. You should be doing 2 miles of a warmup and cooldown before and after the hills, so the workout involves 3 or 4 miles of work. The downhill sprints in the long sets are nearly as important as the uphill parts. Try to run smoothly, without slapping your feet.

MPW: The marathon-pace workout—or MPW, as I call it—should be a 15-minute warmup at an easy pace, then 30 to 60 minutes at marathon pace (MP), followed by a 15-minute cooldown. Make sure you pick a course that best simulates the course you will be racing.

HMPW: The half-marathon-pace workout—HMPW—is the same as the marathon-pace workout, only done at half-marathon pace.

Long slow distance: The LSD run is purely for the purpose of endurance. It increases your aerobic fitness, teaches your body to run efficiently, and helps you build mental discipline. It will give you the endurance to tackle the tempo and speed workouts and recover from them quickly. Long-run pace should be 1 to 1½ minutes slower than marathon pace. Try running the last 3 to 4 miles of your long run at either marathon or half-marathon pace, depending on which program you're following. This will enable you to develop a "negative split" mentality, running the second half of your race slightly faster than the first.

Speedwork: Speedwork will condition your body to run fast on demand. You can do the speed workout on the track or on a road; just make sure the course is accurately measured. Warm up 15 minutes, and cool down 15 minutes. Always jog half the interval distance for recovery.

Classic workouts are mile repeats. It's pretty simple: Run a mile at your 10-K pace, jog a half mile for recovery, and repeat three times.

Yasso 800s are the cornerstone of marathon running. If you want to run a 3:30 marathon, then train to run a bunch of 800-meter repeats in 3 minutes 30 seconds each. Between the 800s, jog 400 meters. Training doesn't get any simpler than this. Begin running Yasso 800s a couple of months before your goal marathon. The first week, do four or five. Each subsequent week, add one more until you reach 10. The last workout of Yasso 800s should be completed at least 17 days before your marathon.

Use 400-meter repeats to keep up some of that leg speed. Twelve times 400 with a 200 recovery is always a great workout.

Tempo runs: For 5-K and 10-K races, warm up 15 minutes, run 20 to 30 minutes at half-marathon pace (HMP), then cool down 15 minutes. Tempo runs can be done on trails or grass.

Taper: Every training plan has a taper in the last segment prior to a race. I find that most runners don't taper enough during those final days. You should run less and rest more to conserve energy for the race. For some runners, just the idea of backing off their mileage seems counterintuitive and they're afraid of losing fitness, but they won't.

Run as many miles as you can on soft surfaces. I recommend doing 70 percent of your running on a cinder, hard-packed, or trail surface.

To run comfortably, remember one word: *breathable*. Breathable fabrics allow perspiration to evaporate from your skin, cooling you off in the heat and keeping you dry. (Cotton, as natural and desirable as it may be, is just about the worst fabric a runner can wear. In the warmer weather, it soaks up sweat and sticks to your skin, and its rough fibers may chafe you.) Wear a lightweight, breathable shirt and shorts made from high-tech fabrics. They're available at running stores everywhere. Microfibers cost more than cotton, but you get a big payoff every time you go for a run. Also, select breathable socks that work well with your shoes, and make sure there are no seams in the toe area that might cause trouble. If for some reason a piece of apparel chafes your skin, apply a lubricating product before you run, such as petroleum jelly, Lube Stick for Runners, or Bodyglide. You may need to carry a small tube with you on longer runs.

Last but not least, don't forget sunscreen. The effects of sunlight on the skin have to be taken seriously. Overexposure to the sun causes wrinkles, precancerous growths, and malignant melanoma.

THE PERFECT 10 (5-K AND 10-K)
FOR NEWBIES

DAY	CYCLE 1
1	Tempo run: 15 min warmup, 20 min faster pace, 15 min cooldown
2	Rest or cross-train
3	3 mi easy
4	Speedwork: 3 Yasso 800s
5	Cross-train
6	4 mi easy
7	5 mi easy
8	LSD: 5–6
9	Rest day
10	4 mi easy

DAY	CYCLE 2
1	Tempo run: 15 min warmup, 20 min faster pace, 15 min cooldown
2	Rest or cross-train
3	3 mi easy
4	Speedwork: 3 Yasso 800s
5	Cross-train
6	4 mi easy
7	5 mi easy
8	LSD: 5–6 mi
9	Rest day
10	4 mi easy

DAY	CYCLE 3
1	Tempo run: 15 min warmup, 25 min faster pace, 15 min cooldown
2	Rest or cross-train
3	3 mi easy
4	Speedwork: 4 Yasso 800s
5	Cross-train
6	4 mi easy
7	5 mi easy
8	LSD: 6–7 mi
9	Rest day
10	4 mi easy

DAY	TAPER 5-K AND 10-K
1	2 mi easy
2	Cross-train
3	Rest day
4	Track: 2 Yasso 800s
5	Cross-train
6	Rest day
7	Rest day
8	2 mi easy
9	Rest day
10	Race day

Follow cycles 1, 2, and 3 twice, then follow the taper.
You must start the program 70 days prior to the race date.

Newbie: those just starting out
Seasoned: experienced runner
Hard-Core: most ambitious

THE PERFECT 10 (5-K AND 10-K)
FOR SEASONED RUNNERS

DAY	CYCLE 1
1	Tempo run—HMPW: 15 min warmup, 20 min HMP, 15 min cooldown
2	Rest or cross-train
3	4 mi easy
4	Speedwork: 6 Yasso 800s
5	Cross-train
6	3 mi easy
7	5 mi easy
8	LSD: 5–7 mi
9	Rest day
10	5 mi easy

DAY	CYCLE 2
1	Tempo run—HPMW: 15 min warmup, 25 min HMP, 15 min cooldown
2	Rest or cross-train
3	3 mi easy
4	Speedwork: 12 × 400
5	Cross-train
6	4 mi easy
7	5 mi easy
8	LSD: 6–8 miles
9	Rest day
10	4 mi easy

DAY	CYCLE 3
1	Tempo run—HMPW: 15 min warmup, 30 min HMP, 15 min cooldown
2	Cross-train
3	5 miles easy
4	Speedwork: 3 1-mile repeats
5	Cross-train
6	5 mi easy
7	3 mi easy
8	LSD: 8–10 mi
9	Rest day
10	4 mi easy

DAY	TAPER 5-K AND 10-K
1	4 mi easy
2	Cross-train
3	Rest day
4	Track: 3 Yasso 800s
5	Cross-train
6	4 mi easy
7	Rest day
8	3 mi easy
9	Rest day
10	Race day

Follow cycles 1, 2, and 3 twice, then follow the taper.

You must start the program 70 days prior to the race date.

THE PERFECT 10 (5-K AND 10-K)
FOR HARD-CORE RUNNERS

DAY	CYCLE 1
1	Tempo run: 15 min warmup, 30 min faster pace, 15 min cooldown
2	Rest or cross-train
3	5 mi easy
4	Speedwork: 5 Yasso 800s
5	Cross-train
6	6 mi easy
7	5 mi easy
8	LSD: 6–8 mi
9	Rest day
10	5 mi easy

DAY	CYCLE 2
1	Tempo run: 15 min warmup, 35 min faster pace, 15 min cooldown
2	Rest or cross-train
3	5 mi easy
4	Speedwork: 6 Yasso 800s
5	Cross-train
6	5 mi easy
7	6 mi easy
8	LSD: 7–9 mi
9	Rest day
10	5 mi easy

DAY	CYCLE 3
1	Tempo run: 15 min warmup, 40 min faster pace, 15 min cooldown
2	Rest or cross-train
3	6 mi easy
4	Speedwork: 6 Yasso 800s
5	Cross-train
6	6 mi easy
7	6 mi easy
8	LSD: 8–10 mi
9	Rest day
10	5 mi easy

DAY	TAPER 5-K AND 10-K
1	5 mi easy
2	Cross-train
3	3 mi easy
4	Track: 4 Yasso 800s
5	Cross-train
6	5 mi easy
7	Rest day
8	3 mi easy
9	Rest day
10	Race day

Follow cycles 1, 2, and 3 twice, then follow the taper.
You must start the program 70 days prior to the race date.

THE PERFECT 10 HALF-MARATHON
FOR NEWBIES

DAY	CYCLE 1
1	Tempo run—HMPW: 15 min warmup, 20 min HMP, 15 min cooldown
2	Rest or cross-train
3	3 mi easy
4	Speedwork: 3 Yasso 800s
5	Cross-train
6	3 mi easy
7	4 mi easy
8	LSD: 4–5 mi
9	Rest day
10	3 mi easy

DAY	CYCLE 2
1	Tempo run—HMPW: 15 min warmup, 25 min HMP, 15 min cooldown
2	Rest or cross-train
3	4 mi easy
4	Speedwork: 4 Yasso 800s
5	Cross-train
6	3 mi easy
7	4 mi easy
8	LSD: 5–7 mi
9	Rest day
10	3 mi easy

DAY	CYCLE 3
1	Tempo run—HMPW: 15 min warmup, 30 min HMP, 15 min cooldown
2	Rest or cross-train
3	4 mi easy
4	Speedwork: 4 Yasso 800s
5	Cross-train
6	4 mi easy
7	4 mi easy
8	LSD: 8–10 mi
9	Rest day
10	3 mi easy

DAY	HALF-MARATHON TAPER
1	Tempo: 10-min warmup, 15-min half-marathon pace, 15-min cooldown
2	Cross-train
3	4 mi easy
4	Track: 2 Yasso 800s
5	Cross-train
6	3 mi easy
7	Rest day
8	3 mi easy
9	Rest day
10	Race day

Follow cycles 1, 2, and 3 three times, then follow the taper.

You must start the program 100 days prior to the race date.

THE PERFECT 10 HALF-MARATHON
FOR SEASONED RUNNERS

DAY	CYCLE 1	DAY	CYCLE 2
1	Tempo workout—HMPW:	1	Tempo run—HMPW:
	15 min warmup, 20 min HMP,		15 min warmup, 25 min HMP,
	15 min cooldown		15 min cooldown
2	Rest or cross-train	2	Rest or cross-train
3	5 mi easy	3	5 mi easy
4	Speedwork: 3 Yasso 800s	4	Speedwork: 12 × 400
5	Cross-train	5	Cross-train
6	5 mi easy	6	5 mi easy
7	5 mi easy	7	5 mi easy
8	LSD: 6–8 mi	8	LSD: 10–12 mi
9	Rest day	9	Rest day
10	5 mi easy	10	5 mi easy

DAY	CYCLE 3	DAY	HALF-MARATHON TAPER
1	Tempo run—HMPW:	1	Tempo: 12-min warmup,
	15 min warmup, 35 min HMP,		20-min half-marathon pace,
	15 min cooldown		12-min cooldown
2	Cross-train	2	Cross-train
3	5 mi easy	3	5 mi easy
4	Speedwork: 3 1-mile repeats	4	Track: 3 Yasso 800s
5	Cross-train	5	Cross-train
6	5 mi easy	6	4 mi easy
7	5 mi easy	7	Rest day
8	LSD: 12–15 mi	8	3 mi easy
9	Rest day	9	Rest day
10	5 mi easy	10	Race day

Follow cycles 1, 2, and 3 three times, then follow the taper.
You must start the program 100 days prior to the race date.

THE PERFECT 10 HALF-MARATHON
FOR HARD-CORE RUNNERS

DAY	CYCLE 1
1	Tempo run—HMPW: 15 min warmup, 30 min HMP, 15 min cooldown
2	Rest or cross-train
3	6 mi easy
4	Speedwork: 4 Yasso 800s
5	Cross-train
6	6 mi easy
7	6 mi easy
8	LSD: 8–10 mi
9	Rest day
10	6 mi easy

DAY	CYCLE 2
1	Tempo run—HMPW: 15 min warmup, 30 min HMP, 15 min cooldown
2	Rest or cross-train
3	5 mi easy
4	Speedwork: 5 Yasso 800s
5	Cross-train
6	3 mi easy
7	4 mi easy
8	LSD: 8–10 mi
9	Rest day
10	5 mi easy

DAY	CYCLE 3
1	Tempo run—HMPW: 15 min warmup, 40 min HMP, 15 min cooldown
2	Rest or cross-train
3	5 mi easy
4	Speedwork: 6 Yasso 800s
5	Cross-train
6	5 mi easy
7	4 mi easy
8	LSD: 12–14 mi
9	Rest day
10	5 mi easy

DAY	HALF-MARATHON TAPER CYCLE
1	Tempo: 15-min warmup, 25-min half-marathon pace, 15-min cooldown
2	Cross-train
3	6 mi easy
4	Track: 4 Yasso 800s
5	Cross-train
6	4 mi easy
7	Rest day
8	3 mi easy
9	Rest day
10	Race day

Follow cycles 1, 2, and 3 three times, then follow the taper.
You must start the program 100 days prior to the race date.

THE PERFECT 10 MARATHON
FOR NEWBIES

DAY	CYCLE 1
1	Tempo run—MPW: 15 min warmup, 30 min MP, 15 min cooldown
2	Rest day or cross-train
3	4 mi easy
4	Speedwork: 4 Yasso 800s
5	Cross-train
6	3 mi easy
7	5 mi easy
8	LSD: 8–10 mi
9	Rest day
10	4 mi easy

DAY	CYCLE 2
1	Tempo run—MPW, 15 min warmup, 35 min MP, 15 min cooldown
2	Rest day or cross-train
3	4 mi easy
4	Speedwork: 6 Yasso 800s
5	Cross-train
6	3 mi easy
7	5 mi easy
8	LSD: 13–15 mi
9	Rest day
10	4 mi easy

DAY	CYCLE 3
1	Tempo run—MPW: 15 min warmup, 40 min MP, 15 min cooldown
2	Rest day or cross-train
3	4 mi easy
4	Speedwork: 6 Yasso 800s
5	Cross-train
6	3 mi easy
7	5 mi easy
8	LSD: 16–18 mi
9	Rest day
10	4 mi easy

DAY	TAPER CYCLE 1
1	Tempo: MPW, 12-min warmup, 25-min MP, 12-min cooldown
2	Rest day
3	4 mi easy
4	Track: 3 Yasso 800s
5	Rest day
6	4 mi easy
7	Rest day
8	4 mi easy
9	Rest day
10	4 mi easy

DAY	TAPER CYCLE 2
1	Tempo: MPW, 12-min warmup, 20-min MP, 12-min cooldown
2	Rest day
3	4 mi easy
4	Track: 2 Yasso 800s
5	Rest day
6	3 mi easy
7	Rest day
8	3 mi easy
9	Rest day
10	Race day

Follow cycles 1, 2, and 3 four times, then follow the 20-day taper.

You must start the program 140 days prior to the race date.

THE PERFECT 10 MARATHON
FOR SEASONED RUNNERS

DAY	CYCLE 1
1	Tempo run—MPW: 15 min warmup, 40 min MP, 15 min cooldown (8–10 mi)
2	Rest day or cross-train
3	6 mi easy
4	Speedwork: 6 Yasso 800s
5	Cross-train
6	5 mi easy
7	8 mi easy
8	LSD: 12–15 mi
9	Rest day
10	6 mi easy

DAY	CYCLE 2
1	Tempo run—MPW, 15 min warmup, 50 min MP, 15 min cooldown (10–12 mi)
2	Rest or cross-train
3	6 mi easy
4	Speedwork: 12 × 400 (8 mi)
5	Cross-train
6	6 mi easy
7	8 mi easy
8	LSD: 15–18 mi
9	Rest day
10	8 mi easy

DAY	CYCLE 3
1	Tempo run—MPW: 15 min warmup, 30 min MP, 15 min cooldown (7–9 mi)
2	Rest or cross-train
3	6 mi easy
4	Speedwork: 4 × 1 mile (9 mi)
5	Cross-train
6	8 mi easy
7	6 mi easy
8	LSD: 18–20 miles
9	Rest day
10	8 mi easy

DAY	TAPER
1	Tempo: MPW, 15-min warmup, 30-min MP, 15-min cooldown
2	Rest day
3	4 mi easy
4	Track: 4 Yasso 800s
5	Rest day
6	4 mi easy
7	Rest day
8	5 mi easy
9	Rest day
10	4 mi easy

DAY	TAPER
1	Tempo: MPW, 15-min warmup, 25-min MP, 15-min cooldown
2	Rest day
3	4 mi easy
4	Track: 3 Yasso 800s
5	Rest day
6	4 mi easy
7	Rest day
8	3 mi easy
9	Rest day
10	Race day

Follow cycles 1, 2, and 3 four times, then follow the 20-day taper.
You must start the program 140 days prior to the race date.

THE PERFECT 10 MARATHON
FOR HARD-CORE RUNNERS

DAY	CYCLE 1
1	Tempo run—MPW, 15 min warmup, 50 min MP, 15 min cooldown
2	Rest day or cross-train
3	8 mi easy
4	Speedwork: 8 Yasso 800s
5	Cross-train
6	7 mi easy
7	8 mi easy
8	LSD: 16–18 mi
9	Rest day
10	8 mi easy

DAY	CYCLE 2
1	Tempo run—MPW: 15 min warmup, 60 min MP, 15 min cooldown
2	Rest day or cross-train
3	8 mi easy
4	Speedwork: 8 Yasso 800s
5	Cross-train
6	7 mi easy
7	8 mi easy
8	LSD: 18–20 mi
9	Rest day
10	8 mi easy

DAY	CYCLE 3
1	Tempo run—MPW: 15 min warmup, 60 min MP, 15 min cooldown
2	Rest day or cross-train
3	8 mi easy
4	Speedwork: 10 Yasso 800s
5	Cross-train
6	7 mi easy
7	8 mi easy
8	LSD: 20–22 mi
9	Rest day
10	8 mi easy

DAY	TAPER
1	Tempo: MPW, 15-min warmup, 35-min MP, 15-min cooldown
2	Rest day
3	5 mi easy
4	Track: 5 Yasso 800s
5	Rest day
6	5 mi easy
7	Rest day
8	5 mi easy
9	Rest day
10	6 mi easy

DAY	TAPER
1	Tempo: MPW, 15-min warmup, 35-min at MP, 15-min cooldown
2	Rest day
3	5 mi easy
4	Track: 4 Yasso 800s
5	Rest day
6	5 mi easy
7	Rest day
8	3 mi easy
9	Rest day
10	Race day

Now that you have adjusted to a 10-day cycle, let's start the 13-month calendar ▶

Follow cycles 1, 2, and 3 four times, then follow the 20-day taper.

You must start the program 140 days prior to the race date.

Bart runs the
Saint Patty's 10-miler
in Allentown, Pennsylvania,
March, 1998

Chapter 19

MARATHON, HALF-MARATHON, 10-K, AND 5-K TRAINING SCHEDULES

If the Perfect 10 doesn't fit your needs, this is a more traditional training format based on a 7-day cycle. In regard to running a marathon, wait until you've been running consistently for at least a year before attempting that distance, and then train for 16 weeks before the race. If you're thinking about doing a half-marathon for the first time, run consistently for at least 6 months before starting the plan. This schedule is similar to the one I send out by e-mail each year to registered participants of the Lehigh Valley Half-Marathon in Allentown, Pennsylvania.

MARATHON

WEEK 1

NEWBIES: 15 MILES TOTAL	SEASONED: 25 MILES TOTAL	HARD-CORE: 35 MILES TOTAL
MON: rest day	**MON:** rest day	**MON:** 5 mi easy
TUE: 3 mi easy	**TUE:** 4 mi easy	**TUE:** 5 mi hills
WED: 4 mi easy	**WED:** 4 mi easy	**WED:** 4 mi easy
THU: rest day	**THU:** 6 mi hills	**THU:** 6 mi MPW run
FRI: 3 mi easy	**FRI:** rest day	**FRI:** rest day
SAT: rest day	**SAT:** 4 mi easy	**SAT:** 5 mi easy
SUN: 5 mi LSD	**SUN:** 7 mi LSD	**SUN:** 10 mi LSD

REST DAYS AND EASY DAYS are mostly interchangeable. This means that those following the seasoned and hard-core schedules who want to take a zero day on Saturday, rather than Friday, should simply switch those days. However, the quality days (hills and Sundays, which will become long runs) should stay where they are.

CROSS-TRAINING is a good idea but should be limited to rest days and easy days. Easy-day cross-training should involve sustained aerobic activity like cycling or an elliptical trainer; rest-day cross-training should be a nonimpact activity like stretching, yoga, or swimming.

HILLS: The seasoned and hard-core schedules call for runs on hills this week. Later in the program, these will become hill repeats; but this week, just pick a run with lots of hills, if possible.

MPW: The hard-core schedule includes a marathon-pace workout. Warm up 1 mile, run 4 miles at marathon pace, then cool down 1 mile.

LSD: Long, slow distance runs are purely for the purpose of endurance. You're going to be on your feet a while to cover 13.1 miles; this is when you get used to it.

MARATHON

WEEK 2

NEWBIES: 17 MILES TOTAL	SEASONED: 28 MILES TOTAL	HARD-CORE: 38 MILES TOTAL
MON: rest day	MON: rest day	MON: 5 mi easy
TUE: 3 mi easy	TUE: 4 mi easy	TUE: 6 mi hills
WED: 3 mi easy	WED: 4 mi easy	WED: 4 mi easy
THU: rest day	THU: 6 mi hills	THU: 6 mi MPW
FRI: 4 mi easy	FRI: rest day	FRI: rest day
SAT: rest day	SAT: 5 mi easy	SAT: 5 mi easy
SUN: 7 mi	SUN: 9 mi	SUN: 12 mi

HILLS: The seasoned and hard-core schedules call for runs on hills this week. Later in the program, these will become hill repeats, but this week, just pick a run with lots of hills, if possible.

MPW: The hard-core schedule includes a marathon-pace workout. Warm up 1 mile, run 4 miles at marathon pace, then cool down 1 mile.

MARATHON

WEEK 3

NEWBIES: 20 MILES TOTAL	SEASONED: 30 MILES TOTAL	HARD-CORE: 40 MILES TOTAL
MON: rest day	MON: rest day	MON: 4 mi easy
TUE: 3 mi easy	TUE: 3 mi easy	TUE: 6 mi hills
WED: 4 mi easy	WED: 4 mi easy	WED: 4 mi easy
THU: rest day	THU: 6 mi hills	THU: 8 mi MPW
FRI: 4 mi easy	FRI: rest day	FRI: rest day
SAT: rest day	SAT: 5 mi easy	SAT: 4 mi easy
SUN: 9 mi	SUN: 12 mi	SUN: 14 mi

HILLS: The seasoned and hard-core schedules call for runs on hills this week. Later in the program, these will become hill repeats; but this week, just pick a run with lots of hills, if possible.

MPW: The hard-core schedule includes a marathon-pace workout. Warm up 1 mile, run 6 miles at marathon pace, then cool down 1 mile.

MARATHON
WEEK 4

NEWBIES: 18 MILES TOTAL	SEASONED: 28 MILES TOTAL	HARD-CORE: 38 MILES TOTAL
MON: rest day	MON: rest day	MON: 4 mi easy
TUE: 4 mi easy	TUE: 4 mi easy	TUE: 7 mi hills
WED: 3 mi easy	WED: 4 mi easy	WED: 5 mi easy
THU: rest day	THU: 6 mi hills	THU: 8 mi MPW
FRI: 4 mi easy	FRI: rest day	FRI: rest day
SAT: rest day	SAT: 4 mi easy	SAT: 4 mi easy
SUN: 7 mi LSD	SUN: 10 mi LSD	SUN: 10 mi LSD

HILLS: The seasoned and hard-core schedules are on hills again this week. Just like last week, this should be the hilliest loop you can find for the distance and shouldn't be treated as an easy run. You'll know you've found the right loop if it's too steep to run easily. Remember to hold form on the downhill as well as the uphill.

MPW: The hard-core schedule includes a marathon-pace workout. Warm up 1 mile, run 6 miles at marathon pace, then cool down 1 mile.

MARATHON
WEEK 5

NEWBIES: 22 MILES TOTAL	SEASONED: 32 MILES TOTAL	HARD-CORE: 43 MILES TOTAL
MON: rest day	MON: rest day	MON: 3 mi easy
TUE: 4 mi easy	TUE: 4 mi easy	TUE: 8 mi hills
WED: 3 mi easy	WED: 7 mi hills	WED: 5 mi easy
THU: rest day	THU: 4 mi easy	THU: 8 mi MPW
FRI: 5 mi easy	FRI: rest day	FRI: rest day
SAT: rest day	SAT: 4 mi easy	SAT: 4 mi easy
SUN: 10 mi LSD	SUN: 13 mi LSD	SUN: 15 mi LSD

HILLS: The seasoned and hard-core schedules are on hills again this week. As usual, this should be the hilliest loop you can find for the distance and shouldn't be treated as an easy run.

MPW: The hard-core schedule includes a marathon-pace workout. Warm up 1 mile, run 6 miles at marathon pace, then cool down 1 mile.

MARATHON

WEEK 6

NEWBIES: 24 MILES TOTAL	SEASONED: 34 MILES TOTAL	HARD-CORE: 44 MILES TOTAL
MON: rest day	MON: rest day	MON: 6 mi easy
TUE: 4 mi easy	TUE: 7 mi easy	TUE: 8 mi easy
WED: 3 mi easy	WED: 7 mi easy	WED: 8 mi MPW
THU: rest day	THU: 8 mi hills	THU: rest day
FRI: 5 mi easy	FRI: rest day	FRI: 8 mi
SAT: rest day	SAT: 6 mi easy	SAT: 7 easy
SUN: 12 mi LSD	SUN: 5-K race— 2 mi warmup, 1 mi cooldown	SUN: 5-K race— 2 mi warmup, 2 mi cooldown

HILLS: The seasoned and hard-core schedules are on hills again this week. As usual, this should be the hilliest loop you can find for the distance and shouldn't be treated as an easy run.

5-K RACE: This is optional for seasoned and hard-core schedules. Don't expect a particularly fast time; the point this week is to go out and enjoy racing.

MARATHON

WEEK 7

NEWBIES: 27 MILES TOTAL	SEASONED: 37 MILES TOTAL	HARD-CORE: 47 MILES TOTAL
MON: rest day	MON: rest day	MON: 5 mi easy
TUE: 4 mi easy	TUE: 4 mi easy	TUE: 8 mi hills
WED: 4 mi easy	WED: 7 mi hills	WED: 4 mi easy
THU: rest day	THU: 5 mi easy	THU: 8 mi MPW
FRI: 4 mi easy	FRI: rest day	FRI: rest day
SAT: rest day	SAT: 5 mi easy	SAT: 4 mi easy
SUN: 15 mi LSD	SUN: 16 mi LSD	SUN: 18 mi LSD

HILLS: The seasoned and hard-core schedules are on hills again this week. As usual, this should be the hilliest loop you can find for the distance and shouldn't be treated as an easy run.

MPW: The hard-core schedule includes a marathon-pace workout. Warm up 1 mile, run 6 miles at marathon pace, then cool down 1 mile.

MARATHON

WEEK 8

NEWBIES: 24 MILES TOTAL	SEASONED: 35 MILES TOTAL	HARD-CORE: 52 MILES TOTAL
MON: rest day	**MON:** rest day	**MON:** 5 mi easy
TUE: 4 mi easy	**TUE:** 5 mi easy	**TUE:** 9 mi hill repeats
WED: 4 mi easy	**WED:** 4 mi easy	**WED:** 7 mi easy
THU: rest day	**THU:** 8 mi hill repeats	**THU:** 9 mi MPW
FRI: 4 mi easy	**FRI:** rest day	**FRI:** rest day
SAT: rest day	**SAT:** 4 mi easy	**SAT:** 6 mi easy
SUN: 12 mi LSD	**SUN:** 14 mi LSD	**SUN:** 16 mi LSD

HILL REPEATS: You're welcome to do hills again this week, but if you feel adventurous, you can try hill repeats. Find a hill that will take you at least 2 minutes to climb, and mark off a "short" repeat (about halfway from the bottom) and a "long" repeat (all the way to the top). Then do a set of short hills: three or four sprints up the short repeat, then a jog back down; a set of long hills: three or four loops of a hard run to the top, a jog back to the top of the short segment and a sprint to the bottom; then another three or four short hills. Adjust the repeats depending on the miles you need; you should be doing 2 miles of warming up and cooling down before and after the hills, so the workout involves 3 or 4 miles of work. The downhill sprints in the long sets are nearly as important as the uphill parts. Try to run smoothly, without slapping your feet.

MPW: The hard-core schedule includes a marathon-pace workout. Warm up 1 mile, run 7 miles at marathon pace, then cool down 1 mile.

MARATHON
WEEK 9

NEWBIES: 30 MILES TOTAL	SEASONED: 41 MILES TOTAL	HARD-CORE: 54 MILES TOTAL
MON: rest day	MON: rest day	MON: Rest day
TUE: 6 mi easy	TUE: 9 mi MPW	TUE: 8 mi easy
WED: 4 mi easy	WED: 3 mi easy	WED: 8 mi, 3 mi repeats
THU: rest day	THU: 8 mi speedwork	THU: 4 mi easy
FRI: 4 mi easy	FRI: rest day	FRI: 9 mi MPW
SAT: rest day	SAT: 3 mi easy	SAT: 5 easy
SUN: 16 mi LSD	SUN: 18 mi LSD	SUN: 20 mi LSD

SPEEDWORK: You don't need a track to do speedwork, but it helps. Don't get spooked by the number of miles on the "repeats" days; they include the warmup and cooldown, and those should be at least 2 miles each way for seasoned and hard-core schedules, leaving 3 miles of actual speedwork. You can make those miles easier by starting your run 2 miles from the track.

MILE REPEATS: This classic workout is pretty simple: Run a mile at your 10-K pace, jog a lap for recovery, and repeat three times.

If you're not running on a track, use a car or bicycle to mark off a mile on a low-traffic road, or run by time. See if you can feel the maximum oxygen pace—it should be at that balance point where you're still comfortable, but even the slightest bit faster would be uncomfortable.

MPW: The hard-core and seasoned schedules include a marathon-pace workout. Warm up 1 mile, run 7 miles at marathon pace, then cool down 1 mile.

MARATHON

WEEK 10

NEWBIES: 32 MILES TOTAL	SEASONED: 43 MILES TOTAL	HARD-CORE: 53 MILES TOTAL
MON: rest day	**MON:** rest day	**MON:** 6 mi easy
TUE: 4 mi easy	**TUE:** 10 mi MPW	**TUE:** rest day
WED: 6 mi easy	**WED:** rest day	**WED:** 9 mi speedwork
THU: rest day	**THU:** 9 mi speedwork	**THU:** rest day
FRI: 4 mi easy	**FRI:** rest day	**FRI:** 10 mi MPW
SAT: rest day	**SAT:** 4 mi easy	**SAT:** 6 easy
SUN: 18 mi LSD	**SUN:** 20 mi LSD	**SUN:** 22 mi LSD

NEWBIES: Sometimes it seems like the seasoned and hard-core programs get all the fun, with speedwork, hills, and more runs per week. The newbie program is based entirely on mileage, with the goal of simply building your endurance to the point that 26-plus miles is an easily reachable or at least attainable distance. So we concentrate more on time on your feet and less on speed. Next time around you can plan on more miles and improve either your time—or how easy your time is.

MPW: The hard-core and seasoned schedules include a marathon-pace workout. Warm up 1 mile, run 8 miles at marathon pace, then cool down 1 mile.

SPEEDWORK: Do 8 Yasso 800s; jog a 400-meter recovery lap.

MARATHON

WEEK 11

NEWBIES: 36 MILES TOTAL	SEASONED: 45 MILES TOTAL	HARD-CORE: 58 MILES TOTAL
MON: rest day	MON: rest day	MON: 6 mi easy
TUE: 6 mi easy	TUE: 4 mi easy	TUE: rest day
WED: 5 mi easy	WED: 7 mi easy	WED: 9 mi speedwork
THU: rest day	THU: 10 mi MPW	THU: 7 mi easy
FRI: 5 mi easy	FRI: rest day	FRI: 10 mi MPW
SAT: rest day	SAT: 4 mi easy	SAT: 6 mi easy
SUN: 20 mi LSD	SUN: 20 mi LSD	SUN: 20 mi LSD

SPEEDWORK: Those on the hard-core schedule are out for some more speed on Wednesday. Now that you've done mile repeats and repeat 800s, do a ladder workout: 1/2, 3/4, mile, 3/4, 1/2. Jog half the distance you just ran between each one. Remember to warm up and cool down.

MPW: The hard-core and seasoned schedules include a marathon-pace workout. Warm up 1 mile, run 8 miles at marathon pace, then cool down 1 mile.

MARATHON
WEEK 12

NEWBIES: 35 MILES TOTAL	SEASONED: 47 MILES TOTAL	HARD-CORE: 58 MILES TOTAL
MON: rest day	MON: rest day	MON: 6 mi easy
TUE: 7 mi easy	TUE: 8 mi easy	TUE: rest day
WED: 7 mi easy	WED: 7 mi easy	WED: 10 mi, mile repeats
THU: rest day	THU: 10 mi, mile repeats	THU: 8 mi easy
FRI: 7 mi easy	FRI: rest day	FRI: 10 mi MPW
SAT: rest day	SAT: 7 mi easy	SAT: 8 easy
SUN: 14 mi LSD	SUN: 15 mi LSD	SUN: 16 mi LSD

SPEEDWORK: You don't need a track to do speedwork, but it helps. Don't get spooked by the number of miles on the "repeats" days; they include the warmup and cooldown, and those should be at least 2 miles each way, leaving 4 miles of actual speedwork. You can make those miles easier by starting your run 2 miles from the track.

MILE REPEATS: This classic workout is pretty simple: Run a mile at your 10-K pace; jog 800 meters or ½ mile.

MARATHON

WEEK 13

NEWBIES: 40 MILES TOTAL	SEASONED: 50 MILES TOTAL	HARD-CORE: 60 MILES TOTAL
MON: rest day	**MON:** rest day	**MON:** 6 mi easy
TUE: 6 mi easy	**TUE:** 6 mi easy	**TUE:** 7 mi easy
WED: 7 mi easy	**WED:** 10 mi speedwork	**WED:** 10 mi speedwork
THU: rest day	**THU:** 6 mi easy	**THU:** rest day
FRI: 7 mi easy	**FRI:** rest day	**FRI:** 8 mi hills
SAT: rest day	**SAT:** 6 mi easy	**SAT:** 6 mi easy
SUN: 20 mi LSD	**SUN:** 22 mi LSD	**SUN:** 23 mi LSD

SPEEDWORK: Do 10 Yasso 800s; jog a 400-meter lap for recovery.

HILLS: And you thought you were off the hills. The hard-core program has 8 miles on hills on Friday.

MARATHON

WEEK 14

NEWBIES: 34 MILES TOTAL	SEASONED: 45 MILES TOTAL	HARD-CORE: 55 MILES TOTAL
MON: rest day	**MON:** rest day	**MON:** 6 mi easy
TUE: 7 mi easy	**TUE:** 8 mi easy	**TUE:** rest day
WED: 7 mi easy	**WED:** 7 mi easy	**WED:** 8 mi, mile repeats
THU: rest day	**THU:** 8 mi, mile repeats	**THU:** 8 mi easy
FRI: 7 mi easy	**FRI:** rest day	**FRI:** 10 mi MPW
SAT: rest day	**SAT:** 7 mi easy	**SAT:** 7 easy
SUN: 13 mi LSD	**SUN:** 15 mi LSD	**SUN:** 16 mi LSD

SPEEDWORK: Now we're coming down to quarters. This week's workout should be 12 times 400 with 200-meter recovery. Jog at least half that distance between repeats to recover.

MPW: The hard-core schedule includes a marathon-pace workout. Warm up 1 mile, run 8 miles at marathon pace, then cool down 1 mile.

MARATHON

WEEK 15

NEWBIES: 24 MILES TOTAL	SEASONED: 32 MILES TOTAL	HARD-CORE: 40 MILES TOTAL
MON: rest day	**MON:** rest day	**MON:** 4 mi easy
TUE: 5 mi easy	**TUE:** 5 mi easy	**TUE:** 7 mi hills
WED: 4 mi easy	**WED:** 4 mi easy	**WED:** 4 mi easy
THU: rest day	**THU:** 6 mi hills	**THU:** 8 mi MPW
FRI: 5 mi easy	**FRI:** rest day	**FRI:** rest day
SAT: rest day	**SAT:** 5 mi easy	**SAT:** 4 mi easy
SUN: 10 mi LSD	**SUN:** 12 mi LSD	**SUN:** 13 mi LSD

REST DAYS: The seasoned and hard-core schedules have an extra rest day this week. Back off on the cross-training at this time.

MPW: The hard-core schedule includes a marathon-pace workout. Warm up 1 mile, run 6 miles at marathon pace, then cool down 1 mile.

HILLS: The seasoned and hard-core schedules call for runs on hills this week—just pick a run with lots of hills, if possible.

EASY DAYS: Make sure they stay easy, even though you're not working as hard on the other days. We're tapering now, and running harder on the easy days won't help. From here until race day, the idea is getting to the race well-rested.

MARATHON

WEEK 16

NEWBIES: 10 MILES TOTAL	SEASONED: 13 MILES TOTAL	HARD-CORE: 18 MILES TOTAL
MON: rest day	**MON:** rest day	**MON:** rest day
TUE: 3 mi easy	**TUE:** 5 mi easy	**TUE:** 5 mi hills
WED: 4 mi easy	**WED:** rest day	**WED:** 4 mi easy
THU: rest day	**THU:** 5 mi easy	**THU:** 6 mi MPW run
FRI: 3 mi easy	**FRI:** rest day	**FRI:** rest day
SAT: rest day	**SAT:** 3 mi very easy	**SAT:** 3 mi very easy
SUN: race day	**SUN:** race day	**SUN:** race day

Enjoy a very easy week in preparation for the race.

REST DAYS AND EASY DAYS: This whole week is about taking it easy, so run very easy on your easy days. You may be antsy, but save that energy for the race.

MPW: The hard-core schedule includes a marathon-pace workout. Warm up 1 mile, run 4 miles at marathon pace, then cool down 1 mile.

HALF-MARATHON
WEEK 1

NEWBIES: 17 MILES TOTAL	SEASONED: 28 MILES TOTAL	HARD-CORE: 38 MILES TOTAL
MON: rest day	**MON:** rest day	**MON:** 6 mi easy
TUE: 4 mi easy	**TUE:** 5 mi easy	**TUE:** 6 mi hills
WED: 4 mi easy	**WED:** 4 mi easy	**WED:** 4 mi easy
THU: rest day	**THU:** 6 mi hills	**THU:** 6 mi HMPW
FRI: 4 mi easy	**FRI:** rest day	**FRI:** rest day
SAT: rest day	**SAT:** 6 mi easy	**SAT:** 6 mi easy
SUN: 5 mi	**SUN:** 7 mi	**SUN:** 10 mi

REST DAYS AND EASY DAYS are mostly interchangeable. This means that those following the seasoned and hard-core schedules who want to take a zero day on Saturday rather than Friday should simply switch those days. However, the quality days (hills and Sundays, which will become long runs) should stay where they are; more on that later in the program.

CROSS-TRAINING isn't necessarily a bad idea but should be limited to rest days and easy days. Easy-day cross-training should involve sustained aerobic activity like cycling or an elliptical trainer; rest-day cross-training should be a nonimpact activity like stretching, yoga, or swimming.

HILLS: The seasoned and hard-core schedules call for runs on hills this week. Later in the program, these will become hill repeats, but this week, just pick a run with lots of hills, if possible.

HMPW: The hard-core schedule includes a half-marathon-pace workout. Warm up 1 mile, run 4 miles at half-marathon pace, then cool down 1 mile.

HALF-MARATHON

WEEK 2

NEWBIES: 18 MILES TOTAL	SEASONED: 30 MILES TOTAL	HARD-CORE: 41 MILES TOTAL
MON: rest day	**MON:** rest day	**MON:** 5 mi easy
TUE: 4 mi easy	**TUE:** 5 mi easy	**TUE:** 7 mi hills
WED: 3 mi easy	**WED:** 4 mi easy	**WED:** 5 mi easy
THU: rest day	**THU:** 6 mi hills	**THU:** 8 mi HMPW F
FRI: 5 mi easy	**FRI:** rest day	**FRI:** rest day
SAT: rest day	**SAT:** 5 mi easy	**SAT:** 6 mi easy
SUN: 6 mi	**SUN:** 10 mi	**SUN:** 10 mi LSD

REST DAYS AND EASY DAYS: If you need to trade rest days for easy days within a week or trade a 3-mile day for a 5-mile day, that's fine. But don't move the quality days (hills, HMPW, or the Sunday long runs), or you won't get enough rest before the next one.

CROSS-TRAINING: If the weather stinks, go ahead and move indoors. Substitute sustained aerobic exercise for easy-day mileage, about the same time (or a little more) than you would spend running.

HILLS: The seasoned and hard-core schedules are on hills again this week. Just like last week, this should be the hilliest loop you can find for the distance and shouldn't be treated as an easy run. You'll know you've found the right loop if it's too steep to run easily anyway. Remember to hold form on the downhill as well as the uphill.

HMPW: The hard-core schedule includes a half-marathon-pace workout. Warm up 1 mile, run 6 miles at half-marathon pace, then cool down 1 mile.

HALF-MARATHON

WEEK 3

NEWBIES: 21 MILES TOTAL	SEASONED: 34 MILES TOTAL	HARD-CORE: 44 MILES TOTAL
MON: rest day	**MON:** rest day	**MON:** 5 mi easy
TUE: 4 mi easy	**TUE:** 5 mi easy	**TUE:** 8 mi hills
WED: 4 mi easy	**WED:** 7 mi hills	**WED:** 6 mi easy
THU: rest day	**THU:** 6 mi easy	**THU:** 7 mi HMPW
FRI: 6 mi easy	**FRI:** rest day	**FRI:** rest day
SAT: rest day	**SAT:** 6 mi easy	**SAT:** 6 mi easy
SUN: 7 mi	**SUN:** 10 mi	**SUN:** 12 mi LSD

REST DAYS AND EASY DAYS: If you need to trade rest days for easy days within a week or trade a 3-mile day for a 5-mile day, that's fine.

HILLS: The seasoned and hard-core schedules are on hills again this week. As usual, this should be the hilliest loop you can find for the distance and shouldn't be treated as an easy run.

HMPW: The hard-core schedule includes a half-marathon-pace workout. Warm up 1 mile, run 5 miles at half-marathon pace, then cool down 1 mile.

HALF-MARATHON

WEEK 4

NEWBIES: 20 MILES TOTAL	SEASONED: 32 MILES TOTAL	HARD-CORE: 39 MILES TOTAL
MON: rest day	**MON:** rest day	**MON:** 5 mi easy
TUE: 4 mi easy	**TUE:** 6 mi easy	**TUE:** 6 mi easy
WED: 3 mi easy	**WED:** 6 mi easy	**WED:** 8 mi HMPW
THU: rest day	**THU:** 8 mi hills	**THU:** rest day
FRI: 5 mi easy	**FRI:** rest day	**FRI:** 7 mi
SAT: rest day	**SAT:** 6 mi easy	**SAT:** 6 easy
SUN: 8 mi	**SUN:** 5-K race— 2 mi warmup, 1 mi cooldown	**SUN:** 5-K race— 2 mi warmup, 2 mi cooldown

HMPW: The hard-core schedule includes a half-marathon-pace workout. Warm up 1 mile, run 6 miles at half-marathon pace, then cool down 1 mile.

HILLS: The seasoned and hard-core schedules are on hills again this week. As usual, this should be the hilliest loop you can find for the distance and shouldn't be treated as an easy run. Next week we'll start thinking about repeats on the hills.

5-K RACE: This is optional for the seasoned and for the hard-core. Don't expect a particularly fast time; the point this week is to go out and enjoy racing.

HALF-MARATHON

WEEK 5

NEWBIES: 24 MILES TOTAL	SEASONED: 36 MILES TOTAL	HARD-CORE: 49 MILES TOTAL
MON: rest day	**MON:** rest day	**MON:** 5 mi easy
TUE: 6 mi easy	**TUE:** 7 mi easy	**TUE:** 9 mi hill repeats
WED: 4 mi easy	**WED:** 7 mi easy	**WED:** 7 mi easy
THU: rest day	**THU:** 8 mi hill repeats	**THU:** 9 mi HMPW
FRI: 5 mi easy	**FRI:** rest day	**FRI:** rest day
SAT: rest day	**SAT:** 4 mi easy	**SAT:** 6 easy
SUN: 9 mi	**SUN:** 10 mi LSD	**SUN:** 13 mi LSD

HILL REPEATS: For the last 4 weeks, you've headed for a really hilly loop for your hill workouts (if you're scheduled for them). You're welcome to do that again this week, but if you feel adventurous, you can try hill repeats. Find a hill that will take you at least 2 minutes to climb, and mark off a "short" repeat (about halfway from the bottom) and a "long" repeat (all the way to the top). Then do a set of short hills: three or four sprints up the short repeat, then a jog back down; a set of long hills: three or four loops of a hard run to the top, a jog back to the top of the short segment and a sprint to the bottom; then another three or four short hills. Adjust the repeats depending on the miles you need; you should be doing 2 miles of warming up and cooling down before and after the hills, so the workout involves 3 or 4 miles of work.

The downhill sprints in the long sets are nearly as important as the uphill parts. Try to run smoothly, without slapping your feet.

HMPW: The hard-core schedule includes a half-marathon-pace workout. Warm up 1 mile, run 7 miles at half-marathon pace, then cool down 1 mile.

LSD: Long slow distance runs are purely for the purpose of endurance. You're going to be on your feet a while to cover 13.1 miles; this is when you get used to it.

HALF-MARATHON

WEEK 6

NEWBIES: 25 MILES TOTAL	SEASONED: 38 MILES TOTAL	HARD-CORE: 50 MILES TOTAL
MON: rest day	**MON:** rest day	**MON:** 5 mi easy
TUE: 6 mi easy	**TUE:** 7 mi easy	**TUE:** rest day
WED: 4 mi easy	**WED:** 6 mi easy	**WED:** 10 mi, mile repeats
THU: rest day	**THU:** 8 mi, mile repeats	**THU:** 6 mi easy
FRI: 6 mi easy	**FRI:** rest day	**FRI:** 9 mi HMPW
SAT: rest day	**SAT:** 5 mi easy	**SAT:** 5 easy
SUN: 9 mi	**SUN:** 12 mi	**SUN:** 15 mi LSD

SPEEDWORK: You don't need a track to do speedwork, but it helps. Don't get spooked by the number of miles on the "repeats" days; they include the warmup and cooldown, and those should be at least 2 miles each way for seasoned and 3 for hard-core, leaving 3 or 4 miles of actual speedwork. You can make those miles easier by starting your run 2 or 3 miles from the track.

MILE REPEATS: This classic workout is pretty simple: Run a mile at your 10-K pace, jog a lap for recovery, and repeat three or four times.

If you're not running on a track, use a car or bicycle to mark off a mile on a low-traffic road, or run by time. See if you can feel the maximum oxygen pace—it should be at that balance point where you're still comfortable, but even the slightest bit faster would be uncomfortable.

HMPW: The hard-core schedule includes a half-marathon-pace workout. Warm up 1 mile, run 7 miles at half-marathon pace, then cool down 1 mile.

HALF-MARATHON

WEEK 7

NEWBIES: 25 MILES TOTAL	SEASONED: 40 MILES TOTAL	HARD-CORE: 52 MILES TOTAL
MON: rest day	MON: rest day	MON: 5 mi easy
TUE: 5 mi easy	TUE: 6 mi easy	TUE: rest day
WED: 4 mi easy	WED: 6 mi easy	WED: 10 mi speedwork
THU: rest day	THU: 9 mi speedwork	THU: 7 mi easy
FRI: 6 mi easy	FRI: rest day	FRI: 10 mi HMPW
SAT: rest day	SAT: 6 mi easy	SAT: 5 easy
SUN: 10 mi LSD	SUN: 13 mi LSD	SUN: 15 mi LSD

NEWBIES: Sometimes it seems like the seasoned and hard-core programs have all the fun, with speedwork, hills, and more runs per week. The beginner's program is based entirely on mileage, with the goal of simply building your endurance to the point that 13-plus miles is an easily reachable or at least attainable distance. So we concentrate more on time on your feet and less on speed. Next time around you can plan on more miles and improve either your time—or how easy your time is.

HMPW: The hard-core schedule includes a half-marathon-pace workout. Warm up 1 mile, run 8 miles at half-marathon pace, then cool down 1 mile.

SPEEDWORK: Do 6 Yasso 800s. It's pretty simple: Run ½ mile or 800 meters at your 10-K pace, jog a lap for recovery, and repeat 6 times.

LSD: Long slow distance runs are purely for the purpose of endurance. You're going to be on your feet a while to cover 13.1 miles; this is when you get used to it. If you can, consider starting your long runs at the same time the race starts.

HALF-MARATHON
WEEK 8

NEWBIES: 24 MILES TOTAL	SEASONED: 38 MILES TOTAL	HARD-CORE: 50 MILES TOTAL
MON: rest day	**MON:** rest day	**MON:** 5 mi easy
TUE: 6 mi easy	**TUE:** 6 mi easy	**TUE:** rest day
WED: 5 mi easy	**WED:** 7 mi easy	**WED:** 9 mi speedwork
THU: rest day	**THU:** 9 mi tempo	**THU:** 7 mi easy
FRI: 5 mi easy	**FRI:** rest day	**FRI:** 10 mi HMPW
SAT: rest day	**SAT:** 6 mi easy	**SAT:** 6 easy
SUN: 8 mi	**SUN:** 10 mi	**SUN:** 13 mi

SPEEDWORK: Those on the hard-core schedule are out for some more speed on Wednesday. You've done mile repeats, and repeat 800s lets you work on a ladder: ½, ¾, mile, ¾, ½. Jog half the distance you just ran between each one. Remember to warm up and cool down.

HMPW: The hard-core schedule includes a half-marathon-pace workout. Warm up 1 mile, run 8 miles at half-marathon pace, then cool down 1 mile.

HALF-MARATHON
WEEK 9

NEWBIES: 23 MILES TOTAL	SEASONED: 36 MILES TOTAL	HARD-CORE: 46 MILES TOTAL
MON: rest day	MON: rest day	MON: 6 mi easy
TUE: 5 mi easy	TUE: 7 mi easy	TUE: 8 easy
WED: 5 mi easy	WED: 8 mi speedwork	WED: 10 mi speedwork
THU: rest day	THU: 7 mi easy	THU: rest day
FRI: 5 mi easy	FRI: rest day	FRI: 8 mi hills
SAT: rest day	SAT: 6 mi easy	SAT: 6 easy
SUN: 8 mi LSD	SUN: 10-K race	SUN: 10-K race

SPEEDWORK: Do 6 Yasso 800s. It's pretty simple: Run ½ mile or 800 meters at your 10-K pace, jog a lap for recovery, and repeat 6 times.

HILLS: And you thought you were off the hills. The hard-core program has 8 miles on hills on Friday.

HALF-MARATHON
WEEK 10

NEWBIES: 22 MILES TOTAL	SEASONED: 31 MILES TOTAL	HARD-CORE: 43 MILES TOTAL
MON: rest day	**MON:** rest day	**MON:** 4 mi easy
TUE: 4 mi easy	**TUE:** 5 mi easy	**TUE:** 6 easy
WED: 3 mi easy	**WED:** 4 mi easy	**WED:** 8 mi speedwork
THU: rest day	**THU:** 8 mi HMPW	**THU:** 5 easy
FRI: 5 mi easy	**FRI:** rest day	**FRI:** 8 mi HMPW
SAT: rest day	**SAT:** 4 mi easy	**SAT:** rest day
SUN: 10 mi LSD	**SUN:** 10 mi LSD	**SUN:** 12 mi LSD

MILEAGE: Those on the hard-core schedule in particular will notice the reduced mileage. That should give you the energy for some faster speed sessions.

SPEEDWORK: Now we're coming down to quarters. This week's workout should be 10 quarters. Jog at least half that distance between repeats to recover.

HMP: The hard-core schedule includes a half-marathon-pace workout. Warm up 1 mile, run 6 miles at half-marathon pace, then cool down 1 mile.

LSD: Long slow distance runs are purely for the purpose of endurance. You're going to be on your feet a while to cover 13.1 miles.

HALF-MARATHON

WEEK 11

NEWBIES: 18 MILES TOTAL	SEASONED: 24 MILES TOTAL	HARD-CORE: 33 MILES TOTAL
MON: rest day	**MON:** rest day	**MON:** rest day
TUE: 4 mi easy	**TUE:** 5 mi easy	**TUE:** 6 easy
WED: 4 mi easy	**WED:** rest day	**WED:** 7 mi repeats
THU: rest day	**THU:** 7 mi repeats	**THU:** 5 easy
FRI: 5 mi easy	**FRI:** rest day	**FRI:** 7 mi HMPW
SAT: rest day	**SAT:** 5 mi easy	**SAT:** rest day
SUN: 5 mi	**SUN:** 7 mi LSD	**SUN:** 8 mi LSD

REST DAYS: The seasoned and hard-core schedules have an extra rest day this week. Back off on the cross-training at this time.

REPEATS: 2 miles each for the warmup and cooldown, then two 1-mile repeats at 10-K pace. Jog at least half that distance between repeats to recover.

EASY DAYS: Make sure they stay easy, even though you're not working as hard on the other days. We're tapering now, and running harder on the easy days won't help. From here until race day, the idea is getting to the race well-rested.

HMPW: The hard-core schedule includes a half-marathon-pace workout. Warm up 1 mile, run 5 miles at half-marathon pace, then cool down 1 mile.

HALF-MARATHON

WEEK 12

A very easy week in preparation for the race.

NEWBIES: 22 MILES TOTAL	SEASONED: 27 MILES TOTAL	HARD-CORE: 29 MILES TOTAL
MON: rest day	**MON:** rest day	**MON:** rest day
TUE: 3 mi easy	**TUE:** 3 mi easy	**TUE:** 4 mi easy
WED: rest day	**WED:** 3 mi easy	**WED:** 3 mi easy
THU: 3 mi easy	**THU:** 5 mi short repeats	**THU:** 5 mi short repeats
FRI: rest day	**FRI:** rest day	**FRI:** rest day
SAT: 2 mi easy	**SAT:** 2 mi easy	**SAT:** 2 mi easy
SUN: 14 (race day)	**SUN:** 14 (race day)	**SUN:** 15 (race day)

REST DAYS AND EASY DAYS: This whole week is about taking it easy, so run very easy on your easy days. You may be antsy, but save that energy for the race.

REPEATS: 2 miles each for the warmup and cooldown, then 8 short pickups of 40 to 60 seconds at your planned race pace. This isn't going to make you any faster, but it will remind your legs what pace you're planning to run on Sunday.

5-K, 10-K

WEEK 1

NEWBIES: 7 MILES TOTAL	SEASONED: 15 MILES TOTAL	HARD-CORE: 27 MILES TOTAL
MON: rest day	**MON:** rest day	**MON:** 4 mi easy
TUE: 2 mi easy	**TUE:** 4 mi easy	**TUE:** 5 mi hills
WED: 2 mi easy	**WED:** cross-train	**WED:** cross-train
THU: rest day	**THU:** 4 mi hills	**THU:** 6 mi speedwork
FRI: cross-train	**FRI:** rest day	**FRI:** rest day
SAT: rest day	**SAT:** 3 mi easy	**SAT:** 4 mi easy
SUN: 3 mi	**SUN:** 4 mi	**SUN:** 8 mi

HILLS: The seasoned and hard-core schedules have hills. This should be the hilliest loop you can find for the distance and shouldn't be treated as an easy run.

SPEEDWORK: 2 miles each for the warmup and cooldown, then 10 short pickups of 60 seconds at your planned race pace.

REST DAYS AND EASY DAYS are mostly interchangeable. This means that those following the seasoned and hard-core programs who want to take a zero day on Saturday, rather than Friday, should simply switch those days. However, the quality days (hills and Sundays, which will become long runs) should stay where they are.

CROSS-TRAINING should involve sustained aerobic activity like cycling or an elliptical trainer; rest-day cross-training should be a nonimpact activity like stretching, yoga, or swimming.

5-K, 10-K

WEEK 2

NEWBIES: 10 MILES TOTAL	SEASONED: 18 MILES TOTAL	HARD-CORE: 30 MILES TOTAL
MON: rest day	**MON:** rest day	**MON:** 5 mi easy
TUE: 3 mi easy	**TUE:** 5 mi easy	**TUE:** 5 mi hills
WED: 3 mi easy	**WED:** cross-train	**WED:** cross-train
THU: rest day	**THU:** 5 mi hills	**THU:** 7 mi speedwork
FRI: cross-train	**FRI:** rest day	**FRI:** rest day
SAT: rest day	**SAT:** 3 mi easy	**SAT:** 5 mi easy
SUN: 4 mi	**SUN:** 5 mi	**SUN:** 8 mi

HILLS: The seasoned and hard-core schedules have hills. This should be the hilliest loop you can find for the distance and shouldn't be treated as an easy run.

SPEEDWORK: Now we're coming down to quarters. This week's workout should be 10 quarters: 10 × 400 meters with a 200-meter recovery jog. Jog at least half that distance between repeats to recover.

5-K, 10-K

WEEK 3

NEWBIES: 12 MILES TOTAL	SEASONED: 20 MILES TOTAL	HARD-CORE: 33 MILES TOTAL
MON: rest day	**MON:** rest day	**MON:** 6 mi easy
TUE: 4 mi easy	**TUE:** 5 mi easy	**TUE:** 6 mi hills
WED: 3 mi easy	**WED:** cross-train	**WED:** cross-train
THU: rest day	**THU:** 6 mi hills	**THU:** 8 mi speedwork
FRI: cross-train	**FRI:** rest day	**FRI:** rest day
SAT: rest day	**SAT:** 3 mi easy	**SAT:** 5 mi easy
SUN: 5 mi	**SUN:** 6 mi	**SUN:** 8 mi

HILLS: The seasoned and hard-core schedules have hills. This should be the hilliest loop you can find for the distance and shouldn't be treated as an easy run.

SPEEDWORK: Now we're coming down to quarters. This week's workout should be 12 quarters: 12 × 400 meters with a 200-meter recovery jog. Jog at least half that distance between repeats to recover.

5-K, 10-K

WEEK 4

NEWBIES: 8 MILES TOTAL	SEASONED: 16 MILES TOTAL	HARD-CORE: 29 MILES TOTAL
MON: rest day	MON: rest day	MON: 5 mi easy
TUE: 2 mi easy	TUE: 4 mi easy	TUE: 5 mi hills
WED: 3 mi easy	WED: cross-train	WED: cross-train
THU: rest day	THU: 4 mi hills	THU: 6 mi speedwork
FRI: cross-train	FRI: rest day	FRI: rest day
SAT: rest day	SAT: 3 mi easy	SAT: 5 mi easy
SUN: 3 mi	SUN: 5 mi	SUN: 8 mi

HILLS: The seasoned and hard-core schedules have hills. This should be the hilliest loop you can find for the distance and shouldn't be treated as an easy run.

SPEEDWORK: 2 miles each for the warmup and cooldown, then 10 short pickups of 90 seconds at your planned race pace.

5-K, 10-K

WEEK 5

NEWBIES: 11 MILES TOTAL	SEASONED: 19 MILES TOTAL	HARD-CORE: 30 MILES TOTAL
MON: rest day	MON: rest day	MON: 5 mi easy
TUE: 3 mi easy	TUE: 5 mi easy	TUE: 5 mi hills
WED: 3 mi easy	WED: cross-train	WED: cross-train
THU: rest day	THU: 5 mi hills	THU: 7 mi speedwork
FRI: cross-train	FRI: rest day	FRI: rest day
SAT: rest day	SAT: 3 mi easy	SAT: 5 mi easy
SUN: 5 mi	SUN: 6 mi	SUN: 8 mi

HILLS: The seasoned and hard-core schedules have hills. This should be the hilliest loop you can find for the distance and shouldn't be treated as an easy run.

SPEEDWORK: Now we're coming down to quarters. This week's workout should be 10 quarters: 10 × 400 meters with a 200-meter recovery jog. Jog at least half that distance between repeats to recover.

5-K, 10-K

WEEK 6

NEWBIES: 14 MILES TOTAL	SEASONED: 22 MILES TOTAL	HARD-CORE: 35 MILES TOTAL
MON: rest day	**MON:** rest day	**MON:** 6 mi easy
TUE: 5 mi easy	**TUE:** 5 mi easy	**TUE:** 7 mi hills
WED: 4 mi easy	**WED:** cross-train	**WED:** cross-train
THU: rest day	**THU:** 6 mi hills	**THU:** 8 mi speedwork
FRI: cross-train	**FRI:** rest day	**FRI:** rest day
SAT: rest day	**SAT:** 4 mi easy	**SAT:** 6 mi easy
SUN: 5 mi	**SUN:** 7 mi	**SUN:** 8 mi

HILLS: The seasoned and hard-core schedules have hills. This should be the hilliest loop you can find for the distance and shouldn't be treated as an easy run.

SPEEDWORK: Now we're coming down to quarters. This week's workout should be six 800s: 6 × 800 meters with a 400-meter recovery jog. Jog at least half that distance between repeats to recover.

5-K, 10-K

WEEK 7

NEWBIES: 15 MILES TOTAL	SEASONED: 25 MILES TOTAL	HARD-CORE: 38 MILES TOTAL
MON: rest day	**MON:** rest day	**MON:** 6 mi easy
TUE: 5 mi easy	**TUE:** 6 mi easy	**TUE:** 8 mi hills
WED: 4 mi easy	**WED:** cross-train	**WED:** cross-train
THU: rest day	**THU:** 7 mi hills	**THU:** 8 mi speedwork
FRI: cross-train	**FRI:** rest day	**FRI:** rest day
SAT: rest day	**SAT:** 4 mi easy	**SAT:** 7 mi easy
SUN: 6 mi	**SUN:** 8 mi	**SUN:** 9 mi

HILLS: The seasoned and hard-core schedules have hills. This should be the hilliest loop you can find for the distance and shouldn't be treated as an easy run.

SPEEDWORK: Now we're coming down to quarters. This week's workout should be 3 times 1 mile: 3 × 1 mile with an 800-meter recovery jog. Jog at least half that distance between repeats to recover.

5-K, 10-K

WEEK 8

NEWBIES: 12 MILES TOTAL	SEASONED: 20 MILES TOTAL	HARD-CORE: 33 MILES TOTAL
MON: rest day	**MON:** rest day	**MON:** 6 mi easy
TUE: 4 mi easy	**TUE:** 5 mi easy	**TUE:** 6 mi hills
WED: 3 mi easy	**WED:** cross-train	**WED:** cross-train
THU: rest day	**THU:** 6 mi hills	**THU:** 8 mi speedwork
FRI: cross-train	**FRI:** rest day	**FRI:** rest day
SAT: rest day	**SAT:** 3 mi easy	**SAT:** 5 mi easy
SUN: 5 mi	**SUN:** 6 mi	**SUN:** 8 mi

HILLS: The seasoned and hard-core schedules have hills. This should be the hilliest loop you can find for the distance and shouldn't be treated as an easy run.

SPEEDWORK: Now we're coming down to quarters. This week's workout should be 12 quarters: 12 × 400 meters with a 200-meter recovery jog. Jog at least half that distance between repeats to recover.

5-K, 10-K

WEEK 9

NEWBIES: 7 MILES TOTAL	SEASONED: 15 MILES TOTAL	HARD-CORE: 27 MILES TOTAL
MON: rest day	**MON:** rest day	**MON:** 4 mi easy
TUE: 2 mi easy	**TUE:** 4 mi easy	**TUE:** 5 mi hills
WED: 2 mi easy	**WED:** cross-train	**WED:** cross-train
THU: rest day	**THU:** 4 mi hills	**THU:** 6 mi speedwork
FRI: cross-train	**FRI:** rest day	**FRI:** rest day
SAT: rest day	**SAT:** 3 mi easy	**SAT:** 4 mi easy
SUN: 3 mi	**SUN:** 4 mi	**SUN:** 8 mi

HILLS: The seasoned and hard-core schedules have hills. This should be the hilliest loop you can find for the distance and shouldn't be treated as an easy run.

SPEEDWORK: 2 miles each for the warmup and cooldown, then 10 short pickups of 90 seconds at your planned race pace.

5-K, 10-K

WEEK 10

NEWBIES: 4 MILES TOTAL	SEASONED: 8 MILES TOTAL	HARD-CORE: 14 MILES TOTAL
MON: rest day	MON: rest day	MON: 4 mi easy
TUE: 2 mi easy	TUE: 4 mi speedwork	TUE: 5 mi speedwork
WED: 2 mi easy	WED: 2 mi easy	WED: rest day
THU: rest day	THU: rest day	THU: 3 mi easy
FRI: cross-train	FRI: rest day	FRI: rest day
SAT: rest day	SAT: 2 mi easy	SAT: 2 mi easy
SUN: race day	SUN: race day	SUN: race day

HILLS: The seasoned and hard-core schedules have hills. This should be the hilliest loop you can find for the distance and shouldn't be treated as an easy run.

SPEEDWORK: 2 miles each for the warmup and cooldown, then 10 short pickups of 60 seconds at your planned race pace.

Bart leads the pack of the Caribbean Cruise to Run in Antigua. The ship transports runners to six islands for races.

Chapter 20

MUST-DO RACES
NEAR AND ABROAD

The Ultimate Runner's Vacation: Cruise to Run

In some circles, cruises are considered vacations for only the newly wed, the overly fed, and the nearly dead. But Cruise to Run targets an entirely different demographic: active people. This cruise features stops at six Caribbean islands for organized runs and a few races. I was one of the original passengers in 2007 and I returned last year for two reasons: Friesen' and freezing. Organizer Jerry Friesen and his wife, Jody, bend over backward to make sure every runner has a fantastic time, and it's usually cold as heck in Pennsylvania in February. In 2008, we boarded a Princess Cruise Ship in San Juan, Puerto Rico, and sailed to Barbados, Saint Lucia, Antigua, Tortola, and Saint Thomas, where we went on morning runs and spent the rest of the day exploring, swimming in the clear waters, and enjoying the amenities of the cruise ship. The ship features a fitness center and Cruise to Run offers exercise classes and running clinics, a movie theater, comedy club, and great restaurants.

Coolest Host City: Austin Marathon, Texas

If you like eclectic downtowns, you'll love Austin—its slogan is "Keep Austin Weird." The town is loaded with funky bars, speak-easies, great restaurants, and all sorts of music venues, including Zilker Metropolitan Park, home to outdoor concerts, gardens, and the famous Barton Springs, where the water temperature is a tepid 68°F all year long. The race is always held on Presidents' Day weekend, so you get an extra day to hang out in a city where it seems everyone runs. Even on 100°F days in summer, the Town Lake Trail is packed with runners. I consider Austin the top running city in the United States. The marathon route is a looped course with gradual climbs and descents. For breakfast, head to Magnolia Café, where a sign outside reads "Sorry we're open."

Best Cult Race: Catalina Marathon, California

This race is 26 miles off the coast of Long Beach on Catalina Island. It's completely rural, with no spectators but plenty of buffalo. I call it a cult marathon because it seems that so many people who run it return year after year, including me. Every March I get Catalina Fever. Former marathon world-record holder Steve Jones caught the fever a few years ago and returns every year. He runs the race 2 hours slower than his 2:07 world record time and crosses the finish line saying, "It doesn't get any better than this." And it doesn't. It feels like a family reunion—but one you want to attend. The course is mostly trail and jeep roads through the interior of the remote island. It's a hilly, challenging marathon but worth the trip because of the collegial feel and the catamaran boat ride to the start in Two Harbors.

Most Romantic: Rome Marathon

You start at the Colosseum and pass the Spanish Steps, Trevi Fountain, the Vatican, and lots of stunning piazzas, each more breathtaking then the last. There are also more cappuccino stands per mile than any other race. I know because I stopped at most of them. My wife and I ran this marathon the day after we got married, and you can't help but fall in love with the Eternal City. About 12 of the 26 miles are on cobblestone streets, but there's no need to worry. The uneven surface has been worn smooth by automobiles.

Most Scenic: Big Sur Marathon, California

I always tell people this is the one marathon they have to do once in their lives because it boasts some of the most majestic views in the Western world. The course runs from Big Sur to Carmel, and the first 5 miles start in the redwoods. From there you work your way through farmland to the Pacific coast. The jaw-dropping moment arrives at the halfway point, when you go over the Bixby Bridge, 260 feet above sea level. There's always a guy there in a tuxedo playing a baby grand piano. I don't think this course is as tough as some runners believe. I posted a 2:54 there at the age of 46 after having run four marathons in the previous 9 weeks.

Most Scenic Urban Marathon: Twin Cities Marathon, Minneapolis–Saint Paul

Many runners, including me, believe this is one of the best-organized marathons in the country. They deliver on every promise, including natural beauty. This race is in the Land of 10,000 Lakes, and it seems like you pass 9,999 of them. The foliage is amazing, right up there with anything you'll see in New England. The finish line is in front of the state capitol in Saint Paul, and parts of the course are along the mighty Mississippi River. You'd never know you're in a city of 400,000 people, except they're all out cheering for you.

Best-Kept Secret: Savannah River Bridge Run, 10-K and 5-K, Georgia

This challenging course goes out and back over Savannah Bridge, a 600-foot span. Savannah drips with Southern charm, from preserved antebellum mansions to Spanish moss on live oak trees. The city is full of quaint shops, first-rate restaurants and a lively nightlife. There are 22 squares dating back to 1733 when the city was first built by General James Edward Oglethorpe. But the nicest part is the people, who practice Southern hospitality with the same devotion as the original inhabitants. The race started in 1991 and now offers a Double Pump so runners can do both the 10-K and 5-K, meaning they cross the bridge three times. The postrace party includes beer and a Southern favorite, Brunswick stew. There's also live music and a climbing wall.

Biggest Challenge: Pikes Peak Marathon, Manitou Springs, Colorado

Bring your oxygen mask for this one—starting altitude is 6,295 feet. The turnaround point is at the top of the mountain at 14,110 feet, for an elevation gain of 7,815 feet. Then you retrace your steps and head back down to Manitou Springs, a small mining town at the base of the mountain. It's the greatest challenge in marathon running, but you can always adjust your pace for the altitude. Loose gravel and occasional tree roots on the trail make it even more of a challenge, but running up this pristine trail is worth posting a slower time. Humidity is only at around 15 percent every year, and you can't beat the view from the top.

Most Regal: Royal Victoria Marathon, Vancouver Island, British Columbia

I think Victoria is the prettiest town in North America. With ivy everywhere, it feels very British—and you can have an Indian curry buffet every afternoon at 3:00 p.m. and high tea as well. Laura and I stayed at the Empress Hotel and felt like royalty because everyone treated us so well. Plus, the whole town gets into the race—it's the biggest event of the year. It's the first race I ever attended where the race director shook the hand of every finishing runner. The race announcer calls out all the runners' names— including personal records and next of kin—as they cross the finish line.

Most Historic Marathon: Athens Marathon

Every marathon geek should retrace the steps of the original Greek marathon. In 490 BC, a messenger named Pheidippides ran from Marathon to Athens to announce the town's victory against the invading Persian army. According to legend, after delivering the news, the foot soldier collapsed and died. That hasn't stopped legions of marathoners from retracing Pheidippides' journey. But it's not for the faint of foot—it's a tough course. I did the first half of it with legendary runner Jeff Galloway in the mid-1990s, and the finish line is on the track where the 1896 modern Olympics were held. That alone was worth the trip.

Best Aid Stations: Marathon du Médoc, France

In what other marathon do they ask you whether you prefer red or white wine at an aid station? They also serve water, but when you're running through the grounds and vineyards of the Bordeaux region of France, why would you want H_2O? There are more than 20 catered wine-tasting stops that also serve oysters, cheese, pâté, and steak. No one's in a hurry to finish, and race organizers award the first- and last-place winners their weight in grand cru, a regional wine. About 90 percent of the people run in costumes. The prerace pasta dinner is in a château, and everyone receives a bottle of Médoc at the finish. The party continues into the night with a fireworks show.

Best Race Experience: Hood to Coast Relay, Oregon

This 197-mile relay is like Woodstock for runners. Instead of sitting in a field getting stoned and listening to rock music, you travel a total of 197 miles, but you run only roughly 17 of them. The race starts at the base of Mount Hood, takes you through old-growth forest, and finishes on the beach in the coastal town of Seaside. Teams are made up of 12 members, and each runner completes three legs. The average finish is 26 hours, and when you're not running, you're most likely sleeping in a field, riding in a van with your buddies, or drinking latte at a coffee stand. The postrace party on the beach is out-of-control fun.

Best Course to Set a 10-K PR: Monument Avenue 10-K, Richmond, Virginia

Runners of similar abilities start in waves of 1,000, fueling competitive spirits on a fast course. Bands play at every quarter mile, upping the energy level of the runners. More than 25,000 people participate, and runners are grouped by a previous race's finish. Monument Avenue was named one of the country's 10 Great Streets by the American Planning Association. Six historic monuments are on the street including five that pay tribute to the Civil War and one to tennis player Arthur Ashe, a son of Richmond.

Best Excuse to Go to Hawaii: The Honolulu Marathon

The marathon starts at 5:00 a.m. with a fireworks display on the beach, and from there it just gets better. The course runs through

Waikiki Beach past Diamond Head, an extinct volcano and the iconic image of Honolulu. The race finishes at Kapiolani Park, a block from the ocean. The water stops are staffed by surfers and beach bums. Your finishing medal is a shell necklace placed around your neck by a native Hawaiian dancer in a grass skirt. Even if you run a 5-hour marathon, you're lying on the beach by 10:00 a.m.

My Wife's Favorite Race: Western States Endurance Run, California

The Western States is often called the Super Bowl of ultra running, a 100-mile torture test starting at Squaw Valley (site of the 1960 winter Olympics) and ending in Auburn. My wife, Laura, was the third female overall finisher in 2001. I've never done the race, but it's a prestigious one to have under your belt, and that's what you get if you finish in under 30 hours. The top finishers get a cougar trophy. If you finish under 24 hours, you get a silver belt buckle, and those completing the race in under 30 hours get the bronze. The trail along rugged passes follows those used by gold and silver miners in the 1850s. The course has 15,540 feet in ascents and 22,970 feet in descents.

Best Race to Watch Friends: Carlsbad 5000, California

This unique 5-K race is done in nine heats throughout the day. Runners are grouped by gender and age, so there's a chance you could run and then watch your spouse or friend race in a different heat. That doesn't happen in any other race. The last heat of the day is made up of the best 5,000-meter runners in the world. So by noon, when all 12,000 runners are done with their heats, they get to be spectators for the fastest 5,000 meter runners in the world. It's also a PR course. Sixteen world records have been set here. Afterward, it's a party by the sea. Carlsbad is the perfect-size village: small enough that everything shuts down for the race but large enough to host great restaurants, bars, and coffee shops for all the runners.

Best Bragging Rights: Mount Washington Road Race, New Hampshire

There's only one hill in this race, but it's the entire 7.6-mile course. You run up the Mount Washington auto road, which has an average grade of 11.5 percent, with sections reaching 18 percent. The finish line has a 22 percent grade—that's like trying to run up the side of a building. It's so steep, your nose scrapes the road in front of you. Finishers are awarded a bumper sticker that spoofs the traditional "This car climbed Mount Washington" sticker. This one says "The driver of this car ran up Mount Washington." It's one of my most memorable races not only because I love running up hills but also because I'm a weather buff, and Mount Washington attracts the most extreme weather conditions anywhere in the United States. It's also home to the highest wind speed ever recorded—the gauge broke at 230 miles per hour. Some years the weather at the start is 70°F and brilliant sunshine, but the finish line can be shrouded in a hailstorm with freezing temperatures.

Best Bling: Berwick Run for the Diamonds, Berwick, Pennsylvania

The top seven male runners receive diamond rings, and the top seven women get diamond pendants for finishing this 9-mile race held for the past 99 years on Thanksgiving Day. In 1998, I missed winning a diamond ring by 3 seconds. But despite the opulent prizes, the race is a campy slice of Americana, with all race festivities held in the basement of the town's Elks Lodge. When you pick up your race number at 9:00 a.m., the bar stools are filled with old-timers downing shots and drinking beer, but they still wish you luck in the race. The course is brutal, a 2-mile hill with steep downhills. Spectators line the course in droves, and every house you run by is filled with people screaming.

Bart's Favorite Race: Garden of the Gods, Colorado Springs

This 10-mile course takes place in Garden of the Gods, a public park in Colorado Springs. The course meanders past imposing red rocks such as Kissing Camels, a 320-foot-tall sandstone formation that looks like two dromedaries with their lips touching. People come from around the world to see the natural beauty of the red cliffs. At the start of the race, temperatures are usually in the low 60s but can quickly rise into the 70s and 80s. I ran this race in 1989 while attending the Road Runners Club of America Convention and almost caught my running idol, Don Kardong, no longer in his prime, near the finish. Kardong finished fourth in the 1976 Olympic marathon in Montreal. My strong finish meant I had paced myself well considering the high altitude of the course.

Oldest Race in North America: Around the Bay 30-K, Hamilton, Ontario

The first running of this race was in 1894, 3 years before the Boston Marathon existed. The start and finish lines have changed over the years, but the majority of the course, circumnavigating Hamilton Bay, remains. Rich in history, a lot of runners use it as a tune-up for Boston. Hamilton is an old industrial steel town and reminds me of my Bethlehem, Pennsylvania, roots. Runners receive a gold, silver, or bronze finishing medal based on their race time.

Best Bridge Race: Cooper River Bridge Run 10-K, Charleston, South Carolina

This point-to-point course offers spectacular views from the Cooper River Bridge, which spans 2½ miles and connects Charleston to Mount Pleasant. My favorite spot is at Patriot Point, where the aircraft carrier USS *Yorktown,* nicknamed the *Fighting Lady,* is docked. With over 30,000 participants, it's one of the largest races in the country. Charleston is a great vacation getaway, with access to beaches, southern cuisine, and historical landmarks.

Fastest Marathon Course in the Country: California International Marathon, Sacramento

This is the fastest course I've ever run in the United States. In 1998, I posted a 2:42, at age 43, my fastest time as a master. The course begins at Folsom Dam near Folsom Prison, where Johnny Cash performed his hit "Folsom Prison Blues" in 1968. The course runs through the suburbs and follows an old mining trail. It finishes on the steps of the state capitol in downtown Sacramento. Don't run this one for scenery—run it for speed.

Most Diverse Race: ING New York City Marathon

Runners from 130 countries participate in this race, not counting the thousands of foreigners who call New York home. Being surrounded by people from so many different parts of the world gives you a sense of inclusiveness and the diversity of the running community. The race starts on the Verrazano-Narrows Bridge, one of the most picturesque starting lines in the world. The course passes through the culturally diverse neighborhoods of Brooklyn, the Hasidic Jewish community of Williamsburg, and into Queens, where runners cross over the 59th Street Bridge into Manhattan, where throngs of enthusiastic fans line First Avenue. There's a jaunt through Harlem as runners head back to Central Park, finishing in front of the Tavern on the Green, a famous restaurant. The race travels through the city's five boroughs and is the only time you can go through these neighborhoods on foot without the menace of vehicles.

Best Winter Getaway: Miami Tropical Marathon

This one's at the end of January, when all marathoners should head south for the winter. The race starts at 6:00 a.m., when it's a cool 60°F, but the day usually warms up by the time you finish. About 1½ miles into the race, you run on a causeway adjacent to docked cruise ships, and the passengers come out on the deck to cheer. They're enthusiastic fans, but the best-looking ones are on Miami Beach, where the art deco lights of the strip glow in the dawn. There, a bunch of Paris Hilton look-alikes trying to leave the bars get trapped by marathon traffic, so they end up staying to cheer for the runners. After the race, everyone hits South Beach.

My Favorite Hometown Race: Lehigh Valley Half-Marathon 5-K and Kids' Race

Most people wouldn't think of the Lehigh Valley as a hotbed for running, but it's home to *Runner's World* and one of the best half-marathons in the country. The race started in the 1970s as a marathon, but it became a half-marathon in the 1980s, when the shorter distance gained popularity. The course passes through four beautiful city parks, including the Little Lehigh Parkway, where runners cross a covered bridge before the stadium finish. About 20 bands line the course to inspire runners. The race always hosts a top athlete for the weekend festivities and pasta dinner. Past celebrities have included Joan Benoit Samuelson, Billy Mills, John Bingham, Ryan Hall, Sarah Reinertsen, and Jeff Galloway.

It's also cutting edge when it comes to race organization. In 2001, when Neal Novak and I were race directors, the half—then called the *Runner's World* Half-Marathon—was the first race in the country not to print an entry form, requiring all runners to register on-line. We also emailed every runner a weekly training schedule, which may be why the race always has such a high finish rate and few injuries.

In 2002, we personalized the race giving every runner a name and not just a number. For the first time in racing, we added the first and last names on every race bib, an innovation that's now become standard in the industry.

INDEX

Boldface page references indicate photographs.
<u>Underscored</u> references indicate tables.

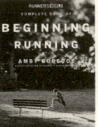

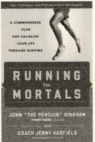

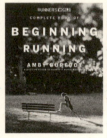

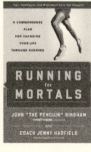
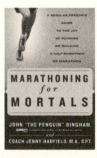